D1224827

WATERWORKS

MAY 04 1983

Michael Hackleman

WATERWORKS

An Owner-Builder Guide to Rural Water Systems

DOLPHIN BOOKS   *DOUBLEDAY & COMPANY, INC.*
Garden City, New York
1983

BOOK DESIGNED BY SYLVIA DEMONTE-BAYARD

Library of Congress Cataloging in Publication Data

Hackleman, Michael A.
Waterworks.

References: p. 161
Includes index.
1. Water-supply, Rural.   I. Title.
TD927.H3   628'.72
ISBN: 0-385-17559-0   AACR2
Library of Congress Catalog Card Number 82–45289

14.95

ACKNOWLEDGMENTS

This book has energy beyond that which was expended in writing it. At this point, it is potential; its real power is not unleashed until you use the information, transforming the words into tools that shape a water system. Giving it that potential, however, was not the result of a singular effort. At the very least, it is a gathering of knowledge won from working through different situations with many people; since the knowledge has been gleaned from the experience of a lifetime, it's difficult to give credit where credit is due.

Other efforts are more easily pinpointed. Again, Harold Moskovitz found a home for the idea. Over some cold brew, Charlie and Steve Acker brought hard experience to bear on a fledgling outline and, along with Steve Heckeroth (Fig. 4–20) and Ted Keck (Figs. 1–10 and 4–27), supplied a number of photos (Figs. 3–1, 3–3, 4–19, 5–8 through 5–11, 6–2, 6–5, 6–10, and 6–13 through 6–16). T. J. Byers wrote up a fine account of the principle, construction, and operation of the "Waterwatch," a water-level monitoring system of his own design.

Some heavies were involved, too. I particularly appreciate the permission given by the American Association for Vocational Instructional Materials to use many of the excellent drawings, charts, and tables from their own book, *Planning for an Individual Water System* (see Figs. 1–6, 1–7, 2–9, 3–5, 3–6, 4–2 through 4–6, and 4–34). Likewise, from the California Water Resources Center at the University of California, Davis, came permission to reproduce a few drawings from Murray Milne's *Residential Water Re-Use* (see Figs. 3–8 through 3–10). And thanks to the folks at Peace Press for an okay to use drawings and photos from some of my own books—*The Homebuilt, Wind-Generated Electricity Handbook, At Home with Alternative Energy,* and *Better Use of: Utility-Supplied Electricity and Low-Voltage DC in the Home and Shop* (see Figs. 1–9, 1–13, 1–14, 3–7, 4–28, and 6–11).

Finally, closer to home, some very appreciated typing, proofing, and production work from Ginny Abert and last-minute typing from Valerie Fall. And—I've saved the best for last—love, patience, and support from Vanessa and the loving antics of our fine sons, Brett and Glenn, who know that what I need after a long day of typing, proofing, paste-up, and drawing is to be crawled all over!

CONTENTS

CONTENTS

CONTENTS

INTRODUCTION

Water is precious. A necessity of life. Unfortunately, most people are city-spoiled. That is, as long as one has made the initial arrangements to have it "connected" and continues to pay the utility bill, further thoughts of water are limited to occasional inconveniences such as leaky faucets or sinks that don't drain. It's all summed up in the nightly weather report with, "Sorry, folks, I've got some bad news for you. Another rainy weekend!"

In a more rural area, though, there's no water main to connect to, so getting water is left to the individual user's efforts. Some relief may be found in the Yellow Pages, which list companies that drill wells; the same people often supply, install, and service the equipment that, with the proper electrical hookup, can approach the same "I-don't-have-to-think-about-it" convenience of a city water supply. It's not a sure thing, however. Dry or low-producing wells, the effects of drought on water levels, and the "do-without" consequences of a utility blackout all serve to bring home the point that country living, even after the large initial expense, can be inconvenient. Without knowing the alternatives, many people come to accept this, along with poor roads, inadequate police and fire services, and long distances to the nearest shopping center, as a fact of rural life. It need not be.

Moreover, these shortcomings don't lie in wait for the unwary alone. Even those who seek out information before buying property or before developing it have no single source of information for the many options available. Manufacturers' pamphlets don't help much either—each company beats its own drum, and it's left to the individual to wade through the mass of information, evaluate all the claims, determine what's been left unsaid, and somehow apply it all to his or her own particular situation. It's the classic case: How do you ask questions about something that you don't know anything about? Too often what little information is available focuses on hardware for specific parts of the system, rather than the whole. Moreover, the subject never touches on combined systems, ignoring the well-known fact that no one energy source or method can do it all, all of the time. As a consequence, the owner typically acquires an understanding of the final water system by reading an owner's manual—after the system is installed and the bill has been paid.

This book will explore the factors peculiar to rural water systems. While acknowledging that any system will work, it concentrates on those that work best for a given set of circumstances. Ultimately, however, only the specific user can make the decision, because he or she is the person who knows the situation best. This book will explore, in layperson's terms, the physics of water as well as—the types of systems available, how they work, and the hardware involved; only then can the individual match his needs and wants with water availability and energy sources.

The *breadth* of the treatment will allow the prospective buyer to scrupulously evaluate manufacturer equipment claims (knowing when you're *not* being ripped off is just as important as knowing when you *are*) and to get the best deal with a contractor for the system installation. The *depth* of the treatment will arm the do-it-yourselfer with sufficient detail for every factor involved in the successful selection, installation, and operation of a water system unique to his or her own situation.

Anyone you'd care to ask about water systems will have something to say on the subject—what's best, what you need, what you don't want to do, and so on. Ask and ye shall receive. If you find reassurance in this, you're welcome to it. Realize, however, that none of these people (including myself!) has to *live* with the system you install.

Similarly, answers that come easily probably aren't worth much. Also, one shouldn't forget the maxim, "There ain't no such thing as a free lunch" (TANSTAAFL). Nevertheless, low-yield energy sources and low-capacity water sources abound. By choosing a system that processes water efficiently, we can make better use of their availability. The book's emphasis is on water systems that do the most for the least expenditure of money, energy, or personal effort.

There's no way to keep this subject from some technical consideration. However, it's a waste of time to write a book that nobody can or will read or understand. Let's make a deal: I won't assume that you know anything about math, physics, engineering, hydraulics, and electricity if you won't assume that what I've written is over your head.

The standard water system found on the farm or rural homestead is powered by utility-supplied electricity, which I find amazing. Here are some folks who buy land, build their home, farm, or shop, grow their own food, boast about their independence, and—in direct contradiction—choose to "rent" the energy needed to make it all work! If the money paid out for utility-supplied electricity were building some kind of equity in it, I'd understand. But it isn't; irrespective of how long you've done business with a utility company, skip one month's payment and you'll get a nasty letter, threatening disconnection. Besides, every dollar spent for utility-supplied electricity is an automatic vote in favor of whatever the utility company wants to do. If you don't like the way they're spending it—on nuclear power, for example—that's tough. Think about it.

Don't misunderstand me—I'm not opposed to utility power. Utility-supplied power has its place, but the attitude it perpetuates does not. It's still dirt-cheap energy, but that's changing fast and continuing to use it as though it will never end is dangerous—at the very least it compromises the environment, and at the worst it may lead to global war. We need not look any farther than our pocketbook to see the attractiveness of many alternatives.

Finally, you may have noticed that neither the title nor the subtitle of this book contains the word "complete." There are two reasons for this. One, I have never found a book that boasted completeness to be *really* complete. And secondly, to include everything on the subject of water systems would be a senseless duplication of good information already in print. So, when I've found a good book on related subjects I've referred you there. That keeps this book under ten pounds (and under a hundred bucks), and allows me to spend more time on material for which there is no other source.

WATERWORKS

Part I

SUBSTANCE

What sets the well-designed water system apart from others? Versatility? Functionalism? Efficient use of water and energy? No, the hallmark of a well-designed system is simple: it cannot be improved upon. You might find its *equal*—that allows for personal preferences—but you can't find its *better*. And this perfection is rooted in two characteristics the system's substance and shape—the materials used and their unique arrangement.

In this section, we will talk about the substance of a water system—the functions, processes, and materials of every system.

1

WATER AND ENERGY

The lifeblood of a water system is the water itself. If it is to sustain you and perform the uses you will put it to, the water source must be carefully selected lest it also become a source of concern. But water found in nature is "wild"; transforming it into a form that will satisfactorily do the things we ask of it requires energy. This is the system's heart. The system's energy source must also be selected so that the two, water and energy, merge in a hard-working symbiotic partnership that will demonstrate again and again how wise it was to expend the effort toward this end.

SOURCES OF WATER

There are many potential sources of water for use in the rural water system. Among the more promising sources are streams, springs, ponds, and wells. On a bigger scale there are rivers and lakes, and even the ocean itself. If one is clever enough, it's even possible to collect the falling rain.

Access is everything. Right off, some of these potential sources may be eliminated from the list—you either have them or you don't. With others it may be a "sometimes it's there and sometimes it's

not" situation. Finally, some sources can only be listed as "probables," particularly if there's no visual evidence of their presence. The extremes are interesting. It would be just as rare to find a piece of property that boasted *all* of these sources as one where *none* of them existed. So it's safe to start with the assumption that there's at least one source available to any piece of land and a strong possibility of more than one.

Each source of water is unique. But if it is to find a place as the source of water for a water system, it must pass a test. It's not difficult to list some of the questions we would be likely to ask of it. However, let's first look at some of the characteristics of each source that both define it and help distinguish it from the other sources.

Ocean

The ocean is the source of all water. Indeed, the first step in the earth's hydrological cycle pulls water from this vast reservoir and dumps it inland. But the water always returns, finding its way back to the ocean. For this reason, coastal farms are likely to appear near these outlets and make use of

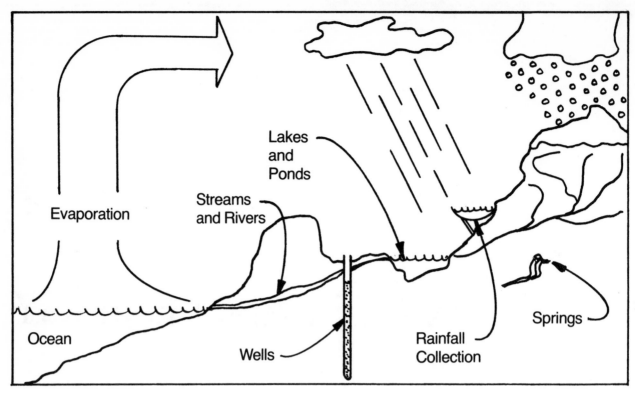

Fig. 1–1 There are eight basic water sources.

the fresh water before it mixes with its saltier cousin. So-called "hostile" coastlines are those without these small streams; for a lack of water, they are uninhabited. "Water, water, everywhere, nor any drop to drink," says Samuel Coleridge's ancient Mariner.

But it need not be so. While it is energy-intensive to distill seawater into fresh water with conventional energy sources, wherever solar energy is available, fresh water may follow. True, countless other favorable factors would be needed to make it a practical endeavor, but using solar power to distill seawater into fresh water should not be ruled out.

Rivers and Streams

Rivers and streams represent a good source of water. Indeed, they are mere reflections of the "river" of water that flows in the sky which, as part of the hydrological cycle, brings water inland from the oceans. Streams tend to vary more in flow rates, helping shed immediate rainfall, whereas rivers typically display a delayed runoff of rain and are fed by a seasonal release of water locked in snowcaps or glaciers.

All rivers have their birth as streams and creeks, so size is the basic difference between a stream and

a river. The sheer number of streams needed to supply one river indicates the higher probability of finding a stream on a piece of land than a river. Beyond these size differences, use the term that best suits you when describing any water flowing across your own land.

Springs

Springs are magical—water flows from the ground, in a trickle or a copious flow of unusual clarity and purity. The actual source of the water varies. It may be the reemergence of a stream that has gone underground. Quite often a seasonal stream is only a *portion* of an underground run of water that, because of sheer capacity, sometimes shows itself aboveground as overflow. Springs may also be the result of a tear in the fabric of the water table itself, when internal pressure "bleeds off" the excess water. In particularly dry regions, the water in some springs may come from a very great depth.

Lakes and Ponds

The flow of water in a river or stream may be temporarily interrupted by large depressions in the ground which must be filled before the journey is again resumed. If it's a big depression, we call it a lake; a smaller one is simply a pond.

Sometimes a lake or, more frequently, a pond is not supplied just by a stream or river; in fact, it may receive a major portion of its water from a spring. There are a number of ways to determine whether this is indeed the case (see "Siting the Water Source," Chapter 5). If a pond is one of several water sources available to you, you may want to defer some decisions until you've positively established the pond's true source of water.

Shallow Wells

So far the discussion has centered on natural water sources (although it is possible to build a lake or pond). However, if the water is not so readily accessible, a shallow well is one way to get at it, particularly if you know it's just below ground level. And while a shallow well can be dug with machinery designed expressly for that purpose, it also can be hand-dug. To achieve any depth over a few feet, the well must be wide enough to allow working room for at least one person; traditionally, a shallow well may be 3 to 4 feet in diameter (see Fig. 1–4). Because of the extreme danger to the digger in the event of a cave-in, these wells are limited to a maximum depth of 25 to 30 feet. Though much deeper wells of this diameter are possible if more sophisticated digging equipment is applied, in this book a shallow well will be considered one that does not surpass 25 feet in depth (see Fig. 1–5).

Deep Wells

A deep well may be needed to reach groundwater; the range extends, for our purposes, from 25 feet to several hundreds of feet. Wells to several thousands of feet are not uncommon, but at the going rate few private individuals could afford to drill to such depths.

The diameter of the hole that's drilled to reach water is as varied as the depths to which one might need to drill to reach water. Naturally, the larger the hole, the higher the cost. But while small

Fig. 1–2 Ponds will store water and supply good fishing too.

Fig. 1–3 A water source may be just below ground level.

Fig. 1–4 A backhoe digs a shallow well.

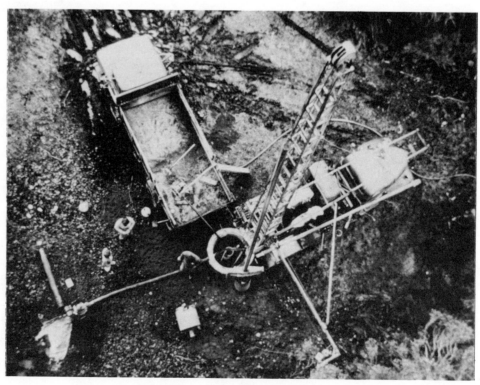

Fig. 1–5 A large-bore drilling rig.

and large holes alike can *reach* water, the difficulty of extracting it (or housing the equipment designed to do this) increases significantly as the diameter drops below 6 inches. A compromise is indicated; it will be easier to find the optimum diameter once a water-extraction system is selected and size of the equipment available from local well-drillers is determined (see "The Deep Well," Chapter 5).

Rainfall

Precipitation initially supplies the water for streams, rivers, lakes, ponds, springs, and wells. However, in whatever form—rain, snow, hail, sleet, or condensation—rainfall is a potential source of water in itself.

A clue to the means whereby rainfall can be tapped as a water source is supplied by nature; streams and rivers, at the persistent urging of gravity, channel the runoff from rainfall to lower elevations. Damming one of these sluices is, in effect, a means of rainfall collection. Another crude but inexpensive way to duplicate this effect is to dig a trench across a slope in the path of runoff, terminating the lower side in some type of storage.

Serious collectors of rainfall are both practical and innovative, merely channeling rain shed by rooftops and their edge-mounted gutters into storage such as a cistern for later use. A surprisingly small amount of roof area will yield thousands of gallons of very clean water each year (see Fig. 1–6). Rainfall measurements are taken by a number of agencies and records extend back for fifty years or more; using these figures and allowing for a 20 to 30 percent loss due to splashing, overflow, and initial washdown of the rooftop, a remarkably accurate determination of capacity may be assessed for any rooftop and the cistern it serves (see Fig. 1–7).

Combinations

There is a strong tendency in the United States for individuals to establish one strong source of water at a particular site and, damn the expense, set up the entire water system around it. This approach to water-system design is, quite frequently, practical. However, many areas don't experience such hardy water sources. And where they exist, the supply diminishes as populations expand and the use of

Figure 1-6
Net Yield of Water for Cisterns per Square Foot of Catchment Area

Minimum Annual Rainfall	Water Yield (sq. ft.)*
(inches)	(gallons)
10	4.2
15	6.3
20	8.3
25	10.5
30	12.5
35	14.6
40	16.7
45	18.8
50	20.8

*Adjusted for 30% water loss to leakage, splash, roof washdown, and evaporation.

water increases. Given the diminishing availability of *pure* water sources, the notion of "one source, one system" becomes both foolish and dangerous. It's foolish because most situations have access to at least two water sources. It's dangerous because single-source systems are inherently vulnerable to the possibility, however remote, that the source will dry up. Even a temporary stoppage can be trouble for a system that has made no provisions for such an event.

EVALUATING THE WATER SOURCE

Now that you have the list of probable sources of water, it's time to evaluate them. Each source of water has inherent qualities and limitations. (That's usually phrased as "advantages and disadvantages," but I'd like to avoid those terms because they are not facts, but value judgments, and one person's advantage may be another person's disadvantage.)

Why don't you look at some of those inherent qualities and limitations and decide which is an advantage or disadvantage *to you*.

Figure 1-7
Capacities of Various Sizes of Cisterns

ROUND TYPE (gallons) — Diameter of Round Type (Feet)

Depth in Feet	5	6	7	8	9	10	11	12	13	14	15	16	17	18
5	735	1055	1440	1880	2380	2935	3555	4230	4965	5755	6610	7515	8485	9510
6	882	1266	1728	2256	2856	3522	4266	5076	5958	6906	7932	9018	10182	11412
7	1029	1477	2016	2632	3332	4109	4977	5922	6951	8057	9254	10521	11879	13314
8	1176	1688	2304	3008	3808	4696	5688	6768	7944	9208	10576	12024	13576	15216
9	1323	1899	2592	3384	4284	5283	6399	7614	8937	10359	11898	13527	15273	17118
10	1470	2110	2880	3760	4760	5870	7110	8460	9930	11510	13220	15030	16970	19020
12	1764	2532	3456	4512	5712	7044	8532	10152	11916	13812	15864	18036	20364	22824
14	2058	2954	4032	5264	6664	8218	9954	11844	13902	16114	18508	21042	23758	26628
16	2342	3376	4608	6016	7616	9392	11376	13536	15888	18416	21152	24048	27152	30432
18	2646	3798	5184	6768	8568	10566	12798	15228	17874	20718	23796	27054	30546	34236
20	2940	4220	5760	7530	9520	11740	14220	16920	19860	23020	26440	30060	33940	38040

SQUARE TYPE (gallons) — Length of Sides of Square Type (Feet)

Depth in Feet	5	6	7	8	9	10	11	12	13	14	15	16	17	18
5	935	1345	1835	2395	3030	3740	4525	5385	6320	7330	8415	9575	10810	12112
6	1122	1614	2202	2874	3636	4488	5430	6462	7584	8796	10098	11490	12974	14534
7	1309	1883	2569	3353	4242	5236	6335	7539	8848	10262	11781	13405	15134	16956
8	1496	2152	2936	3832	4848	5984	7240	8616	10112	11728	13464	15320	17296	19378
9	1683	2421	3303	4311	5454	6732	8145	9693	11376	13194	15147	17235	19458	21800
10	1870	2690	3670	4790	6060	7480	9050	10770	12640	14660	16830	19150	21620	24222
12	2244	3228	4404	5748	7272	8976	10860	12924	15168	17592	20196	22980	25944	29068
14	2618	3766	5138	6706	8484	10472	12670	15078	17696	20524	23562	26810	30268	33912
16	2992	4204	5872	7664	9696	11968	14480	17232	20224	23456	26928	30640	34592	38756
18	3366	4842	6606	8622	10908	13464	16290	19386	22752	26388	30294	34470	38916	42500
20	3740	5380	7340	9580	12120	14960	18100	21540	25280	29320	33660	38300	43240	48444

Access

Access implies on-site presence. While much may be hidden from the eyes, if you don't have it, you don't have it. So if you're inland, strike the ocean as a (direct) source. The same goes for streams, ponds, springs—a walk of the land will quickly reveal whether they're there or not. If they are, list them as probables; the same goes for any source that is intermittent, such as seasonal streams. However, don't confuse "don't know" with "definitely not." For most properties, the evaluation of this single criterion—access—will cut the list of possible water sources in half.

Ease of Development

On a scale of one to ten, make a preliminary evaluation of the relative ease or difficulty of developing any probable water sources. In a way, this is an availability rating. If you can walk right over and scoop it up, it gets a high rating. If you don't know, give it a question mark. Be honest and accurate.

Water and the Law

Access to, and availability of, water is not equivalent to the legal right to use it. Just because a stream flows through your property does not mean that you can take any of it for any purpose you wish. In some instances it may be permissible to take the water for household use or for a small garden, while other usages such as irrigation of fields, watering of livestock, and power production may be prohibited. In some places, this may even apply to a spring that starts on your own property but that passes over the property line.

Legal use of water is defined as "riparian," "appropriative," or both. The first acknowledges the need to share water, and the second is "first come, first served." It's beyond the scope of this book to cover all of the possibilities in sufficient detail. But it's up to you to fend for yourself. Water rights are not always clearly designated in the property deed, nor are they automatically part of the title search that commences once a property is in escrow. Little wonder, then, that people buy a piece of land only to discover sometime after the sale that their right to the water on their land is restricted or pro-

hibited. For this reason, any property that has an unusual abundance of water that has not been developed should be treated as suspect in this matter; if you want the water, make its legal use part of your conditions of sale, or keep on looking.

Susceptibility to Contamination

Supposedly, the United States has the purest water in the world. However, it's only a matter of time before that standing changes; we are, after all, working *very* hard at it—and, unfortunately, succeeding. The use of grade AAA water in toilets and the use of streams and rivers as industrial waste-disposal systems are evidence of this.

All surface waters are subject to pollution. They're easy to abuse, too; the evidence of dumping garbage, sewage, and chemicals is quickly carried away. With each passing mile, the list of contaminants grows: airborne pollutants brought down by the rain; fecal matter from animal stock, camper owners, and improperly installed and maintained septic systems; minerals washed from tailing (the material left over from mining operations) and landscaping projects. . . . The list is long and deadly, the probability of contamination higher with each passing mile.

In all fairness, it should be indicated that the flowing motion of a stream or river has a purifying action; the more the riverbed turbulates the water —makes it tumble, swirl, and spray—the greater the effect. However, as with all filters, whether natural or man-made, there's a finite capacity to purify. Beyond that limit, the water only transports the pollutants.

Lakes and ponds are in the same predicament as the rivers and streams that feed them. However, unlike their nomadic cousins, their still waters are not always able to pass the problem on downstream somewhere; instead, the suspended material precipitates and coats the bottom. Left undisturbed, the polluted material is quickly covered by other suspended material. However, if the inrush of water feeding the pond or lake normally stirs up the sedimentary layers, watch out. Those who harvest the rich silt from seasonal ponds should take note; they may get much more than they bargain for.

Springs and wells are least affected by contamination, even though their water percolates down through the soil from the surface, because the soil itself is an excellent filter. In fact, the water doesn't have to go very far at all; with some soil types, a few feet is sufficient to remove most of the contaminants. For this reason, water from springs and wells is some of the purest available. However, this water is also exposed to mineral deposits, and other substances, and their concentration in the water may exceed levels acceptable for human consumption.

Collected rainfall is also quite pure. The first few minutes of rainfall should purge the air through which it passes of contaminants; furthermore, this same water will flush the actual collection system (a rooftop?) of any other particulates. But, while this source altogether bypasses the type of exposure experienced by streams, rivers, ponds, lakes, springs, and wells, it is also devoid of the beneficial trace elements found in these sources. If used as the only source of drinking water, its sterility actually could be unhealthful.

These are relative indicators. Until proved otherwise, water from any source should be considered suspect, tested, and if need be, treated for the presence and relative concentration of a host of elements, minerals, pollutants, and bacteria (see "Water Quality," Chapter 3).

Any source of water exposed to the open air may also be contaminated by nuclear fallout; whether it's from testing or an actual war or the failure of a nearby nuclear power plant, the effect is the same. Naturally, rivers, lakes, streams, and ponds are easily contaminated by fallout. Again, springs and wells are the least affected. However, a big part of this is "cover." An open spring box or open storage of well water defeats the natural protection of these sources from contamination. As for a system using rainfall collection—do I really need to comment?

Proximity to Usage

A potential water source should be rated according to its distance from the point where the water is needed. This evaluation assumes that the building site has already been established. If it has not, pick some "possibles" and evaluate the potential sources accordingly. Precise distances are not required; a simple comparison between two or more sources is sufficient for now. In the final analysis, it's conceivable that developing a less accessible source closer at hand may be preferable to the cost or relative difficulty of transporting water from a readily available water source.

Elevation

The elevation of each water source relative to the usage site should be noted. Higher ratings go to sources that are higher than the usage site; lower ones go to those that are lower. Note any reservations. Lower ratings are assigned to high-elevation sources that are too far away, are not in line of sight, or are traversed with gullies or other inhospitable terrain. Approximate these elevations above or below the level of the usage site; a more accurate calculation or measurement may be obtained for these distances using several techniques if the need for precision warrants the effort.

Capacity

Any water source has a capacity. This refers to the maximum amount of water it will deliver under any condition, and it's usually described in some convenient term such as gallons per minute (gpm) or gallons per hour (gph). Depending on the source in question, there is always some means of approximating or measuring the source's capacity. If there's a need to deliver water to an application at a *higher* rate than that available from the source, there are a couple of tricks that may help. But that's all they are—tricks. Capacity is inherent in the water source itself and it exists *irrespective of our knowing it.*

Measuring capacity is rarely a difficult task (see "Capacity" in Chapter 5). However, such a measurement represents an instantaneous reading. Measure it later—by the hour, day, week, month, half year, or year—and you're likely to come up with as many different values as the actual number of readings taken. Why?

Simply stated, capacity varies. Rainfall, snowpack, seasons, drought or unusually wet periods, earthquakes, evaporation, seepage, increased usage, and higher population densities will, to some degree, influence capacity. No water source is exempt from the effects of some of these conditions. Minor fluctuations are of no concern; the variance in the readings one will obtain from any one source over a period of time, however, is evidence enough that we're not talking about insignificant differences.

If we took the readings at regular intervals over the span of a year, we'd know both the minimum and maximum values of capacity. A fail-safe tactic, then, is to build your system based on the lowest figure obtained. Naturally, this is inefficient; severe conservation measures might be required. It's also short-lived. Since this system can't cope with higher amounts of water, it must bleed it off. Believe me, nothing halts water conservation like seeing water running to waste! Another tack—basing your system on a capacity figure halfway between the minimum and maximum readings—makes more sense, but it introduces an element of risk; voluntary conservation will be needed during the drier portions of the year. A saner and safer course might be to select a rating closer to the minimum and between one fourth and one third the maximum.

In any event, it is impractical to wait long enough to take readings over a period of a year just to obtain figures and then extrapolate a reasonable design capacity. A better and faster means of obtaining a sound answer is to discover exactly what factors are responsible for the variance in the capacity of any water source. This has a fourfold effect. One, it helps select the best time to take the reading. Two, it indicates what can affect the accuracy of the reading. Three, it permits adjustment of the reading to a figure useful in system design. And four, it indicates what can affect the specific source(s) you use; this assures a quick response to a crisis and implementation of conservation techniques or alternate water sources. It beats waiting until the effect is felt and it's too late. A fish has no exclusive claim to being stranded high and dry.

Capacity Variance Factors

Let's look at the factors that may affect the capacity of each of the potential water sources—river and stream, lake and pond, spring, well, and rainfall.

THE MEASUREMENT

Whatever the technique used for measuring the capacity of a water source (see Capacity Measurement Techniques, Chapter 5), it should be performed with skill. To some extent this means selecting a measurement technique that is appropriate to the source involved. Next, always choose as large a time frame as permissible—anything timed in seconds, or portions thereof, includes a larger degree of possible error than something timed for half a minute or more. Then, no matter what pains you took to do it right, repeat the measurement. An accurate reading is a repeatable one.

USE

A variance in capacity may be attributable to a variance in the *use* of the water. How many times have you heard someone claim that there's less water available during the summer than in the middle of winter? There are other factors that affect this, but one that's frequently forgotten is that there's a greater *need* for water in the summer—for cool showers, the watering of orchards and gardens and such—than in winter. This doesn't constitute a *real* change in capacity, but it sure feels like one.

An influx of new residents in the immediate vicinity will inevitably bring about a greater usage of water, decreasing the supply of some sources. Or there may be very little change; even a new well or spring development nearby will not necessarily tap your own supply. At worst, the water table may drop and a stream dry up; depending on the types of water rights in your area, you may or may not be able to do something about it. More drilled wells in the immediate area will inevitably lower the water table further, and your well could dry up. Unfortunately, subsurface water is not nearly so well protected in a legal sense as streams or rivers may be; the difficulty of proving that any specific well is responsible for the loss of others is obvious.

If you are still in the developing stage, this might be a case against a spring or well development, particularly if there's the potential for a lot of new wells or a few high-consuming wells (as for industry or business) in the vicinity in the years ahead. Naturally, the smaller the parcel of land, the higher the probability of some effect from a neighboring well near the property line; sitting snugly in the middle of even a piddling forty acres is buffer enough against interference in most instances.

EVAPORATION

Water left standing in the open will be sucked up by the air as water vapor. This is called evaporation. The rate at which water evaporates depends on the dryness of the air, the temperature of the ambient air and water, the amount of water exposed (the surface area), and the amount of air movement (wind speed). While it varies with the situation, any kind of pond, lake, or reservoir (a man-made pond or lake) will suffer evaporation losses. So, if this is the source for a water system or the storage for water taken from other sources, evaporation must be taken into account in estimating its capacity.

Water standing in spring boxes, wells, covered tanks, or cisterns (closed reservoirs) also experiences some losses due to evaporation. However, since less air is in contact with the water under these conditions, smaller losses are incurred.

Spring- and stream-fed ponds and reservoirs may show little capacity variance due to evaporation losses; these may be offset by input. On the other hand, ponds or reservoirs that are filled by a seasonal stream—that is, one that runs for only a portion of the year—must hold their own against losses other than normal use, such as evaporation or seepage. In these cases, evaporation becomes a critical factor in water source or water storage capacity.

There's little one can do about evaporation from an existing pond. A new pond, on the other hand, can be designed to minimize losses. Start with the pond's shape: it should be relatively deep in proportion to its surface area. Retaining the volume but halving the surface area will halve the evaporation losses.

A second tactic is to site the pond out of the direct rays of the sun; taking advantage of shade trees or natural shading from hills will help. Know the sun's path through the sky during the summer months. If natural shade is not available, build it! If it's too expensive to shade the reservoir altogether, erect a structure that will shade the water for at least a portion of the day.

Under the worst possible conditions—very dry air, lots of wind, a hot and sunny day—the amount of water lost to evaporation is actually measurable. To see this, find a pond and stick a ruler in the mud. Take a reading in the morning of a high-evaporation day and another that evening. I've measured a ¼-inch loss in one day strictly from evaporation. (This test assumes that no other water is being taken from the pond.) With a big pond, it adds up quickly. For example, with a circular pond 50 feet across, a ¼-inch drop adds up to 306 gallons lost per day! That's 2,140 gallons a week—in one month, a staggering 64,223 gallons sucked up by evaporation. It doesn't take many months to dry up a pond at that rate!

If nothing else, knowing the effect of evaporation should indicate the futility in simply damming up a section of a creek in the merry belief that this is an automatic guarantee of water through the hot summer. And, as the levels sink, you won't be lured into an assumption that it's "seeping away" and throw more money into solving *that* problem. Of course, you could be losing water both ways—to evaporation and seepage—but each inflicts losses that no conservation techniques will dent.

SEASONAL VARIATION

A dry creekbed in the middle of summer may be a raging stream during winter. Measuring the level of water in a well will invariably lead to higher readings in the dead of winter than those taken in the fall. That comes as no surprise to most people; winter may bring cold and misery, but it also brings precipitation. In the form of sleet, rain, hail, or snow, it's still water. And as the water makes its way over and into the land, the water table rises, the creeks begin to flow or flow more profusely, and ponds fill.

Any measurement of capacity must take into account the season in which it's taken. A water system designed around a reading taken at the end of summer is never going to want for water, while a system based on a reading in the spring of the year may find itself in trouble by summer's end.

How much difference will exist between the two readings? Unfortunately, it's too situational to generalize; however, the capacity rating used for system design will probably be something below the average of these two readings.

Fortunately, we don't always have to be exact with these figures. It is helpful to have some numbers for system design, but we must not lose sight of the fact that capacity does vary. Inevitably that means that sometimes there will be too much water and at other times too little water for our needs. A good system can easily handle the rare instances where there's too little source capacity, but it's a versatile system that is able to make use of the instances where there's "extra" water. It's not always cost-effective to take advantage of extra water (increase in capacity) just because it's there; however, a system that permits you to do so is better prepared to handle the unplanned event that is a threat to any water system.

One limitation of end-of-summer capacity measurements is that the source may have just temporarily run out of water. Not only is a measurement impossible (a zero reading requires no measurement), but an otherwise good source of water may be hidden as well. However, don't be put off by a really low reading; besides the fact that it's the reliability of the source that's important, take some consolation in the fact that the reading you've obtained probably represents the lowest it will ever be.

RAINFALL

While winter is normally characterized by an abundance of water and summer by a lack of it, rainfall occurs in varying amounts throughout the year. So rainfall at other than seasonal times is a bonus and its absence a penalty to some water sources. Few water sources will note a measurable difference in capacity from a light rain, even if it's over a period of several days. If the rain is heavy, however brief it may be, the ground may not absorb it rapidly enough and runoff will occur. In this event, even seasonal streams may flow and ponds will fill.

This event should be treated solely as a bonus to a system, and if it's able to capture it, this bonus will permit an extra ration to the garden and a long shower for yourself. However, no system should be designed around such a chance occurrence. Accordingly, whenever a measurement of capacity is taken after any such freak event, the reading must be adjusted accordingly.

Cloudbursts and heavy rainfall runoff may be considered for their water potential, in addition to a system's own reliable water source, if they occur often but aren't predictable enough to depend on. Here the gain must be weighed against the cost of establishing some means of collection, and possibly storage, of the runoff. Since heavy runoff is characterized by turbidity (suspended particles like silt, organic materials, etc.—see "Water Quality," Chapter 3), a secondary storage setup is recommended, even if it's only temporary. This recognizes that while filters to eliminate water turbidity do exist, the best overall means of controlling this condition is to let the water "pool"; once immobilized, the suspended particles simply settle to the bottom of the holding tank.

Springs and wells are unlikely to experience any immediate increase in capacity due to rainfall. If the rainfall is short-lived and comes down hard, there will be no increase, since the water will escape along the surface. A long, slow rainfall will raise the water table, but it will take time for the water to reach it through the earth. Any measurements from either a spring or well that are taken a few days to a few weeks after a long, steady rainfall may affect a capacity measurement; the reading should be adjusted accordingly.

OTHER FACTORS

Other factors will affect either capacity or our measurement of it. For example, even a small earth tremor can alter the water-bearing strata and hence a developed water source. While it's more common for a spring or well to be "lost" to such an event, it is also possible for it actually to *increase* the capacity of a well or spring or, in the extreme, to cause new springs to emerge. Larger earthquakes can also effect these changes, but in addition may damage access to water—for instance, by shearing a drilled well. This is less likely to occur if the well has been "cased" (lined with steel pipe), but even then this threat cannot be eliminated altogether.

Unseasonably dry or wet years will affect capacity, and consequently any system where the designer/builder estimated water availability too high. While it is silly to design a system for the worst possible circumstances, it's also foolish to expect that they can't happen. The earth has experienced uncommonly good weather for the past fifty years, but that cycle is about to end; what we typically refer to as freak weather may, in the years to come, represent the norm. Simple confidence that "riding it out" is all that's required is a common but often fatal attitude to circumstances beyond our own control. On the other hand, rationing what is still available will substantially reduce the hardship of most events anyone is likely to experience.

Leaks in the system can quickly reduce capacity and have the owner shaking his or her head in wonder as to what's happening. If the capacity is suddenly reduced, it's common to forget the possibility that there is a leak somewhere. If it's a real breach in the system, it's usually blatant—a flooded basement, a pond where the garden used to be, a neighbor's complaint about the river flowing down the driveway. Slow leaks, however, are difficult to discover and pinpoint. An annual check of the level in some part of the storage system should be conducted to rout out such leaks. Any outflow with the valves closed for a period of time will be sufficient evidence; then comes the grueling search for the culprit. New construction in the vicinity of pipes is the first suspect. While it's always irritating to break a waterline when trenching, fencepost-holing, etc., that's not nearly so bad as just nicking the thing, *not* getting a gusher to tell you it's happened, and burying the evidence!

Final Comments on Capacity Variance

The intermittent nature of any wildly fluctuating water source motivates people to seek other, more reliable sources. But in the cost/benefit ratio—taking into account such factors as dollars, time, skills, knowledge, reliability, simplicity—don't rule out extensive or occasional use of variable-capacity sources. *No* source is a guaranteed, long-term thing. Fortunately, anything that might affect capacity only influences *some* of the potential water sources at any given site. Therefore a multiple-source water supply is preferable to one seemingly strong source. If nothing else, permit options in the final design and sketch out a few details for connecting up to an alternative source should you need to. A preplanned course of action in an emergency is a whole lot better than merely reacting to the situation.

Specific Uses

We'd all prefer to have grade AA water or better, but with the sources available to us that may not be possible. Water purification beyond some token filtering is costly, complex, and difficult to maintain, and should always be avoided. However, too often a water source that's only slightly tainted is crossed off the list in favor of one that delivers purer water at a significantly higher cost in development, transportation, or complexity.

A large part of the difficulty in this thought stems from a tradition—lumping all of our water uses together as needful of the same *level* of water purity. That is, we demand drinking-water quality in the toilet!

Understandably, we *will* want a high level of purity in water used for drinking, cooking, dishwashing, bathing, and some gardening, but other needs—agricultural, watering stock animals, washing clothes, treating sewage, watering lawns or washing cars, storage in case of fire, and so on, do not require "perfect" water. The two groups overlap and may even be separated into other "shades" of water purity (see "Multiple Use of Water," Chapter 3). Only the ready availability of pure water has prevented more extensive implementation of "gray-water" systems.

Other than the cultural stigma attached to gray-water use, the main objection to multiple uses of water has been the need for duplication of pipe runs and sufficient planning to ensure that the various levels of water do not unwittingly merge. For existing systems requiring retrofits, the objection is valid and duly noted. However, for new systems it's so much baloney—the cost of the extra material and designwork is very competitive with the higher need for water and the energy required to pump it from supply to use. Since pure-water sources are decreasing and the cost of energy is increasing, a system that favors low water use (characteristic of multiple-use systems) also uses less energy. While some will disagree over whether or not a gray-water system is presently cost-comparative, none will disagree that in the long run it is the best system.

Cost

So many of us have taken water for granted so long that when it comes time to shell out some money for a water system, we're shocked at the cost—we might be talking about thousands of dollars! Striving to keep the costs to a minimum is natural, and any system should be cost-effective. However, it's unwise to concentrate too long or heavily on cost right away; otherwise, we end up letting this factor lead us through the myriad of decisions, and down the line we end up paying for it in some other way. Maybe the ultimate cost will be too high in intangibles—dissatisfaction, for example, or time and worry, adjustments in lifestyle, a lack of versatility in the system. Sometimes, though, we're talking about hard cash—repairs, refits, modifications for every little new thing that's added to the system, extraordinary maintenance, the cost of consumable materials such as filters and chemicals, those monthly energy bills. Rarely do our troubles stem from ignorance; too often, we know these things exist. If we had the power really to minimize them as effectively as we're able to convince ourselves of their supposedly minimal effect, we'd have something!

Good design can significantly reduce the impact of the initial cash outlay for a system. For example, an honest appraisal of what's needed right now and what can wait until later gets things going with a reduced cash outflow; planned "add-on" always costs less than modifications that weren't anticipated from the start. Another merit of this approach is that it permits a "weathering" of the system. Changes do occur, so the water system you designed as a result of reading this book may have a different feel once you start living on your land a year from now. And whatever changes are implemented at that point may seem ridiculous, ineffectual, and even uncommonly naïve a year later. People change, situations change, and both affect the system. A wise course of action takes that into account. Design it, build the portion you can afford, and build in sufficient leeway for changes as they're needed or when you will have the money. You get what you pay for. Remember: the bitterness of poor quality is remembered long after the sweetness of low cost is forgotten!

ENERGY SOURCES

Water is, among other things, a mass. In the earth's gravitational field, it has weight. At sea level, it comes to 8.33 pounds per gallon. Draw a gallon from a spigot and lug it up a few flights of stairs, and thereafter you won't think of a gallon of water as an insignificant weight.

As with anything that has weight, if we want to move water from one place to another we must use energy to do it. Lugging water about in buckets wouldn't tickle anyone's fancy; the human race is basically lazy. However, we're also equipped with a brain that allows us, in lethargic repose, to undertake a study of the matter and develop alternative schemes.

Terms

Any discussion of energy sources is marred if the terminology is vague or muddled. For example, I like to ask people the source of their electricity. I get a variety of answers. One might be "wind power." Another answer is "a standby generator." A common one is "the local utility company."

What's wrong with these answers? The first one —wind power—describes a genuine energy *source*, also referred to as a "prime mover." Gravity, moving water, human and animal power, wood and fossil fuels (oil, diesel, gasoline, propane, methane, and coal) are other true energy sources.

The second answer—a standby generator—really describes an energy conversion *device;* its job is to transform energy from one form to another, hopefully more useful, form. A standby generator is a twin conversion device; its engine converts chemi-

cal energy (gasoline) into mechanical energy (rotary motion) which, in turn, spins the generator to produce electrical energy. Motors, turbines, and various mechanical devices are other conversion devices. Buckets, transmission wires, and mechanical linkages are used in conjunction with conversion devices, but it would be incorrect to label them as such; they only aid in the *transfer* of energy.

The third answer—the local utility company—is descriptive of an energy *service* that specializes in converting the energy from a number of sources (principally fossil fuels) into one universal energy form—electricity. Or, more specifically, 110- or 220-volt, 60-cycle A.C. By this definition, a local gas station or hardware store might also be considered an energy service if you can purchase gasoline, kerosene, diesel and propane fuel from them.

The distinctions between prime movers, conversion and transfer devices, and services are useful if you are concerned about efficiency. *Energy is lost every time it is either converted or transferred.* There's no avoiding this, but it's nice to keep it to a minimum; fortunately, this problem was discovered a long time ago, and the current state of the art has gotten very good at cutting the losses down to tolerable levels. However, conversion and transfer losses are *cumulative;* and it's not simple addition—they multiply. Therefore, as the conversions and transfers increase between the energy source and the energy application, the losses quickly acquire exorbitant proportions. Good design minimizes the number of conversions and transfers and reduces the cumulative effect by employing an energy source that is only a few steps away from a useful form.

Individual water systems have individual energy needs. Very few are lucky enough to require "no" energy, and some are *unlucky* enough to require energy at every step—extraction, transport, pressurization, and storage. Water that required one or more of these steps to be converted from standing water into useful form for household or farm use is said to be *processed.* That subject is fully discussed in the next chapter, but right now, let's look at the variety of energy sources—the prime movers—that may be set to work processing water.

Gravity

Set a bucket of water upright on the floor and nothing happens; the water will stay in there until it evaporates or starts growing all sorts of things. However, empty the bucket out the window, and its contents will fall until they strike the ground.

So, gravity is first on the list. Whenever and wherever water is high enough to let gravity do all the work, let it! Sometimes even when it isn't high enough, it pays to go out of your way to give it this potential for the benefits it yields over the energy expended in the effort. More on this later.

Human Muscle Power

Water may be processed by human power. This takes two forms. One is through use of the bucket, where a person scoops up the water and walks from the water source to the point of usage. At the rate most families use water today, that's pretty labor-intensive. However, the idea has some merit, and should not be rejected outright. The initial investment is small (one bucket) and the exercise alone should keep anyone fit.

Human power can also transport water through the use of a pump. The hand-operated pump standard (see photo) has been around for a long time, and it's guaranteed to give you strong arm muscles along with the water. A variation on the theme is a pedal-powered water pump. Legs are more powerful than arms, and through suitable linkage, the leg muscles may be put to work pumping water. Admittedly, for all that pedaling the scenery doesn't change much, but at 100 gallons to the "mile," who's complaining?

Animal Power

Prior to the use of fossil fuels, physical labor beyond the capacity of the ordinary man or woman was done by beasts of burden such as horses, oxen, or goats. This is still a good possibility for pumping water wherever any of these animals have been reintroduced to the farm or homestead. However, considering the amount of feed these critters can consume, centering any water system totally around animal power is a doubtful possibility.

Fossil Fuels

Another popular energy source for processing water is fossil fuels. Initially only oil was available, and its use was limited to centralized facilities

Fig. 1–8 Hand pumping is strenuous but rewarding.

where oil-burning turbines drove generators, producing electricity that was in turn transported over wires to the usage site. Once there, the electricity could power electric motors that would supply the needed mechanical motion to operate pumps of various types. Fossil fuels in the guise of utility-supplied electricity are probably the number-one source of energy for water systems in the U.S.A. today.

High-density fuels—propane, diesel, kerosene, and gasoline—derived from fossil fuels may also be purchased for engines powering on-site water-processing equipment. However, the cost and noise factors usually limit this usage to backup systems for use only during emergencies when the primary system isn't functioning.

Waterpower

Moving water is also an energy source, whether it's a river or a waterfall; either way, this energy may

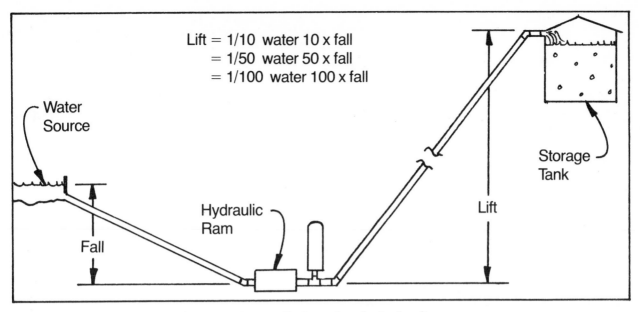

Lift = 1/10 water 10 x fall
    = 1/50 water 50 x fall
    = 1/100 water 100 x fall

Water Source

Fall

Hydraulic Ram

Lift

Storage Tank

Fig. 1–9   An installation using the hydraulic ram.

be captured by a variety of novel mechanical or electrical devices that will, in turn, pump a portion of this water (or water from another water source) to places far away or higher up—anywhere the water would not flow of its own accord. The simplest device available is the hydraulic ram (see Fig. 1–9), which uses the energy of water to pump a small portion of the water to a higher point; theoretically it would pump $\frac{1}{10}$ of the water 10 times as high as the waterfall, $\frac{1}{100}$ of the water 100 times as high, and so on, although pump inefficiencies reduce this amount somewhat. If a landowner has access to a river but either has no legal right to use any of its water or chooses not to, the dual-acting hydraulic ram (see photo) is useful, since this will use the energy of the river's water to pump water from another source such as a spring or well to the appropriate place.

Waterwheels and turbines will also pump water directly. More often, however, they are connected to other devices that supply mechanical or, in the case of generators, electrical energy.

Natural Gas

The decomposition of organic materials under certain environmental conditions produces natural gas. At the utility company level, this gas is often processed to produce propane, which has a higher energy yield per cubic foot than natural gas and is easier to liquefy. Back on the farm, however, natural gas may be produced from animal or agricultural waste in a digester. Methane is the desired

Fig. 1–10   A homemade hydraulic ram.

end product, but it is produced in company with other gases and substances; in this mix, it's called bio-gas.

Detectable amounts of bio-gas may be produced from a remarkably small amount of organic material, but for application in a water system, sufficient bio-gas must be produced to power a small internal-combustion engine. This in turn can directly operate a water-pumping mechanism or produce the electricity to power a motor that will move a pump. This requires an enormous amount of animal or agricultural waste. Nevertheless, where the right conditions exist, and in view of the increased cost and decreased availability of fossil fuels, the production of bio-gas is a viable alternative to on-site energy sources for small, engine-driven water-pumping functions.

Wind Power

Another major source of energy for water processing systems is the wind. Here, one of several types of wind machines extracts the wind's energy and converts it into the mechanical motion needed to work a water pump (see Fig. 1–11). If there's a problem with this setup, another type of wind machine can be used to produce electricity to power a motor connected to a water pump.

As far back in recorded history as you'd care to go, wind has been harnessed to pump water. In some areas the wind is constant enough and hard enough to guarantee water processing around the clock. However, in most areas it is not; for this reason, any system that uses the wind's energy for water extraction and transport must be equipped with sufficient storage to satisfy demand during periods of low or no wind.

In the early 1900s there was a definite need for water pumping in very remote areas for livestock and agriculture. To meet this need, private companies developed wind machines that were simple, rugged, and virtually maintenance-free. Even the later introduction of electrically powered motors and oil, kerosene, or gasoline engines could not stem this industry—after the initial investment, there was no further operational cost with a wind machine. Closer to the farmhouse, these wind machines did yield to the high-capacity electrical pumps, but the mere presence of the old towers and wind machines today is proof enough that the farmer or rancher wasn't inclined to let them go altogether. Even in disuse, these reliable machines are hard to part with.

Fig. 1–11 The windsail is ideally suited to water pumping.

Fig. 1–12 This small, water-pumping wind machine seemed to have no trouble keeping the big cattle tank full.

Fig. 1–13 Bigger wind machines are needed for low-wind areas or larger water needs.

Fig. 1–14 Long neglected, this 10-foot water-pumping wind machine awaits restoration and raising.

SELECTING THE ENERGY SOURCE

Selecting the energy source for a water system is an interesting process; however, unless compelled to do otherwise, most people make this decision without much thought. The common attitude is, "It's done this way. It's the only way I know how to do it. I don't want to hassle with it." Nevertheless, we all have very definite expectations of the chosen source—reliability, availability, low cost, simplicity, ease of installation. These factors do not occur by themselves, so it's a whole lot easier to struggle with them now on paper than later, after the system is installed and the undesirable qualities are built in.

For your own water system, each potential energy source—gravity, muscle power (human or animal), fossil fuels, natural gas, water, or wind—should be evaluated in terms of energy needs, reliability, availability, access, independence, complexity, and cost (initial and ongoing). If you have no prejudice in the matter, this becomes a straightforward process of elimination, followed by a simple choice if more than one source emerges unscathed. If you do have preferences (most of us do), this process may help you select a secondary, or backup, energy source. Is that necessary? Judge for yourself.

Energy Needs

A prime factor in selecting an energy source is its ability to handle our system's *needs* in processing water. Irrespective of how much that amounts to, you want to keep this to a minimum. A system's need for energy is ongoing, and since energy in any form costs something, both dollars and "sense" dictate using as little as possible.

Now is as good a time as any to introduce the concept of TANSTAAFL. That's short for "There ain't no such thing as a free lunch." Don't expect something for nothing. No energy source is free. What about gravity? True, gravity is everywhere; however, if the water source on the property is too low relative to the usage site, you can't put gravity to work unless you first expend some other form of energy to lift the water high enough for gravity to take over.

If your site doesn't permit you to take direct advantage of gravitational energy, one fact emerges: you have a lot more energy sources to choose from if you can keep the system's energy requirements very low. Water-pumping wind machines, for example, will suffice even in areas of very low wind because they're designed to operate at low wind speeds. This advantage is lost in energy-intensive systems, as would be the case with muscle power, methane, and small-scale waterpower developments. All too quickly, energy sources available on-site are lost in the "big-energy" shuffle.

Reliability

If you move to a rural area and have to develop your own water system, you must deal with many things (this book is a testament to that). However, there comes a time when you will want to squirrel away your drawings, fill in those trenches, and go on with life—in short, *to be done with it*. You will want your system to work reliably ever after.

Reliability is, first and foremost, not having to worry about the system. Open a faucet and you should get water. If the storage tank is low, either it is filled automatically or, through a monitor, you are informed when refilling is needed. Reliability is also continuance. Everything wears out sooner or later, but frequent breakdowns are a symptom of a problem. However minor the defect may be, the effect accumulates until you can't trust the system, and you begin to have visions of its breaking down at a critical time.

Reliability doesn't just happen; if this factor isn't built into the system in its design and equipment, it's doubtful that it will be exhibited during operation. How do you design for reliability? That's easy —follow the *kiss* principle: Keep It Simple, Silly! A system is no better than its smallest or weakest part; if you skimp on *any* aspect of the system, it's going to get you!

Reliability is increased as the number of energy conversions and transfers involved between the prime mover (the energy source) and the application decreases. For instance, a water-pumping wind machine converts the wind's energy to mechanical energy (rotary motion) and then into a reciprocating action (up and down motion) which, via a long rod, works the water pump. This amounts to *one* energy conversion and *two* simple energy transfers.

If the water system is based on a submersible pump powered with utility-supplied electricity, how many steps are involved? Since most of this electricity comes from oil- or coal-burning power plants, the coal or oil must be found, extracted, processed, transported to the power plant, and burned. The resultant heat produces steam, which drives turbines coupled to electrical generators. The manufactured electricity travels through power lines to your land, where it drives an electric motor which in turn operates a pump. That's *six* energy conversions and *four* energy transfers.

Now, I ask you—which system is more reliable?

Availability

Availability has a time frame; what has been available in the past and is now may not be available in the future. Many people don't like to think about that—it smacks of doomsday—but there's no avoiding it. The world is running out of oil, natural gas, and coal; the experts may not agree on when our supplies of these natural resources will be exhausted, but it *will* happen. This is the time of plenty, and chances are pretty good that it won't happen in our lifetime. However, long before the fuels run out, the ripples of the shortage will make themselves felt. Will it affect your water system? That's not a question that I'm asking you; it's one that you might want to ask yourself.

Independence

An offshoot of availability is a personal decision involving independence; however gregarious we are, most of us would like to gain control of our individual lives to the extent that that is both possible and healthful. The convenience of utility-supplied electricity, then, might be shunned for the independence to be gained by using available on-site energy sources to which no meters are attached.

This is a common fantasy. Independence is not negotiable; you can't buy it. A system you don't understand and can't fix only transfers the responsibility for fixing anything that goes amiss. Independence comes when *you* take on the responsibility for the system—its maintenance, correct operation, and at least minor repairs. If you won't or can't take this responsibility, save yourself a lot of misery and let someone else do it. When it comes right down to it, you might as well stick with the local utility company; they *are* professional people, and service-related trouble on their side of the meter is free of charge.

Complexity

The connection between reliability and complexity has already been established; certainly the fewer the component parts, the less there is to go wrong. However, it's also true that complex systems are easier to operate than simple ones. Why? Essentially, automation takes the burden of decision-making away from the human user; given the sheer number of factors at work, to choose the correct response for any given set of circumstances requires an extensive monitoring and control setup.

There's nothing inherently evil about complexity; any increase in vulnerability arising from the number of parts is easily offset if the owner/operator understands how it's all supposed to work. Supposedly, then, it's easy to troubleshoot and isolate malfunctioning components. However, this makes the individual an *integral* part of the system. The alternative is to set up a simple system and retain the decision-making aspect yourself.

Cost

It's sometimes difficult to separate the energy costs from the system costs. For example, the use of some variable, intermittent, or low-yield energy source demands a provision for water storage (tank, cisterns, etc.). However, there are other reasons that might prompt an individual to use a storage system or to install a much larger size than what's required for simple utilization of the energy source itself.

Without getting into actual dollars and cents, we can establish a few associations. One concerns the initial cost versus the ongoing cost. Utilizing available on-site energy sources—that is, wind energy and water energy—seems at first prohibitively expensive: all the money is up front. By comparison, a utility-powered submersible setup comes with a lower initial price tag. However, there's a string attached: it all runs on specialized energy that must be purchased in monthly installments. The "string" is suddenly an umbilical cord. Given the high tax write-off percentages (up to 60 percent in some states) for solar, wind, water, and other so-called "alternative energy"-based systems, one doesn't have to look more than a few years down the line to see the payoff in dollars saved.

It was an enlightening experience to start up my water-pumping wind machine and be told that the *last* time the company made a major change in the design was 1933! What does this have to do with cost? Quite a bit, actually. If you're to spend hard-earned dollars on equipment, it's nice to get built-in quality, ruggedness, and craftsmanship (even several generations ago, the workmanship was superb). Manufacturing dollars spent on equipment of an older design go into materials, whereas with newer equipment the manufacturer must pay off tooling, designwork, and advertising to inform the public that the product exists.

Multiple Energy Sources

Just as it's good to have more than one water source, it's good to have more than one energy source.

Any energy source or service can suffer a temporary interruption; how well the system will fare during this period is a matter of design and luck. Minimizing the "luck" part is, of course, desirable; systems that apply all of their energy to processing water in such a way that it may thereafter assume energy-free (gravity) flow and pressurization (see "Gravity Flow" and "Gravity Pressurization," Chapter 2) are prepared for such eventualities. However, some owners may find the price tag for this brand of security a little steep.

An alternative is the system that utilizes two or more energy sources; while either may be interrupted at any time, the probability that they would be simultaneously is mighty low. Add a third energy source and you can bet your nest egg that you'll have at least one of the three sources operational at any given moment.

Now, contemplating the use of *two* energy sources when you haven't even picked *one* may seem a bit much at this point. No problem. Pick one, design the system around it, and install it. Use it that way for a while. Keep thinking about that alternative, though; which is the right one may not really become clear until later anyway.

The only important thing you should do before installing a water system when you think a system with two (or more) energy sources might be a good idea is to leave that option open. For example, it's always nice to avoid duplicating any more of the equipment than is necessary; knowing beforehand what additional source might be used will help you select equipment that may also accommodate the other energy source when (or if) it's added (see "The Gold System," Chapter 6). This is not always possible; some energy sources use mutually exclusive equipment. Nevertheless, the systems can be tied together (see "The Silver System," Chapter 6), and forethought will at least identify where the systems can be joined. Then even if the "mate-up" plumbing is not installed initially, you can keep this area of pipe accessible and otherwise unencumbered for it later.

If two energy sources are intended, why not select one that's free, provided you have the equipment to harness it? I can *understand* a system that has a gasoline-fueled standby generator backing up a utility electricity-powered submersible pump, but I can *appreciate* a submersible setup with a wind energy backup. A focus here is the word "backup." If the wind machine doesn't supply a major portion of the system's energy needs during the year, at least it didn't cost anything, other than the initial expense of building it. The same cannot be said for the standby generator. Besides, why rule out the possibility of a pleasant surprise? Wind machines do pay their own way, and if it produces more than 50 percent of the energy needed, you can then say that the utility-supplied energy is the "backup" for your water system!

Of course it's even nicer when you have a free energy source backing up another free source—for example, a hand pump backing up a wind pump. This is a noble thought but, alas, it's seldom practical. The situation where *one* freebie is available in generous amounts is rare; the fantasy of finding *two* free energy sources in stiff competition for the primary spot borders on delirium!

Sample hybrid systems—ones using multiple energy sources—are illustrated and discussed in Chapter 6.

2

WATER PROCESSING

The water source and the site where the water is used are frequently separated by some distance; however, even if they weren't, having water at the usage site does not automatically guarantee water flow from faucets, spray from showers, or a full toilet bowl. If we want this capability, then the water must be "processed" into useful form.

Processing water involves as many as four functions: extraction, transport, storage, and pressurization (see Fig. 2–1). Normally they're lumped together; the standard utility-powered water system based around the submersible pump performs them simultaneously. This *is* convenient. However it's also wasteful and inappropriate. Each function is distinct. Consequently, a better system would be one that acknowledges the differences in functions and accommodates their needs individually.

WATER TRANSPORT

Water transport evolved when individuals found that it really wasn't all that convenient to plunk oneself down in a stream somewhere and let water come to you. Oh, it had its advantages—fresh running water without plumbing, a convenient waste-

disposal system, and no water bills to pay. But there were inconveniences too. There was no way to shut it off. Also, there was no way to vary the flow—if there wasn't enough, that was too bad. And what about those neighbors who'd moved in upstream? Or a flash flood?

For transporting water from the stream, someone invented the bucket; for small water needs and short distances, it was great. Farther away from the stream, it helped to have subservient women, strong kids, and a slave or two.

In a last-ditch effort to fight the labor-intensive water traffic each day, someone channeled his energy into some thoughtful observance of the stream and stream bed itself and duplicated it, diverting some of the water to the campsite. Some less observant copycats also dug ditches, but couldn't get the water to flow. Why not? Was there magic involved? No—they just didn't understand some basic principles.

Water has mass and weight; moving it, then, requires energy. If it's moved by means of buckets, we're talking about the energy of patient people. In the channel, however, the energy of gravity is harnessed for transport.

Gravity works in one direction: down. To use it

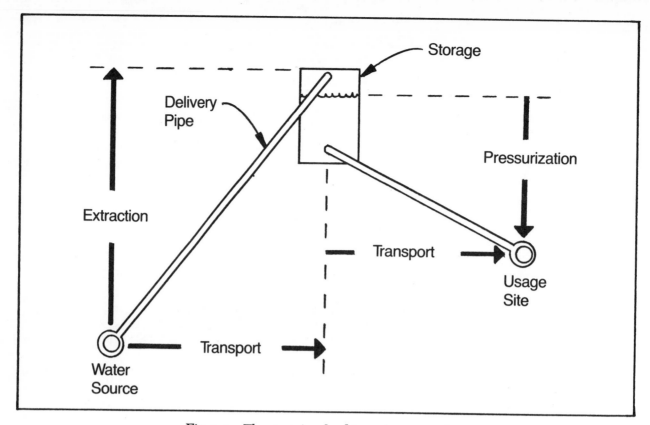

Fig. 2–1   The steps involved in water processing.

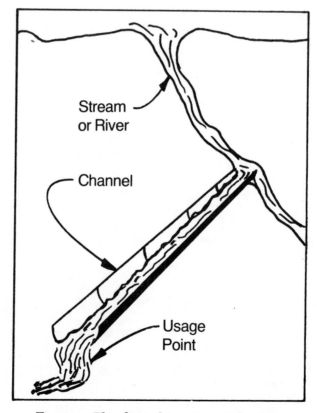

Fig. 2–2   The channel is a man-made river.

for transporting water, then, we must slant the ditch, channel, canal, or aqueduct downward—away from the water source and toward the usage site. Since water is slippery stuff, the angle of this tilt does not need to be very great; we'd easily get flow with a drop of only one foot for each 100 feet of run (horizontal distance). This is called a 1 percent grade. For higher flow rates, the tilt can be increased.

Since the water transported by this method arrives downhill from the point of origin, we must locate the upper end of the channel at a point higher than the elevation of the usage site, right? How much higher depends on the total distance the water must be transported and how high a flow rate we want. If the distances are great but there's no hope of intercepting the water source at a point much higher than the usage site, the slant must be slight and a high flow rate sacrificed; getting a small amount of water to the usage site, after all, is more important than getting a higher flow rate to some point *below* the usage site.

Initially, channels were dug directly into the soil. A problem appeared: the soil absorbed some of the water. This was handled by increasing the slope angle to accommodate a higher flow, minimizing the effect of the loss. Wherever the soil had clay in it, there was less seepage. So if there was clay available, it was used to line the channel. Later, concrete, plastic, or wood lined the channel to prevent water loss enroute.

A great deal of effort is expended to make channels smooth. This acknowledges another aspect of inertia: things in motion tend to stay in motion unless acted upon by other forces. These "other forces" are illustrated in the standard stream bed—rocks, weeds, and the irregularity of the stream bed itself. All of these resist the flow of water, and in channels such obstacles work against high flow rates.

Channels built across hilly terrain are rarely straight; instead, they weave through the countryside. Close inspection shows that they follow the land contour. There are two reasons for this. One, it's an economizing technique, providing the least loss of elevation for the horizontal distance covered. Two, it keeps the flow rate of the water from reaching uncontrollable levels. Consider, for a moment, the way roads are built over high mountain passes. Ever see one that goes straight up and comes straight down the other side? Of course not. If they built them that way, a car or truck would need a new set of brakes after each trip; that as-

sumes, of course, that the vehicle would have sufficiently low gears to climb *up* the steep grades!

Water is not fitted with brakes; let it build up any significant speed and at the usage site you'll have something between a water slide and a waterfall. Merely shutting it off won't help; it will splash over the side of the channel, and your yard will be awash with the spilled water. In some instances, if the horizontal distance between the water source and usage sites is very short while the difference in elevation is large, the use of a channel may require some section that has the effect of a waterfall to help bleed off the effect of gravity. In this instance, you might actually use a rock-filled, rough-contoured channel in the steep section to *increase* the resistive effect on the water in order to slow it down.

If a channel is used to transport water, a transit or other surveying tool will be needed to lay it out; without such a tool there's just no way to plot your channel to keep a uniform flow. For example, if you want a 2 percent grade—2 feet of fall in 100 feet of run—you must assure an even gradation or the finished channel will only be able to support an appreciably smaller flow than it should. So with 24 inches of drop over 100 feet of length, we'd need a drop of 2.4 inches for *each* 10-foot section; that's 2.4 inches after 10 feet, 4.8 inches after 20 feet, etc. Not exactly something that can be "eyeballed," is it? Whatever the technique employed, it must be accurate or the results will be disappointing.

Open channels are beset by a major problem—flotsam. The deep-running or swiftly moving water conveys everything that can be carried away: rocks of all sizes, grit, sediment, careless children, toads that leap before they look, and other unmentionables. Inserting screens helps somewhat, but this only sugarcoats the problem, since you still must clean the screen. This age-old problem does have an age-old solution: cover the channel (this is the forerunner of pipe). Immediately the overall sanitation and debris problem is lessened.

The use of a channel for water transport is limited by some of its own characteristics, but there's one limitation it can't surmount: if the usage site is level with or higher than the water source and any distance separates the two, the channel can get the water close but not *to* the usage site. Also, the slope must not be too steep between the usage and source sites if the water is to arrive at anything other than breathtaking velocity.

It's primarily for this reason that channels have been replaced by pipe. However, for all the advan-

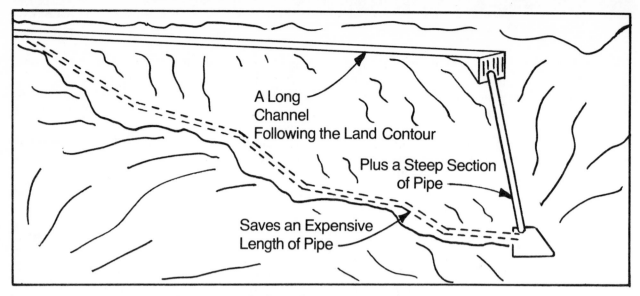

A Long Channel Following the Land Contour

Plus a Steep Section of Pipe

Saves an Expensive Length of Pipe

Fig. 2–3 Both channel and pipe can be used in an installation.

tages of pipe over channel as a means of water conveyance, it would be an error to consider the channel as nothing more than a waterlogged relic of yesteryear. In view of the expected rise in price of all kinds of pipe in the years to come, it may be more cost-effective to use channel for a portion of any long distance separating the water source and the usage site and then use pipe to handle the last part. Such "hybrid" water transport usually offers the advantages of both the channel and pipe, while at the same time effectively canceling out the limitations associated with either.

Pipe is portable channel. Whereas the use of channel involves working the site to meet the necessary requirements, pipe is made in factories in an easily-assembled form. Pipe comes in a variety of sizes (to handle varying flow rates), standard lengths (to keep it manageable) and materials; pipe made from copper, steel, or plastic is readily available. All types of pipe can be cut to any desired length or, through the use of couplers, extended to any dimension over the length of one standard section; depending on the type of pipe used, the sections are joined by screwing, gluing, or soldering. Pipe and its characteristics are discussed fully in Chapter 4.

All in all, pipe can do everything that channel can do and then some. For example, pipe can easily transport water down sharp inclines. Moreover, by attaching the appropriate fitting—a valve—the water flow may be stopped. If that's attempted at the lower end of a channel, the water will overflow.

The real uniqueness of pipe as opposed to channel is that its use is essential to the delivery of water to a usage site that is *above* the water source. But that's covered under "Water Extraction" later in this chapter. First let's examine water pressurizing, an odd effect that is not exhibited by the channel but that occurs when we transport water downhill via the pipe.

Energy and Transport

Transporting water horizontally does not require much energy. Even in a gravitational system, less than one degree of slope will permit water movement in a channel or pipe without further assistance. In fact, even in a perfectly horizontal pipe or channel, water will flow until it's all at the same level in the pipe. So there's demonstrably not much resistance on the part of water to flow, or once flowing, to keep flowing. If any energy is consumed in transporting water horizontally, it is only to overcome the resistance of the channel or pipe itself.

WATER PRESSURIZING

Water pressure is essential. If you have it, water gushes out of faucets. If the pressure is weak, the water trickles, and if it's gone, no water flows.

As soon as we started using pipe for transporting water and screwed a valve onto the end, we could stop water flow. Once the valve was shut, the pipe would fill with water. Opening it would always

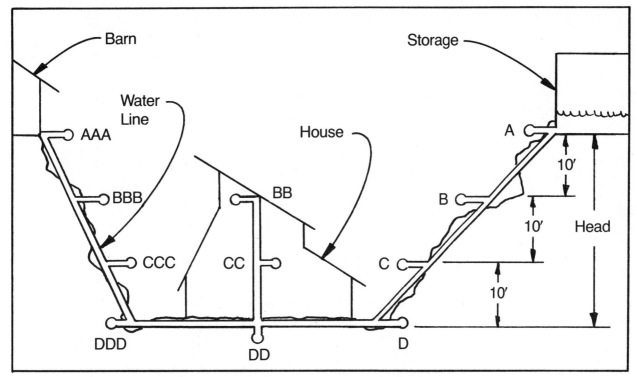

Fig. 2–4 An understanding of water flow and pressure is essential to system design.

produce a gush of water. After some initial flow, there was a more stable and less forceful flow.

This was our first taste of water pressure. Water was not available in such a forceful state from the channel, but once it was enclosed in the pipe, something happened—and continued happening as long as the water that was taken out of the pipe did not exceed the amount of water coming into the pipe from the water source.

To help describe water pressure, let's look at a typical situation where gravity provides the force. Let's say that we connect a pipe between a water source located high on a hill and a modest, two-story house in the valley. Then we run another pipe between the house and a barn that is up a hill on the other side of the house (see Fig. 2–4). Next, let's locate a number of valves—faucets, if you will —along the pipe. Finally, let's install a pressure gauge (see photo). This is a device that connects a pressure-sensitive diaphragm to a needle free to move across a scale; the higher the pressure, the greater the deflection. The pressure gauge is equipped with a fitting that can be screwed onto a faucet at any location so that we may read the pressure at that point.

Now, what might we observe about this arrangement?

Fig. 2–5 A pressure gauge.

1. When faucet AAA is turned on, water fills the entire pipe grid. Let's say that AAA is at precisely the same level as the water source, as verified by an accurate altimeter or surveying instrument. Note that the water level at point A and point AAA would be the same. This verifies the adage, "Water seeks its own level."

2. When the pressure gauge is attached first at point A, then at points B, C, and D, correspondingly higher pressures are noted. Does pressure vary with the length of pipe? It would seem so until we take readings at the other faucets in the system. Then we will discover that the pressure readings at points B, points BB, and BBB are identical. And that the pressure readings at points C, CC, and CCC, while higher than the readings at points B, BB, and BBB, are also identical.

This is pretty strong evidence that pressure is *not* related to the length of pipe or to the angle of the pipe. Instead, pressure is directly related to the *vertical distance* between the level of water and the point of measurement. (Read that over; it's important.) This is the *depth* of the water; in water systems, this distance is called the "head," and it's measured in feet.

3. Pressure is linear. That is, if we compared the readings on the pressure gauge, we'd note that the reading at point C is twice the value of that taken at point B; since point C has twice the head, it has twice the pressure. The same holds true for point D, which has three times the head of point B and three times the pressure reading.

4. Water is virtually incompressible. That means that while you can pressurize it, you can't reduce its volume (water is very different from air in this respect).

If this is true, an odd conclusion can be drawn. The pipe connecting the water source with the house (between points A and D) is longer than the pipe connecting the house to the barn (between points DDD and AAA). So, if the pipes are the same diameter inside and water is truly incompressible, there must be more water in the pipe between points A and D than in the pipe between points DDD and AAA. This would be confirmed if the water were actually drained out of the pipes and measured; and yet, the pressure reading at points D and DDD are identical.

The conclusion? Pressure is not related to an *amount* of water—the number of gallons—but, again, only to the *depth* of water in any combination of vessels and pipes (see Fig. 2–6).

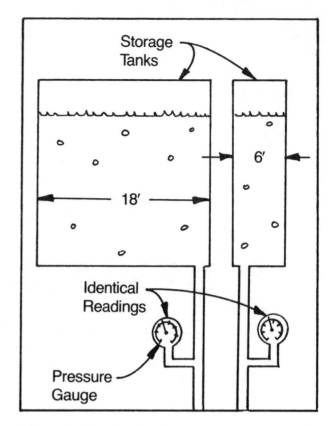

Fig. 2–6 The depth of water, not its weight, determines pressure.

5. Since pressure is a force and force can be measured, we can measure pressure. First let's establish the units we'd use. A common one is pounds per square inch; to save breath and writing, that's psi. Metric fans will describe pressure in terms of kilograms per square centimeter or square meter: ksc or ksm. Take your pick.

A really accurate instrument will measure the water pressure at a depth of one foot at .433 psi. At two feet, that's .866 psi. We'd get 1 psi at a depth of 2.4 feet. A depth of 10 feet would measure 4.33 psi and thirty feet of depth would be roughly 13 psi.

A check of the figure of .433 psi per foot of depth can be verified by converting the weight of one cubic foot of water (62.4 pounds) to that weight per square inch at its bottom. Since there are 144 square inches in a square foot, dividing 62.4 pounds of water by 144 square inches yields .433 pounds per square inch.

6. Looking at the drawing, note that, just as pressure increases when the depth of water in-

creases, it decreases as the depth of water decreases. So, if we want a gush capability at any specific faucet, there's a limit to how high the faucet can be located and still retain some of the pressure that's available at the lowest point.

So far everything we've done with this setup has involved only pressure readings in a static state, with no water flow. What happens if we look at it in a dynamic state—with the water flowing? Well, let's try it. Open the faucet at point B; out comes the water in a steady flow. As we might suspect, it's a heavier flow at point C than at point B, and the largest flow occurs at point D.

But suppose we leave the pressure gauge on the faucet as we open it and let water come out. At point B, it's unlikely that we'll notice anything significant—the reading just flickers when we open the faucet. At point C, we see a discernible decrease in the pressure reading. Not large, but definite. At point D the decrease is even greater. How about point CC? Point CCC? Each time the faucet is turned on at a greater distance from the water source, the pressure reading decreases further.

This jump isn't an all-at-once drop from the no-flow pressure reading. There is a flicker as we slowly open the valve, but the actual drop occurs as we open the valve more and more. If you took the time to open each value in even increments—say, a quarter of a turn at a time—you'd notice that the drop in the reading occurs at the greatest rate in the last few quarter turns before the valve was fully open.

What's happened? One answer is that the pressure is "reduced," but that's an inaccurate appraisal of the situation. After all, as far as we can tell, the force of gravity hasn't lessened. Nor has the water level dropped. And since the faucet is still in the same place relative to the level of water, the pressure can't have changed. However, since the pressure reading has decreased, we *can* say that we have "lost" some pressure. Where did it go?

Water flowing in a pipe is impeded by the close surroundings. Even if the inside of the pipe is very smooth and uniform in shape, the portion of water directly in contact with the wall is fractionally slowed down by the slightest irregularity. As a result, water that flows by the slower-moving water is also slowed. Obviously, the water at the very center of the pipe is flowing the fastest. So we have layers of water flowing over other, slower-moving layers. That creates friction, and friction makes heat (most of which goes toward warming up the

water a slight amount), and since friction resists the force of pressure, it decreases the pressure force.

Well, that's the theory anyway. And the theory is easy to prove. Suppose we had used larger pipe. The effect on our gauges would be very noticeable; even point BBB would show a drastic reduction in pressure when a valve was opened all the way.

This is a good point at which to make some other observations. To do it, we need a bucket. Place the bucket under the faucet at point BBB. And, for a moment, let's put the smaller pipe back in. Open the valve all the way and time the filling of the bucket. Write it down. Now put the larger pipe back in and repeat the test. Note the time. Now compare the two readings. It took less time to fill the bucket with the larger pipe, didn't it?

Walk down to point CCC and again fill the bucket with water and time it, first for the smaller pipe and then for the larger pipe. Same thing happens, doesn't it? With the larger pipe, the bucket fills faster. Also compare the fill time for the larger pipe at point BBB and the one taken for it at point CCC. The time at point CCC is shorter, isn't it?

What have we learned?

1. If the pipe size is increased, not so much pressure is lost as when smaller pipe is used; this is verified by the readings at points BBB and CCC.

2. If the pressure is greater at a faucet, water flow is increased. Since it took less time to fill the bucket at CCC than it did at BBB, the higher flow rate occurs, for large *or* small pipe, with higher pressure.

3. The higher the flow rate, the greater the pressure loss. Readings taken with every quarter turn of the handle on a faucet show the fastest decline in pressure in the last few quarter turns before the valve is fully open. This occurs with both large and small pipe. If you measured enough combinations of pressure, pressure drop, and pipe size, you'd find that an interesting relationship emerges. *Pipe resistance to water flow increases as the square of the flow rate.* In other words, double the flow rate through any size of pipe of any length and the resistance to that flow will be increased four times. A fourfold increase in flow yields a sixteenfold increase in pipe resistance!

Does it matter? Do we *need* water pressure? Yes —all this talk about pressure is not abstract. With pressure, we have flow at varying rates. Without it, sprinklers and nozzles won't work. Some washing machines won't operate satisfactorily if there's little or insufficient pressure.

But how much pressure are we talking about? Ask a dozen people that question and you're likely to get a dozen different answers. However, they'd range between 25 and 60 psi. Can we narrow it down? Yes—the standard is 30 to 35 psi.

Before you accept that as *your* standard, I'd like to invite you to visit my farm. We have a gravity pressure system; our water flows from a storage tank located up a hill some 200 feet away from the house. The bottom of the tank is approximately ten feet above the elevation of the top of our house. That puts the head at 30 feet and the pressure at a piddling 13 psi. The majority of visitors wonder how we "make do" with so little pressure. I like to invite them to turn on one of our outside faucets. When that water starts blasting out of there, churning up the dirt and leaves, their eyes go wide! Some are amazed, and others are downright suspicious; usually I have to take them up the hill and show them that, indeed, there's no pressurizing pump—it's strictly gravity flow. How do I do it?

In a culture where electricity is (momentarily) cheap and pipe is expensive, small pipes are generally used in water systems; at high flow rates, this results in horrible pressure losses. To compensate, high-pressure pumps are used. The trouble starts when people naïvely install the same *size* of plumbing in their low-pressure system; with such high-pressure losses, there's no performance. *Only by installing larger pipes can high flow rates and satisfactory pressure be sustained.*

Pressurizing Pumps

We'd need only a foot of head to get water transport on level ground, but even if people could install larger pipe and accept our own 13 psi as a satisfactory amount, 30 feet of head would be required to get the same water pressure. In this light, the setup we have on our land is ideal. But how many people have a piece of land where the water source (or storage tank) is located high enough above the usage site to permit both gravity flow and gravity pressurization? A far more representative situation is where the usage site and the water source are at the same level, or something in between these two situations. At best, the water might transport itself (with the slightest head), but there wouldn't be sufficient head to pressurize the water. At worst, there'd be no gravity potential whatsoever, and we'd need another energy source to both transport and pressurize the water.

Fig. 2–7 Large pipe assures adequate flow even at 13 psi.

Irrespective of the energy source, the hardware that accomplishes both water transport and pressurization in lieu of gravity is the force pump. It's also called a pressure pump, water pump, or lift pump. By whatever name, it exerts a force that will push water along through a pipe. As previously indicated, this is no chore; transporting water is neither difficult nor energy-intensive since it moves water perpendicular to the force of gravity. Only resistance of the pipe itself will fight this effort. However, transporting water is actually a *byproduct* of the process of pressurizing (see Fig. 2–8) the water; it takes a very strong force pump to push the water very hard and fast. When the pump's *sole* function is to pressurize and transport water, I'll refer to it as a pressurizing pump.

A pressurizing pump is quite small, uses little energy, and doesn't cost very much. One with a working pressure of 30 psi and a pumping capacity of 10 gpm (gallons per minute), enough for all household uses, would cost under 100 dollars.

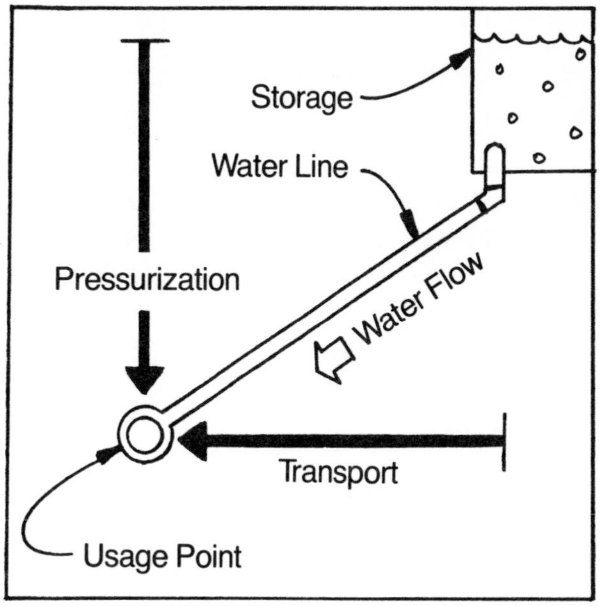

Fig. 2–8　Transport is a byproduct of gravity pressurization.

WATER STORAGE

As squirrels put away nuts for the winter, one should tuck away some water for a time of greater need. Actually, all water is "stored." (All water is also recycled; the planet has only what it started with.) Some water sources, notably ponds and lakes, automatically include the provision of storage. Streams and rivers use the storage of snowpack or, like springs and wells, water stored in the ground. Out of the group of potential water sources, only rainfall carries no inherent storage capacity, save for the reliability of the hydrological cycle itself!

Natural water storage is great, but the individual water system may not be able to take advantage of it. In a way, this is defined by the source's capacity to replenish itself when water is removed. But it may need time; its connection with the great water "warehouse" may not be all that great.

Artificial water storage can aid in this situation, buffering the source's inherent capacity against the widely varying flow rates characteristic of any water usage. The actual storage technique used—pond, lake, reservoir, cistern, tank, etc.—is situational. There are many reasons why someone might use water storage (of whatever type). Even though water storage could gobble up a good chunk of the money allotted for a water system, it's not unusual to find water storage as an integral part of some system that doesn't *need* it, but nevertheless includes it for the practical and versatile features it exhibits.

What are they? In a nut shell, water storage is useful in normal usage, source variance, energy availability, gravity flow, gravity pressurization, fire fighting, blackouts, and other emergency situations. Now, more detail.

Normal Usage

In normal usage, the *rate* at which water is consumed is situational; different functions—washing clothes, showering, dishwashing, flushing a toilet, irrigating—need water at varying flow rates. Any water source, however, has a capacity which, in a broad way, may be defined as a rate of flow. If the highest rate of usage exceeds the capacity of the source, there's a problem. Without storage, the user must either avoid higher-than-capacity flow rates (and anything that needs them for proper operation) or develop another water source with sufficient capacity to handle the highest usage rate. With storage, however, the water source is able to provision the system against high-usage rates during those times when they're not present. So it's a case of pumping "low and long" from source to

Figure 2-9
Fixture Flow Rates

	GPM
HOUSEHOLD	
Bathtub	8
Clotheswasher	8
Dishwasher	2
Shower	4
Sink, Bathroom	2
Sink, Kitchen	4
Sink, Laundry	6
Swamp Cooler	1
Toilet	3
OTHER	
Car Washing	5
Fire Fighting	
— just started	10
— cool adjacent buildings	10
— stop a well-developed fire	500–1000
Irrigation, Garden	5
Irrigation, Lawn	5

storage, and from storage to usage, delivering water "high and short" as needed.

This is a neat trick. Through proper application of storage techniques, even a water source with an extraordinarily small capacity may be useful. However, like all tricks, once past the smoke and mirrors, there's no magic involved; we're only shuffling one aspect of water—rate of flow. This does not increase the source's capacity; in the end, the ledger must balance. The total usage of water (in gallons) in a twenty-four-hour period cannot exceed the source's capacity to store that much water during the same time period.

Source Variance

The capacity of the water source may seem steady when compared with, say, the rates at which we might use the water daily, but in a larger time frame it may be subject to larger variations. This can be unnerving. (All of the factors that will influence capacity are itemized and thoroughly discussed in "Evaluating the Water Source" in

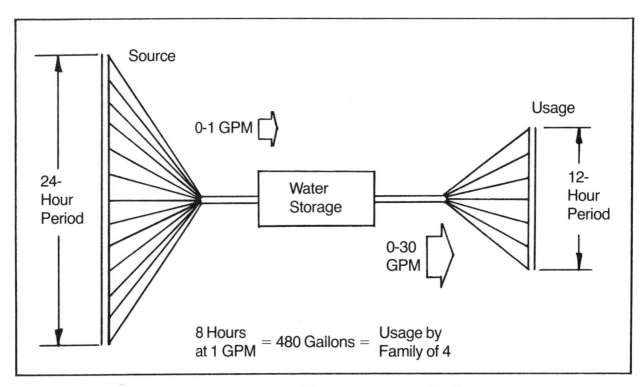

Fig. 2–10. A low-yield water source can handle high flow rates and daily volumes through the use of storage.

Chapter 1; if you've leapfrogged here and missed that section, I suggest you read it now.)

The ability of storage to handle the variances in the capacity of the source, in addition to the fluctuations of usage, depends largely on the water source itself; some are less susceptible to variance than others. There are two concerns here. One is the ability of the source, in its varying capacity, to handle the total usage in *any* time frame—daily, weekly, monthly, or annual. And even if your source could handle it, could you afford the money and space to rig up enough storage to carry water from the water-rich months of the year over to the water-poor months?

Most systems need only concern themselves with building a small reserve so that, given a diminished but steady flow of water in the worst periods, all usage needs can be met. Naturally, with the dollar looming overhead, we may end up skimping. And somewhere lurks the possibility that the highest use may occur simultaneously with the lowest capacity. Ergo, no water. If this is about to occur, however, it's easy enough simply to exercise some basic conservation to ride out the crisis. In many ways that makes more sense than trying to conceive of every eventuality, designing the system ac-

cordingly, and having to foot the bill for all that protection.

Gravity Flow

The particulars of gravity flow have been covered extensively in the section "Water Transport" in this chapter; however, even if the water source is not located at an elevation higher than the usage point, it may be possible to site water storage there. If the terrain is cooperative, this may involve a hillside location; if it's all flatland or your usage site is located at the highest point, this advantage may be weighed against the cost of slightly elevating, say, a storage tank to achieve gravity flow. While this would not necessarily eliminate the need to pressurize the water for some uses, the extra five to ten feet of head (over direct delivery to usage) would not represent any real burden for the pump that must extract and transport the water to storage. Additional uses such as gardening and watering livestock might well be served with this unpressurized water, thus eliminating the need for a pump large enough to pressurize all the water (see Fig. 2–11).

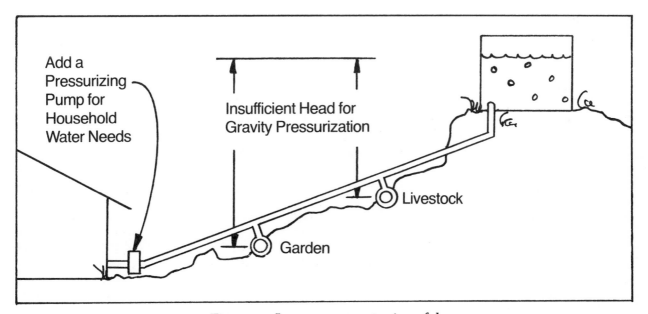

Add a Pressurizing Pump for Household Water Needs

Insufficient Head for Gravity Pressurization

Livestock

Garden

Fig. 2–11 Low-pressure water is useful.

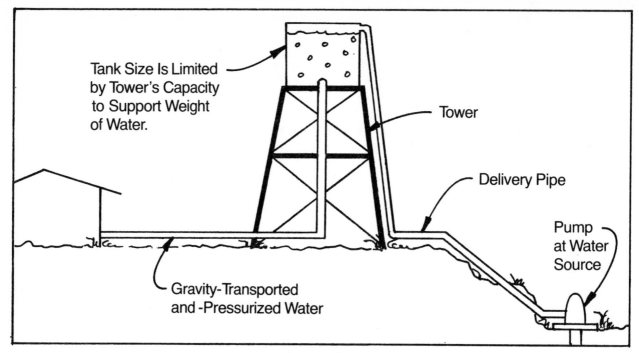

Fig. 2–12   A water tower aids in water processing.

Gravity Pressurization

The merits of gravity pressurization of water for usage have been extensively detailed in "Water Pressurizing" in this chapter. They show how lucky those few are who own a piece of land where the water source is high enough above the usage site to benefit from natural (gravity) pressurization of water. However, by storing water *everyone* can be a winner. No matter how far down the hill or under the ground the water may be, we can always lift it higher than the usage site to a storage site situated to allow gravity pressurization.

Admittedly it helps to have a nearby hillside of the right height. If the usage site is located at the highest point or the land is flat, another option is to use a tower to raise a storage tank to the necessary elevation (see Fig. 2–12). Of course, the cost of the tower alone might tempt you to discard the idea altogether. *Don't do this!* If a system has gravity transport and pressurization, the only energy required will be that applied to extraction and, perhaps, some transport.

A "demand" system installed in identical circumstances must extract, transport, and pressurize water at the highest usage rate; this requires energy use at high rates and large pipe to avoid pressure loss at the higher flow. The store system, on the other hand, lets the position of the tank handle peak usage needs—high flow rates, pressurization, etc.—while it permits low-energy extraction (and the utilization of energy sources that are low-yield

in nature) of water through (possibly) smaller pipe. The additional energy required to boost the water the extra distance to storage (to take advantage of gravity pressurization) should be considered, but at such a low rate of flow it's not likely to be significant.

The potential for the store system in this situation is exciting but, alas, not always realizable; to ignore the relevant factors and impose a system that doesn't fit the situation is foolhardy if not outright expensive. But consider it—it may work after all.

Energy Availability

The amount of energy available for water processing is a major voting block in the issue of storage. It's not difficult to see which way the vote will be cast under some conditions. If, for example, the source capacity cannot handle the largest rate of flow in usage, storage will be required. However, if the source capacity is sufficient to handle demand, the issue of energy must be addressed next. If its availability is high, the system design may follow a number of paths. If, however, the availability is *low*, storage will be required as a means of stockpiling water against high usage needs. Additionally, this circumstance favors the location of storage in such a way as to use gravity for transporting and pressurizing the stored water for use.

Fire Fighting

No structure, rural or urban, is completely free from the threat of fire. In the city water is supplied by buried mains; except for the very worst of conditions, then, water is available for fire fighting from taps about the house itself, indoor and probably outdoor, and from nearby hydrants.

A rural home or farm, however, does not enjoy the same availability of water since it's often supplied by individual wells or springs. Even if fire trucks can respond quickly enough to be effective, there are no convenient hydrants to which they may attach hoses. Accordingly, many are designed to carry their own supply of water. Obviously the aid they render is minimal if the fire is not completely doused before they run out of water. Imagine the plight of the owner who must watch a nearly quenched fire grow in strength once again as the tanker truck must rush off to a nearby pond or water main to recharge.

Grass, brush, and forest fires also menace the rural homestead. As the fire draws nearer, several things become apparent. One is that the fire trucks are otherwise engaged, trying to stop the fire itself. Where possible, they will try to save structures, but if saving yours leaves the fire to threaten others, let's face it—your structure is expendable. Again, the limitation on the amount of water they can carry will also be a factor. In the midst of the confusion, you as an owner may be shocked to discover that you have no water. Any water system that is dependent upon utility electricity for water extraction, transport, or pressurization may be without that vital power during any kind of brush, grass, or forest fire. Why? Because most power poles are wooden, and if they're in the path of the fire, they burn too!

Water storage is fire insurance. Where the system design has sited water storage for both gravity transport and gravity pressurization, hoses and sprinkler systems will still be functional when electric power is lost during a fire. Even a system normally in need of electricity for water transport and pressurization from storage may be saved; several measures may be taken to accomplish this task when utility power fails (see Fig. 6–22). In any instance, the presence of stored water assures the replenishment of a fire truck's dry tanks. Even if the fire fighters can't use your fittings, they usually have the equipment to draw water from your tank through a hose they carry for just that purpose.

Of course it's of little use to anyone with a stor-

age tank if the aforementioned fire occurs at a time when the tank is low or empty. Keeping a tank topped off all the time, however, is neither practical nor always possible. This is particularly true in systems that use a wind machine for pumping water. However, a compromise may be struck. How about designating a certain portion of the tank (one half? one fourth?) as a reserve for fire fighting only? A simple plumbing modification (see Fig. 2–13) will handle normal usage. In the event of a fire the valve is opened; the water reserve is now available.

There's another alternative. If the owners are willing to conserve until more water can be pumped, a sensor (a float-operated microswitch) may be positioned in the tank at a point above the reserve level (see Fig. 6–20). When the level in the tank reaches this point, the users will know they have only so many hundreds of gallons left before they start cutting into the fire reserve. Then

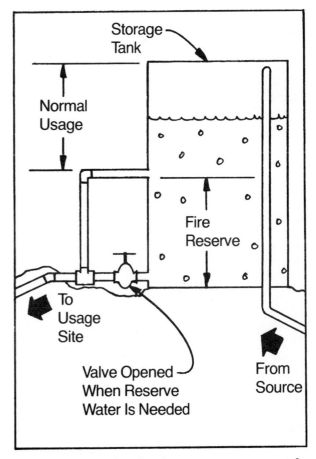

Fig. 2–13 Simple plumbing can assure ample water for emergency needs.

it's their decision whether to initiate a partial or complete refill of the tank or simply ration usage until the primary system fills it again.

Blackouts

In the event of a power failure, the inability to use the toilet, shower, or kitchen faucet is a nuisance. Since gravity is unaffected by such failures, any water system based on gravity pressurization functions perfectly normally in a blackout. Even systems using pressurizing pumps for stored water may be safeguarded from this effect (see "The Silver System," Chapter 6). Finally, stored water with only the potential for gravity flow works well during blackouts; in this light (or lack of it), water at *any* pressure is a joy.

Other Emergencies

Other events may interrupt the normal operation of a water system. Normal maintenance—for example, lubrication and replacement of chemicals and filters—and component failure can render the system inactive for a time. Cataclysmic events such as freak storms and earthquakes, can incapacitate *any* system; those equipped with storage, however, can supply their owners with enough time to cope with other pressing matters and set up some alternative pumping if required.

As with fires, without implementing an actual reserve capacity in the store system there's no guarantee that you'll have a full or partially full tank when an emergency occurs. Don't leave this to luck! Through either automatic functioning or an audible or visual indicator (see "Monitoring Storage," this chapter), a reserve capacity should be protected against being drained off in normal, everyday usage. Common sense tells us that we must be practical; experiencing an emergency tells us that planning isn't the whole answer. How about a middle ground—half of capacity devoted to storage? Granted, even a thousand gallons of water isn't much. But however much water is set aside for fire fighting and other emergencies, it's going to seem like a lot compared with none at all.

Types of Storage

Storage can take many forms. First of all, it may be readily available, as a nearby pond or lake.

With the right kind of terrain, ponds or lakes may be made to take advantage of the presence of streams, rivers, or springs. Wherever there's little hope of channeling surface water into these depressions, a man-made pond may be scraped out of the earth. Another type of storage is the reservoir; while it may be earthen or have its sides and bottom lined with concrete, in this book the term is used to mean uncovered, concrete-lined storage containers.

The same factors that limit the use of ponds and lakes as sources of water apply to their use as storage systems (see "Evaluating the Water Source" in Chapter 1). Reservoirs suffer from the same limitations, so I will not consider them any further for primary water storage. However, any one of the three may faithfully serve as *secondary* water storage. It's somewhat annoying in water-scarce areas to see a sudden shower yield a small flood—all that water going to waste! With secondary storage, a system may take advantage of a freak rain shower without having to depend upon it; the water captured in this manner may be used wherever needed, or a portion of it may be transferred to primary storage (see "Hydraulic Ram," Chapter 4).

The remaining three storage systems—the well, tank, and cistern—are all good candidates for primary water storage.

In-Well Storage

Due to the characteristics of wells (see "The Deep Well," Chapter 5), once water is struck at some depth, the water level may rise significantly. For example, in our own well water was struck at 125 feet and immediately rose to within 40 feet of the surface! Attempting to find a larger capacity (it had tested at 4½ gpm), we drilled the well to 150 feet before we stopped. Since the deep-well cylinder (see "Pumps," Chapter 4) we installed sits at a 125-foot depth, we have 85 feet of "storage" in the well (125 feet minus 40 feet). For a hole 6 inches in diameter, that's approximately 1.5 gallons of water per foot or, for 85 feet, 128 gallons of storage water.

In a way, this was free; we had to drill to 125 feet in order to hit water in the first place. However, had we hit water at 40 feet, we probably would not have drilled more than 25 feet farther. Why? At 10 dollars per foot of drilled well, the in-well storage capacity is costing over 6 dollars per gallon. And whereas we could site the storage tank for both gravity flow and gravity pressurization, the "siting" of the in-well storage is *not* a matter of preference and is, in fact, in the wrong place!

In-well storage has its place. In a "demand" water system, in-well storage serves as a buffer against higher-than-capacity usage while assuring that the inlet to the pump is, at all times, submerged. Unfortunately, for low-capacity wells, the well may need to be drilled extra deep to prevent drawdown—the distance the water level drops during normal pumping—from exposing the pump inlet. At the lower pumping rates characteristic of stored water systems, drawdown is seldom a problem.

Tank Storage

Water may be stored in tanks made of wood, metal (see photo), concrete, or plastic; the plastic and some types of metal tanks can be delivered to the property ready for use. Of course, this is more expensive than building tanks or cisterns on the site.

However, the relatively higher cost of storage may be justified in light of the convenience and the built-in protection against contamination (relative to the cistern). For the qualities and limitations inherent in tanks made of different materials, see "Tanks," Chapter 4.

Cistern Storage

A cistern is normally classified as underground water storage. Since tanks, reservoirs, and cisterns overlap somewhat in definition, for our purposes in this book the cistern is a non-portable concrete tank that is built on-site, is buried or partially buried, using the earth as support for its walls and bottom, and is completely covered (which distinguishes it from a reservoir). By this definition, little or no sunlight reaches the water in a cistern, and with screening the water is not accessible to anything larger than a gnat (unless it's able to open the access hatch!). For more details, see "Concrete Tanks," Chapter 4.

Fig. 2–14 Relatively small welded steel tanks will store thousands of gallons of water.

Characteristics of Storage

Some other good but not so obvious characteristics of storage will manifest themselves at some point; in the interest of saving you some time and money, let's look at a few.

Open versus Closed Tanks

"Closed" tanks are sealed against the atmosphere. They're also referred to as pneumatic, or pressure, tanks. They're small—most don't exceed a 100-gallon volume—and are intended primarily to aid in water pressurization; though found in any system where the water is pressurized, but not by gravity, they are most useful in the "demand" water system. Contrary to popular opinion, pressure tanks are not really intended to store water. (If that were their primary function, they would do it poorly; a 100-gallon tank can supply only about 15 gallons of water under pressure.) For this reason, a pressure tank should never be confused with a tank designed to store water (more on pressure tanks in "Accessories," Chapter 4).

Tanks that serve only to store water are usually open to the atmosphere. This category includes cisterns or steel tanks because, in fact, they're only "covered," not "closed." A tank that stores water should always be equipped with a vent pipe, which permits free movement of air into and out of the tank as the water level falls and rises. Normally this is far from being a problem—the tougher challenge is to make a tank airtight—but an overzealous first-timer might succeed in so restricting airflow as to cause the formation of pressurized air pockets or a vacuum in the tank. Either event is both undesirable and dangerous. Any type of pumping equipment (for water extraction or transfer) that is designed to pump into an "open" head may suffer extensive damage if the vent pipe prevents air release or, worse yet, overflow. The outflow of water in an airflow-restrictive tank creates a vacuum, and it takes surprisingly little vacuum to cave in the tank walls.

Tanks that are completely buried in the ground are most susceptible to airflow blockage, but it's an easy situation to remedy—a vent pipe may be attached at either the input or the output pipe. Luckily, this can double as an overflow pipe. However, since some systems may normally route tank overflow to some other use—gardens, orchards, pools, other tanks—it may be wise to isolate the two functions so that there's no risk of blockage.

Inlet and Outlet

Typically, a tank (hereafter also meant to include cisterns and reservoirs) has the inlet pipe at the top and the outlet pipe at the bottom (see Fig. 2–15). This follows from the days when wind-powered water pumping extracted the water from wells and transferred it directly to storage. However, insofar as pressure is related to the depth and not the quantity of water, it will make no difference to the pumping (and extraction) equipment if the water inlet to the tank is located at the bottom instead of the top—either way, the water gets to the storage tank. It's actually easier to pump water into the bottom of the tank, because at low tank levels there's a few feet less head for the lift pump to push against (see Fig. 2–16). Of course, as the tank approaches its maximum level this difference is negligible.

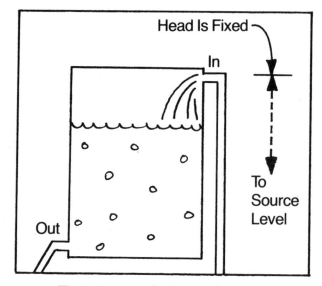

Fig. 2–15   Standard tank plumbing.

One distinct advantage of locating the inlet pipe at the base of the tank may be for the inlet and outlet to *share* the same pipe! This is *very* situational—the source and usage sites should be on the same side of the tank—but considering the cost of pipe nowadays, in avoiding duplication significant sums of money are saved. If there's a potential for gravity flow (pressurization) but it means going a distance up a gentle slope, this little trick neatly cuts the length of pipe needed to do the job in half (see Fig. 2–17). Twice the distance for the same

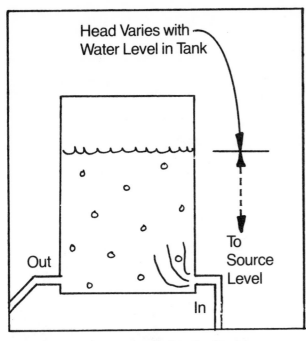

Fig. 2–16 Improved tank plumbing.

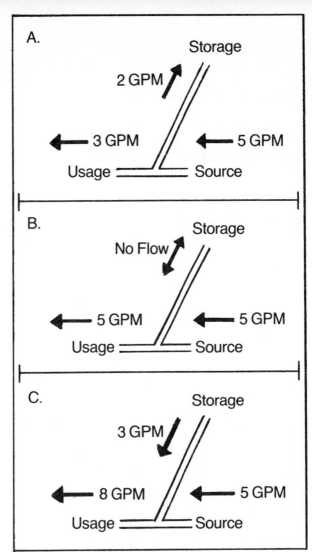

Fig. 2–18 The dynamics of a shared inlet and outlet in one pipe.

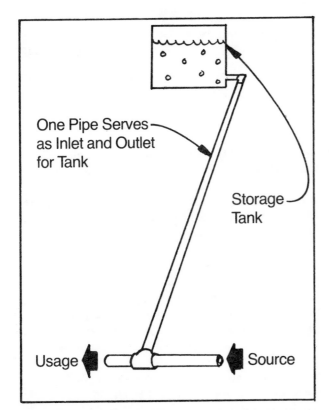

Fig. 2–17 Combining pipe functions can save money.

money or the original distance for half the cost—take your pick!

There's often some confusion about the operational characteristics when the inlet and outlet pipes are combined. For example, what happens when water is being used at the same time water is being extracted and transferred to storage? How can the water flow up and down the common pipe at the same time?

The answer is simple: it doesn't. If the supply rate from the source is greater than the usage rate, all of the usage water comes directly from the supply and the remainder of the supply water is pumped to storage. If, on the other hand, the supply rate is lower than the usage rate, all of the supply water goes toward usage and the remainder comes from storage. As confusing as it may seem, the *water* has no problem with this, and at the usage end, variation in supply or usage rates produces no detectable or undesirable effect. (See Fig. 2–18.)

The combined inlet and outlet pipe arrangement definitely saves money. However, there is one potential problem in using the common pipe idea: the lift pump in the system may "leak," allowing backflow out of the storage tank when not in operation. Theoretically, it doesn't; however, experience says otherwise. A deep-well piston pump (see "Pumps," Chapter 4) has "leathers" (similar to the piston rings in a car engine) which may wear out. If this happens and the pipe that connects the source to storage enters the tank at the top, the only water "lost" back into the well is that which is in the delivery pipe; any water that has reached the tank has already flowed into the tank. Where the inlet pipe is situated at the *bottom* of the tank, the loss could be *all* of the water in the tank.

The leathers can't be checked like the oil level in an engine. Not surprisingly, one learns of their wear (or another similar problem) by waking up one morning to an empty tank; that's definitely not the right way to start the day. Even if there's ample time to replace the leathers right away (You didn't order spares? You were just leaving on vacation?), the worry about the next time it (or something else) causes an equally disastrous loss of water is not conducive to happiness.

There is a simple solution to this problem—a check valve (use a gravity type, not a spring type). By placing it at the outlet from the well, you ensure that no water will be lost back into the well. At fifteen to twenty dollars, the check value is cheap for the worry it will save.

Tank Cleanout

The tank outlet is rarely located in the very bottom of the tank; instead, it is about 6 to 12 inches up the side. Why? Operate the system for a while, then drain the tank and you'll have the answer! The polite name for all of that gunk and muck coating the bottom of the tank is sediment. How did it get there? An open tank or a poorly covered one will always allow dirt, leaves, insects, lizards, and mice into the water system. The incoming water may carry its own sediment, held in suspension, which, in the tranquil waters of the tank, will precipitate. Some minerals as well (see "Water Quality," Chapter 3) will, upon contact with air, precipitate out in a storage tank. Locating the outlet up the side of the tank a wee bit, then, will *always* result in this accumulated debris. Nevertheless, as nasty as it may be to clean out, consider

Fig. 2–19 A plug located at the lowest point of the tank will aid in cleanout.

the alternative. If it's spic and span in your tank, it means that you've been drinking the stuff!

Don't forget to install some means of ridding yourself of the accumulated debris. The simplest setup is to install a cleanout plug in the lowest part of the tank (see photo). Then, when it's time, you drain the tank (or let it drain over a few days' time and turn off the refilling system) and remove the plug. If the tank bottom isn't designed to drain like a bathtub or isn't tilted to ensure removal of all refuse littering the bottom, remove the plug while the water level in the tank is still high; this is a violent event, but necessary to flush out the settlings.

While this technique works, I prefer an additional feature in a storage tank—access. With reservoirs and open-top tanks this is already provided, but for covered or buried tanks it must be added.

If you can squeeze your body into the tank, you can be absolutely certain the bottom is clean—whereas in the purge method, it's blind faith. A bonus, with access, is a visual confirmation that the sediment level is getting a bit thick. There are other advantages in having some access—for wall scrubbing, checking on water turbidity, water level detection, help in removing accumulated debris, and repainting of the interior walls. However, access *demands* control. A hatch with a child-proof locking mechanism is the minimal requirement for keeping out inquisitive children. I shudder at the mere contemplation of anything less!

Overflow

Any type of pump used to store water in an open tank is said to be pumping into an "open head." Therefore if the water *leaving* storage does not keep up with the water coming in, the storage tank may overflow. This is not such a serious event, but it can be messy. Can it be avoided? Yes—prevention is one possibility but it requires, among other things, that we detect the presence of overflow. Another possibility is to put unintentional overflow to some practical use.

PREVENTING OVERFLOW

The first thought about overflow is usually directed at preventing it. If the water system is using a lift pump powered by an electric motor or a gas engine, overflow is easy to stop—just stop the pump itself. If the system is automated, there are two ways to prevent overflow. One is to install a (toilet-type) float valve at the top of the tank (see Fig. 2–20); when the tank is filled, this shuts off the flow of water, preventing overflow. An in-line pressure switch, then, will shut off the electric pump (via the power relay). A small pressure tank is often added to ease the shock of float-valve closure and prevent the pump from starting up with the slightest water usage (see "Pressure Tank," Chapter 4).

A variation on this theme is to use a float-activated electrical microswitch at the top of the tank and have it switch the pump's power relay directly (see Fig. 4–31). This averts the need for a pressure switch and pressure tank in the system, but necessitates the use of wiring to connect the switch to the lift-pump site. Unless it's a retrofit, there's only the question of the wiring cost; the wires may be

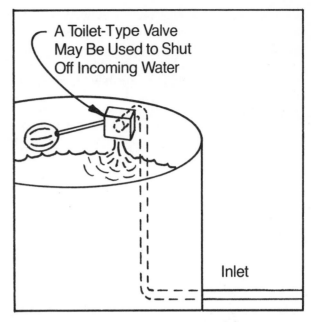

Fig. 2–20   An automatic level control for a storage tank.

buried in the same trench provided for the source-to-storage plumbing.

Electrical pumping equipment that is not automated will require manual shutoff to prevent overflow once the tank is filled. Fortunately, there are a number of ways to know the level of water in the tank (see "Monitoring Storage," below). A word of caution: *never* use a float valve on the tank's inlet pipe. This will prevent overflow, but at the price of burst pipes or a burnt-up motor; after all, how can the pump *know* that it's supposed to shut off?

Non-electrical water-pumping equipment, particularly wind-powered, is not as cooperative in the prevention of overflow; again, merely cutting off the flow of water by a float valve will inflict some damage to a system that has no internal provisions for pumping into a "closed" head. If the distance between storage and supply is small, mechanical disconnect features may be used, but they may be expensive alternatives to simple monitoring and manual startup and shutdown.

OVERFLOW USES

The easiest solution to unintentional overflow is to let it happen, putting the spilled water to some use; however, this applies only to systems that are not using expensive energy to get the water to storage. Some people will put the water in a nearby pond or a thirsty garden or orchard—or, perhaps, another storage vessel. The possibilities would be unlimited, except that physical realities may prevent you from using the water effectively. What if the tank is some distance from anything that might benefit from the water? Extra piping or hose could make overflow an expensive proposition. Besides, how much water are we talking about? Is it hundreds of gallons, or is it thousands? Transforming a garden into something like a rice paddy is *not* a blessing. Finally, taking water out of the ground may affect the water table. How much may be anyone's guess (see "Water and the Law," Chapter 1), but water is a finite resource and letting it go to waste—even if it's not costing any energy or effort—is not a good idea.

MONITORING STORAGE

Monitoring the amount of water contained in storage is important. At the extremes, it's nice to know when overflow is about to occur (if there are no provisions for handling it), or when the tank is empty.

A person can monitor storage simply by walking up to the tank and looking in; but if there's any distance involved, this gets old fast. If storage is in the line of sight of the usage point, a level indicator may be added to the tank (see Fig. 2–21).

A dandy method of monitoring storage, effective in systems with gravity-pressurized water, is to install a pressure gauge at the usage site; then note the reading when the tank is full, and again when it's empty except for the water lines. Thereafter, if the gauge reads at or between these points, you'll know how much water is in storage.

The pressure-gauge method of monitoring is plagued with two limitations. One is that if the pumping equipment is operating, the needle will be all over the place, preventing an accurate reading. Secondly, at only .433 psi per foot of head, a 10-foot difference in the tank's height (between full and empty) is only 4.33 psi. If the difference in elevation between the storage and usage sites is large, this represents a pretty small reading range; many gauges are neither sensitive nor accurate enough to supply such precise information.

If running a few wires between the storage and usage sites is no problem, low- and high-water level sensors may be added to the storage vessel.

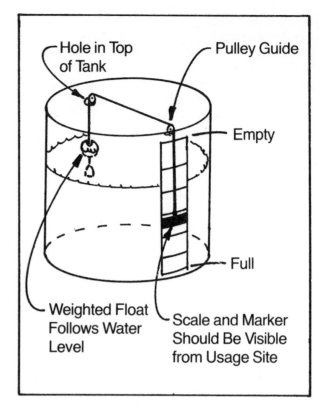

Fig. 2–21 Line-of-sight water-level monitoring.

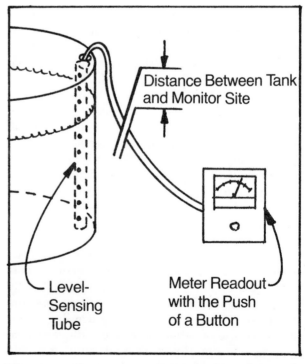

Fig. 2–22 Remote meter monitoring of stored-water levels.

Based on a simple microswitch, these may be connected to audible or visual alarms to indicate the extreme conditions. A limitation of this setup is the wire size used to connect the sensor to the alarm; if the sensor is expected to switch pumps or even power relays, a long run of the correct wire size is going to be expensive.

By far the best method that I have seen for monitoring storage is the "Waterwatch" (see Fig. 2–22), developed by T. J. Byers. Requiring only two wires between the storage and monitoring points, ten equally spaced sensors mounted in the tank supply a monitor meter with ten possible increments of reading, ranging from empty to full (depending on the number of screws covered by the water). The beauty of this design is that the sensors may be spaced apart to fit *any* storage depth. The small circuit has been designed around a 9-volt battery to accommodate any situation; wired as shown, no power is used until the operator pushes the button for a reading. Since $\frac{1}{1000}$ of an amp is the highest current that flows through the wires, only small-sized wiring is needed between the storage and monitoring sites. Constructing, installing, and using the Waterwatch is fully described in "Special Systems," Chapter 6.

Sizing Storage

The amount of normal usage, source capacity variance, energy availability, emergency needs, favorable terrain—all affect the sizing of water storage. So, how much is needed? Sorry, there's insufficient data. But you're one step closer to the answer once you've sketched the preliminary design and selected primary and secondary water and energy sources. Why the second choices? Having water is not equivalent to having *usable* water—that is, having it reliably processed—extracted, transported, stored, and pressurized. Besides, while we can't cut the usage below certain levels, there *is* a way to "fool" the water source into "thinking" that we have! Sound impossible? It's not. And that very subject is up next.

WATER EXTRACTION

While it's handy to have the water source on the same level as or above the usage point, many people are not so fortunate. So whether the water is at the bottom of a hill or at the bottom of a well, the water must be *extracted*. There are basically three ways to extract water; it can be hauled, induced, or pushed.

Hauling

Hauling implies techniques such as buckets pulled up by ropes, the use of a mechanical lever (the hand-cranked winch over an open well), or a mechanical conveyance system that captures, lifts, and dumps the water for immediate or eventual use. For anything other than very small water needs or small distances, this method tends to be labor-intensive unless a renewable source of energy, such as water or wind power, is used.

Induction

Water may be extracted by induction; this is my own term for utilizing the natural forces of both gravity and atmospheric pressure in producing a vacuum (see Fig. 2–23). If you evacuate the air from a pipe with its lower end submersed in water, atmospheric pressure will push the water up the pipe. This is similar to sucking soda through a straw. The better the vacuum, the higher the water will rise.

Extracting water by suction is limited to the amount of force exerted by atmospheric pressure; at sea level this amounts to a limit of 32 (vertical) feet for a perfect vacuum. Since we can't generate a perfect vacuum, the practical limits of suction are about 25 feet, and with each thousand feet above sea level it drops another foot. Elevating water by suction is limited to the type of pump that is able to generate a vacuum or is able to hold its "prime" (which we will discuss later). And the smallest air leak in the pipe will nullify the lifting of water by suction.

One offshoot of extraction by induction is the siphon. Most of us, at one time or another, have had to use a siphon hose (otherwise known as an Oklahoma credit card) to extract gasoline from a car's tank. Those who have tried this and failed are usually in violation of one very important rule of the siphon: once started, the outlet of the hose (or pipe) must be *lower* than the level of fluid at the source. Also, if the fluid level drops below the pipe's inlet, air will enter the system and stop the siphoning effect. To avoid constant re-priming, a faucet may be added (see Fig. 2–24); this will

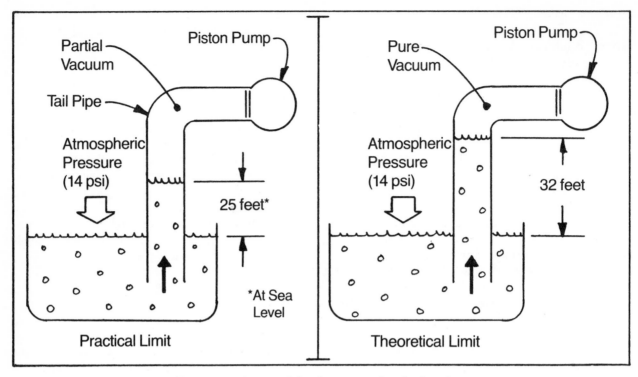

Fig. 2–23 Suction lift of water is handy but limited.

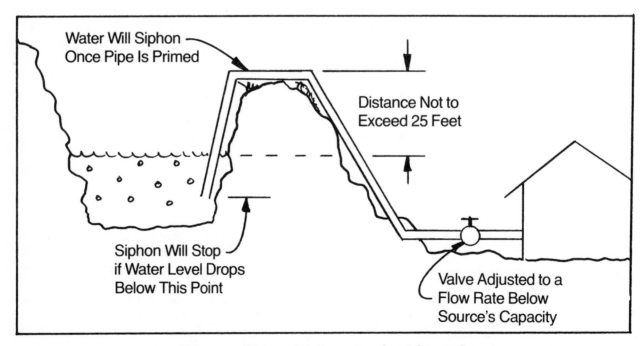

Fig. 2–24 Water extraction using the siphon technique is free.

limit the extraction flow rate to something less than the source's own capacity.

Pushing

Most water systems use the "push" technique for extracting water; here, pumps collect the water and force it upward. If the pump's outlet is open to the air, you get a fountain; confine the forced water to the inside of a pipe, and the water will rise upward to some higher point.

Combinations

Some types of force pump combine several of these extraction techniques in normal operation. For example, the shallow-well pump (see Fig. 2–25) is mounted as high as 25 feet above a water source; still, it is able to suck water up through its inlet pipe and then push it to much higher elevations. Another force pump, the deep-well piston pump (see Fig. 4–21), is technically able to use all three extraction techniques—suction, lift, and push—in

one cycle of its operation. Other types of pumps such as jet or centrifugal can fulfill only one extraction technique under the best of conditions.

The Lift Pump

As previously defined, extracting water is distinguished from both transporting and pressurizing water in that it involves only the vertical component of water processing—moving water straight up. A pump that will force water upward may be called a lift pump to help distinguish it from a pressurizing pump. That's important, because for all practical purposes you couldn't tell them apart —they're both force pumps. In real life, a pressurizing pump will lift water and a lift pump will pressurize water. However, a pressurizing pump's principal job is to pressurize water for use, and transporting it is a byproduct. On the other hand, a lift pump's purpose is to extract water—to get it out of the well (a purely upward motion) or up a hill (which will probably include some horizontal transport as well—see Fig. 2–26). There are pumps that do all three things—extract and transport and

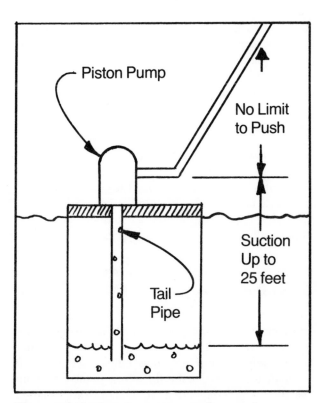

Fig. 2–25 A piston pump can suck or push water.

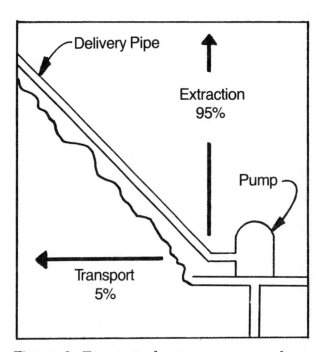

Fig. 2–26 Transport of water consumes only a fraction of the energy used to extract it.

pressurize. But, as we shall soon see, the requirements of these pumps are quite different from those of pumps that work simply to extract water.

A pressurizing pump fights only pipe resistance. A lift pump must fight pipe resistance and gravity. A lift pump, then, must pump harder and faster to overcome the opposition. But how much pressure do we need to fight gravity?

If we want to talk solely in terms of pressure, a partial answer is supplied by referring back to Fig. 2–4. The reason the water reaches all the way up to point AAA is that gravity, working through point A, has pushed the water through the pipe layout up to point AAA. In the process, it pushes *through* point DDD. And the pressure at point DDD has already been established at 13 psi. If we erased the rest of the system and drew in a lift pump at point DDD (see Fig. 2–27), wouldn't it push water to the same height as AAA if it could generate a pressure of 13 psi? The answer is yes.

This helps to establish one of the two major ratings of any lift pump: how much pressure it will develop. *For each foot of height that we want to raise water, we will need a pump pressure of .433 psi*. A 10-foot raise requires 4.33 psi. A 100-foot raise requires 43.3 psi.

If a lift pump located at point DDD generates a little *less* than 13 psi, the water will theoretically rise in the pipe until it's very close to point AAA but no flow will occur. If it generates exactly 13 psi, the water will reach point AAA and flow out of the faucet, however weakly. If the pump generates a little more than 13 psi, there will be a good flow of water from point AAA.

Well, you'd think so anyway. Again, real life intervenes to spoil the best-laid plans; with the first flow, pipe resistance will come into effect and, with higher flow rates, rob us of some of that precious pressure. Nevertheless, system pressure is never difficult to compute. All one has to do is determine the head—the vertical distance between the level of water at the source and any faucet at the usage site—and multiply this figure by .433 psi/foot—pounds per square inch (pressure) per foot (of depth) of water; the answer obtained is the minimum pressure the lift pump must exert if water is to be lifted and flow out of the faucet. Tacking a few more psi to this calculated value should handle pressure losses due to pipe resistance.

A person armed with this information might next flip through the appropriate catalogue in search of a pump with a rating equivalent to, or larger than, the one calculated. But we can't look at the dynamic state of water extraction simply from the standpoint of pressure, because we have no way to convert pressure units into units that describe the rate of flow. Pumps don't just "make" pressure; rather, a pump produces pressure at some particular rate of flow. Use it in different situations and, within limits, it will supply different rates of flow. In a way, we can say that it trades off pressure for flow rates. The higher the pressure (the head) into which it must pump, the less the flow. So, in addition to the pressure needed to combat gravity and losses, all pumps must add service pressurization (see Fig. 2–28).

Water Horsepower

A really good way to get a feel for the dynamic state of water extraction is to look at the energy requirements. Lifting water is akin to lifting weights. Depending on your muscular build, you could lift a small weight from the floor to a point over your head in a certain period of time. Lifting a larger weight through the same distance would probably

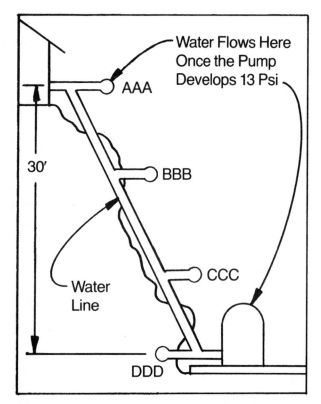

Fig. 2–27 Pump pressure is needed to lift water against gravity.

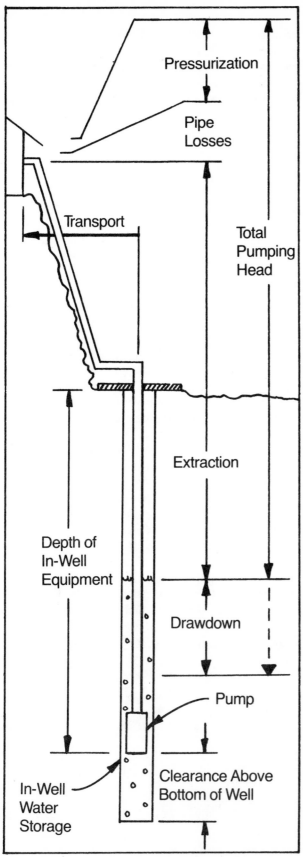

Fig. 2–28 The dynamics of water processing.

take you longer. The range of weights is unimportant; the essence here is that each of us has a built-in capacity for work.

The same goes for pumps—they have design limits. It doesn't matter what type of energy source is connected, they can still only handle a certain work capacity. And as in human weight lifting, we're working with three things: weight, distance, and time. In a water system the precise capacity of any pump may be established by asking three questions. First, how *much* water do we want to lift? Second, how *high* do we want to lift it? And, third, how *fast* do we want to lift it?

The relationship between these three factors—how much, how high, how fast—may be equated to another standard: Horsepower. One horsepower equals 33,000 foot-pounds per minute. If 33,000 pounds is lifted one foot in one minute's time, that's 1 horsepower. If one pound is lifted 33,000 feet in one minute's time, that's also 1 horsepower. If 330 pounds is lifted 100 feet in one minute, that's still 1 horsepower's worth of work.

In working with water, we're used to dealing with gallons, so let's convert the formula. One gallon weighs 8.33 pounds. Dividing 33,000 foot-pounds per minute by 8.33 pounds means that we can lift 3,962 gallons of water a vertical distance of 1 foot, and if we do it in one minute's time, it only consumes 1 horsepower. Let's round off this figure to an even 4,000 gallons of water per minute per foot, changing nothing else. It takes 1 horsepower to lift 400 gpm through a head of 10 feet, 40 gpm through a head of 100 feet, and 4 gpm through a head of 1,000 feet.

It's obvious that, for flow rates in the 4 gpm range, it won't take much horsepower to lift water some pretty hefty distances. However, beware. This figure represents *water horsepower* only. No allowance has been made for any losses; this figure assumes frictionless pipe, a 100 percent pump efficiency, and a perfect conversion of the energy (from whatever source) into the mechanical motion required for pump mechanism. In most instances we must multiply the calculated water horsepower by at least a factor of *two* or *three* to obtain the correct ratings for the pump and related hardware such as electric motors and gasoline engines.

Water Extraction and Energy

At this point the importance of water horsepower is that it takes a *lot* of energy to extract water. For any flow rate, we need a certain amount of energy to push the water against both gravity and pipe resistance. Double that flow rate and the energy required is *double* the original value *plus* the additional energy required to combat the fourfold increase in pipe resistance.

This is a fact. Since energy, particularly in the form of utility-supplied electricity, is still relatively cheap, the only comment some people would register at this point is, So what? Get a bigger pump or use bigger pipe.

However, others will view this relationship in a different light. If higher flow rates result in higher energy requirements and increased pipe resistance, that also means that lower flow rates will need less energy and suffer lessened pressure losses.

It is true that if we pump water at a smaller flow rate, we must also pump *longer* to get the same total amount of water to the same elevation. Doing it quickly prohibits the use of some energy sources (see "Energy Sources," Chapter 1), which simply cannot produce energy at a high *rate*. They are, however, capable of producing energy in smaller amounts over a period of time—long enough, anyway, to get all of the water to the desired elevation. Since the effect of pipe resistance is almost eradicated at lesser flow rates, an additional bonus of slow pumping is the option of using smaller pipe for the long haul.

Only with a well installation is the lift pump pushing water straight up. If, instead, it pushes the water through a pipe up a hillside with a 45-degree slope, a horizontal component of travel is also involved (see Fig. 2–26); by my own definition, that's water transport. In transport, however, the only resistance to flow is that of the pipe itself. So it takes only a small amount of additional energy to pump water through the extra pipe length in the hillside situation. However, at smaller angles—where the vertical component (the head) is small

relative to the horizontal distance the pipe spans—combined with higher flow rates, the energy required for the lift pump may exceed the requirements for pure lift (no transport) by several multiples. Correct pipe sizing, however, is not difficult, as will be seen later, in Chapter 4.

Final Comments

Even though I have separated the functions of water processing into extraction, transport, storage, and pressurization, the two basic types of water system—demand and store—frequently combine these functions in operation. For example, the demand system is inactive except when water is required. Then the system turns on and one pump does everything—extraction, transport, and pressurization (see Fig. 4–31). This *is* convenient. However, it's also inefficient, since the pump requires a rate of energy usage that represents the *highest* rate of water flow (in gpm) needed in the system. Therefore, even at very small flow rates the pump uses energy at a rate that may be *ten times* the amount required to handle that flow!

The other type of system, the store system, wholly separates the functions that are necessary at the water source from those required at the usage site. In this setup, extraction and transport of water from the source may be tailored to source capacity without ignoring the widely varying needs—pressure and flow rates—of the usage point. The buffer that performs this minor miracle is storage. If storage can be sited high enough above the usage site to make gravity pressurization possible, the extraction head is only slightly increased (see Fig. 2–1). If storage is too low for gravity pressurization, a small pressurizing pump may be added (see Fig. 4–31).

3

WATER QUALITY, TREATMENT, AND REUSE

There's nothing sweeter than the first cup of water from a newly drilled well, developed spring, or completed water system. Most rural landowners expect that their water will be pure. Pour it into a clean, clear glass and it may *look* pure. A tentative sip may even reveal that it *tastes* pure.

But purity is not a matter of luck or wishful thinking; the eye-and-tongue test is a carry-over from the days before the discovery of germs. Clean and dirty are not black and white terms, but merely shades of gray. And, as you shall soon see, it saves a lot of effort, money, and energy if we don't generalize the meaning of water quality *or* reuse.

WATER QUALITY

What can be in a perfectly clear drop of water? Bacteria, germs, viruses, parasites, chemicals, ele-ments, minerals, and other matter. The list of names is long, and the effect they can have on humans is pronounced: typhoid fever, dysentery, infectious hepatitis, polio, diarrhea, anthrax, tuberculosis, intestinal worms, poisoning, to name a few.

It makes you want to go out and get the strongest disinfectant you can find and sterilize that drop of water. However, treatment is the *last* resort because, alas, it often only affects the symptom rather than getting at the cause. For example, four out of every five systems that use water treatment would not require it if proper procedures had been followed when the water source was sited and developed.

So things are not always as they appear. However, this is a two-way street; just as "clear" should not be equated with "pure," we must not be too hasty to judge water that is murky, smells or tastes funny, and leaves rings in the bathrub, deposits in pipes, and scale in teapots. Water is the universal

Fig. 3–1 There's nothing quite like the first taste of water from a source you've developed.

presence of one or more of these substances in water is *not* unnatural. It may be repulsive and it might make you fearful, but it is only a *condition* requiring your attention. Treat it as one. As varied as the combinations may be, each condition is known, detectable, and treatable. In many instances it is even preventable; for every system that *experiences* a water-quality-related condition, there's another that actually *creates* a problem. Only when a condition has resisted preliminary efforts to prevent, minimize, or bypass its impact should it be considered a problem in need of a specific solution. Even if it reaches this stage, the answer is not always simply the purchase of the equipment or chemicals of a water treatment system; the cost and complexity of that specific solution alone should motivate the user to exhaust every other alternative before standard water treatment is implemented.

Water Testing

Water is tested by collecting a sample and submitting it to a laboratory for analysis. The sample itself is small—about a cup of water. But what is tested? And how much is it going to cost you? Well, that depends on what you ask for. There are four basic types of test—coliform count, general, full-spectrum, and specific.

The Coliform Test

The coliform test (see Fig. 3–2) is designed to test whether the water is "safe"; implicit is "for human consumption or use." There are dozens of potentially harmful bacteria, and testing for all of them is time-consuming and therefore expensive. If you submit a water sample for a safety check, it should cost under twenty dollars. There's no way they could test for all bacteria at that price. So what *do* you get?

The standard coliform test searches for *E. coli*, a fecal coliform bacteria; this comes from the intestinal tract of warm-blooded animals. It is not in itself dangerous, but whenever it occurs in sufficient quantities, it is an indicator of the presence of the more harmful varieties of bacteria. Conversely, if it's not there, there's very little chance that any of the others are either.

If a test sample yields a high coliform count, have them repeat the test with a new sample; it's

carrier and solvent, dissolving and carrying away all manner of things. For our own convenience let's separate them into two main groups, organic materials and inorganic. Organic matter includes bacteria, viruses, parasites, and other wigglies; even trace amounts of many of these substances can be harmful to humans. When they are present, the water is called "unsafe." Before it is consumed, then, it must *always* be disinfected.

The presence of inorganic materials—elements, minerals, chemicals, dissolved or in suspension—a high or low pH (alkaline or acid), and odors constitutes a "condition." Excessive amounts of inorganic materials can be just as harmful as minute quantities of some organic materials, but for the most part many of these conditions are only a nuisance to humans, coating or eating away at pipes, staining clothes, giving us something less than good-smelling or sweet-tasting water. Water treated for inorganic materials, odors and tastes, and varying pH is said to be "conditioned."

From the start, it's important to realize that the

Figure 3-2
A Lab Report for Water "Safety"

For:

Sample:

Received:

RESULTS OF BACTERIOLOGICAL TEST FOR COLIFORM GROUP

Sample Identification	Coliform *M.P.N./100 ml.	Interpretation (see below)

Interpretation

A. The sample submitted is fit for drinking purposes.

B. The sample submitted shows a slight amount of contamination. We suggest another sample be submitted for examination. The greatest care should be taken so that the water is not contaminated when it is being sampled. In the meantime, the water should be boiled before it is used.

C. The sample submitted shows a high degree of contamination which may be due to sewage pollution. It is unfit for drinking purposes.

If the classification of your water sample is either "B" or "C," the situation may be corrected by pouring a gallon of Clorox or Purex into the well. After 24 hours, the water should be pumped through the system until no trace of Clorox or Purex can be detected. Two days later, another sample of water should be submitted for examination to determine if the contamination has been eliminated. In the meantime, the water should be boiled before it is used.

*Most probable number

very easy to contaminate the sample. As bad as it is to find coliform in the water source, it's even worse to have it *appear* to be present when, in fact, it's not. For less than twenty dollars, verification is cheap.

The General Test

A separate water sample may be submitted for a general test of the water, detecting the presence of other conditions—hardness (dissolved iron, manganese, calcium, etc.), acidity, odors, flavors, and turbidity (suspended particles). This test which ranges between forty and sixty dollars, will identify potential problems and show relationships (see Fig. 3–3); two conditions in combination may require different treatment than either one alone.

The Full-Spectrum Test

A full-spectrum test of a water sample is the high-priced test. It attempts to identify *everything* that's in the water sample submitted. Or if it's set up to test for a wide range of substances, it identifies everything above a certain minimum concentration. The price reflects this effort; expect this test to run at least one hundred and fifty dollars.

The Special Test

If you only want to check a water sample for one substance (besides coliform), it may be possible to get a lab to do it at a substantially reduced price. A lot will depend on how difficult or time-consuming it is for them to do this. However, get a quote. Less effort on their part doesn't always mean less money from you.

Where to Test

A water sample may be tested at a commercial laboratory that routinely does chemical analysis. Finding the one nearest you is no problem; simply contact the nearest sanitation department and ask them where they do theirs. If you want a coliform test *and* either a general or full-spectrum test, you may need two samples; call and ask. In some cases, particularly for the coliform test, the lab may supply the container to lessen the probability of contamination. In either case, follow the instructions *to the letter;* a poorly collected sample is money thrown away.

A few companies that specialize in water treat-

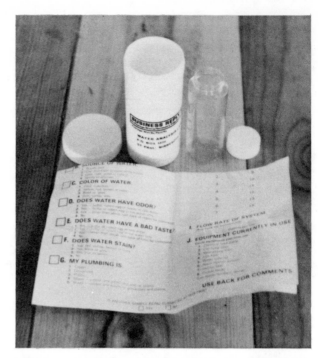

Fig. 3–4 Getting a water analysis is as simple as filling out a form, taking a sample, and mailing it off.

ment systems offer free general testing. This is an obvious sales gimmick; if your water needs treatment, they'll be more than happy to sell you the necessary equipment. There's usually no option to buy, so it can be a good place to take a sample. If there's nobody close offering this service, pop into the nearest Sears store and get a sample bottle and mailer; yep, they offer it, too!

There are several problems, though, with using water-treatment companies for water testing. One is that it's of questionable value: there's no way to verify the results without a professional lab. A second problem is that it's a one-shot deal; unless you can convince them you "blew" the first sample or want it verified, they're going to refuse to do any more free tests. (However, if there's an abundance of these places in your area, you can get a lot of testing done before you run out of places that will do it.) A third problem is that most of these places will not do a coliform test, and that may be the most important one of all.

Test Results

Okay, you've sent in a sample and the test results have been returned. What now? Scan the page and

CLIENT: _____

ADDRESS: _____

SAMPLE#: 9-6506 _____

DATE COLLECTED: 2-26-80

LOCATION: _____

COLLECTED BY: Client

STANDARD MINERAL ANALYSIS

ANIONS:	Mg/L	Meq/L	DETERMINATIONS:	Mg/L
Sulfate (SO$_4$)	250. PPM 23.7	0.49	*VARIABLE* Alkalinity, Total (CaCO$_3$)	98
Chloride (Cl)	250 PPM 18.8	0.53	Ca Hardness (CaCO$_3$)	NO LIMIT 60
Bicarbonate (HCO$_3$)	119	NO LEGAL LIMIT 1.95	Mg Hardness (CaCO$_3$)	NO LIMIT 31
Carbonate (CO$_3$)	25 PPM 0	No LEGAL 0 LIMIT.	Total Hardness (CaCO$_3$)	NO LIMIT 91·
Nitrate (NO$_3$)	45. PPM 2.4	0.04	Total Dissolved Solids (Calc.)	500.00 180
Fluoride (F)	1 PPM 0.16	0.008	pH	NO LIMIT 7.2
			Turbidity (NTU)	5 UNITS
TOTAL		3.01	Elec. Cond. (Micromhos)	900 275
CATIONS:			OTHER:	
Calcium (Ca)	24	(No LEGAL LIMIT) 1.20	Radioactivity Gross Alpha:	
Magnesium (Mg)	7.5	(NO LEGAL LIMIT) 0.62	15.0 PCI/L Activity= 0.00 PCi/1	
Sodium (Na)	20.00 18	(NO LEGAL LIMIT) 0.78	Error = 1.14 PCi/1	
Potassium (K)	1.7	0.04		
Manganese (Mn) Total	.05 3.1	---		
Iron (Fe) Total	0.3 7.8	---		
TOTAL		2.64		

Fig. 3-3 A general test report of water conditions.

you'll see chemical notations, lots of numbers, and strange words. Data. By itself, it's meaningless. Two things will help—a unit of measurement, and standards.

The unit of measurement used depends on the substance in question. For coliform, it's usually the MPN (most probable number) per 100 ml (milliliters) of sample. Alkaline or acid water is defined according to pH with neutral defined as pH 7.0. Anything below 7.0 is acid, and anything above is alkaline. Dissolved or suspended particles, minerals, or elements are listed in ppm (parts per million) or mg/l (milligrams per liter). All define the relative concentration of the substance in the water sample.

Once the counting is done, the figures obtained may be compared against a standard. Naturally, the standards vary according to the substance. A bit of a surprise comes with the discovery that these standards vary depending on the county, state, or country in which you live. Why? Experts don't always agree on what's safe. The closest they come is with coliform; most agencies would like to see only a 1 to 6 count of *E. coli* bacteria per 100 ml. With other substances it seems to be a matter of taste (no pun intended)—that is, the essential criterion is the extent to which it's a nuisance to *you*. The recommended procedure is to use the water and determine for yourself if it does or does not constitute a nuisance as is. If it doesn't, fine; if it does, do something about it.

You don't have to work without some sort of reference. Good reports will show both the sample concentrations and the standard concentration for each substance tested. If there is no legal or safe limit, either that item will be blank or they'll indicate that no standard exists. Excessive readings are frequently pointed out. If you hand-delivered or hand-retrieved the report from the lab, you may be able to snag someone who will interpret it for you. Be nice—you've paid for analysis, not consultation. If this effort fails, try the nearest public health facility.

A problem with either of these methods is that it's difficult to ask questions about something you know nothing about. So a better deal might be to check appropriate literature at the local library (see "References" at the end of the book) and make your own decisions about this.

WATER TREATMENT

Treatment Tactics

If the water you've sampled doesn't "pass" the test, what do you do? Start treatment? It would seem so—but we're not at that stage yet. No, it's better to formulate some tactics and isolate the problem. Here's a possible strategy:

1. Take another sample. This is surprisingly effective if there's some question about the validity of the analysis or if you simply don't like the answer you got. For example, a standard request by the testing laboratory following a water sample that shows a high coliform count is for you to submit another sample. It's easy to contaminate the sample during collection.

2. Use another testing facility. If the first test was free but gave poor results, pay for a second one at a good lab in the hopes of getting a better readout. If you paid for it the first time, you can still try another lab; anything other than coliform tests, however, are rarely inaccurate, so don't get your hopes up. Then, too, most laboratories can't afford to be sloppy in their work, particularly if you've paid the blue-cheese price. However, the question is academic until you either accept the findings or ask for verification with another sample submitted to the same, or another, lab.

3. Flush out the water system. Don't forget that the purpose of the coliform test is to determine whether the water source is contaminated. If the sample is collected after the water has traveled through pipes, tanks, and pumps, it could be contaminated by bacteria that thrive in these enclosures. A simple chlorination flush of the system (see Glossary) will eradicate this possibility. If the next sample shows the same high coliform count, the source is at fault; if it doesn't, it will be vindicated.

If the water source is undeveloped, there's obviously nothing to flush, right? Wrong! Spring water which "pools" or water standing in a well can nurture bacteria. Again, the application of chlorine will kill what's presently there, and provided that you can drain the spring's pool or pump the well's water free of the chlorine water, a new sample might be free of the coliform.

Eliminating the Source of Contamination

If the water is contaminated, the next question should be: Can I eliminate the source of contamination? This is particularly valid if a chlorine flush of the source or system yields a much improved test result in the second water sample. If contamination happened once, it could happen again. Often, though, this is the result of a poorly sited or badly installed system; *any* water source is susceptible to contamination during and after development. Again, it helps to know what can contaminate the water and what methods can be used to minimize or avoid the circumstance. Installing well seals, allowing for proper drainage, and siting the source away from animal-use areas or septic systems (even old ones) will help.

The pipes that carry water from the source to the usage area may also be sources of contamination. Steel pipe (galvanized or iron) yields cadmium and lead from the galvanizing. Copper pipe leaks lead from the solder and cadmium from the copper itself. Plastic pipe exudes cadmium, lead, and polymers from the plastic stabilizers and cement used to join the pipes. Slightly acid or very "soft" water tends to leach these chemicals from all of these types of pipe. I guess there's something to be said for "primitive" societies that use bamboo pipe.

Using Another Water Source

No water source is free from the possibility of contamination or conditions that might make its use objectionable. However, some sources are less susceptible than others to contamination (see "Evaluating the Water Source," Chapter 1). If you've the option, develop one of these instead. However, don't forget to test the alternative water source too.

Treatment of Unsafe Water

Water that contains more than standard amounts of coliform bacteria should be treated; if it isn't, illness or even death could result. There are presently four methods used to treat "unsafe" water—pasteurization, ultraviolet exposure, chlorination, and superchlorination—see table (Fig. 3–5) and "References" for more information on these methods.

A basic premise still very much in evidence today is that bacteria are "bad" and chemicals, particularly if they kill bacteria, are "good." However, data on the long-term exposure to chemicals—that is, chlorine or iodine—indicates that treating water with chemicals may be a case of using a lesser evil. For this reason, I'm reluctant to even suggest the use of chemicals to combat water-related problems. However, if no other treatment method is practical, chemicals should be used.

Standard treatment of water in need of purification involves equipment using chemicals or replaceable filters inserted in-line somewhere between the water source and the usage site. An alternate to this method is the "pinpoint" technique of water treatment. This acknowledges that there is no real need to treat *all* of the contaminated water, but only that portion that may be ingested—that is, water for drinking, cooking, and dishwashing. In this instance the *E. coli* count should not exceed 1 in 100 ml. Other applications—bathing, food crops, washing clothes—can safely handle an *E. coli* count of 2.2 per 100 ml. Irrigation of orchards, lawns, and gardens can handle a 23 per 100 ml count. These are *tough* standards. In fact, it's been suggested by various health agencies that some of these standards are too strict; ones that are three to fifteen times these concentrations have been proposed. Considering the rather low percentage of water ingested daily per person, a "pinpoint" treatment of "unsafe" water makes a lot of sense; by leaps and bounds, it reduces the initial cost, maintenance, and chemicals required to make water safe.

Water Conditioning

Water conditioning handles all other water treatment needs—softening hard water, neutralizing acid or alkaline water, filtering out suspended matter, eliminating odors or odd tastes, and so on. Again, water treatment consists of equipment and the chemicals or replaceable filters needed to perform the various tasks. Both the size and the sophistication of the equipment are directly related to the speed with which the treatment must be performed (the rate of water flow through the system) and the total volume involved. Higher flow rates and large volumes, then, mean increased cost. However, as with water disinfection, there is no need to treat *all* of the water in the system or, in this case, *every* condition.

The wide range of effects exhibited by various

Figure 3-5
A Comparison of Water Disinfection Methods

DISINFECTION METHODS

	SIMPLE CHLORINATION	SUPERCHLORINATION-DECHLORINATION	ELECTRIC PASTEURIZATION	ULTRAVIOLET RADIATION
Effectiveness Under Normal Conditions				
FOR KILLING BACTERIA	Effective.	Effective.	Effective.	Effective for clear water.
FOR KILLING VIRUSES	Effective with some viruses. Complete effectiveness has not been determined.	Effective with many viruses. Complete effectiveness has not been determined.	Effective with many viruses. Complete effectiveness has not been determined.	Effective with many viruses. Complete effectiveness has not been determined.
SPEED OF KILL (Bacteria)	Requires at least 20 minutes contact time with minimum chlorine residual of 0.2 to 0.5 ppm.	Requires about 10 seconds contact time with minimum chlorine residual of 5 ppm. (Longer contact times—5 to 7 min.—effective with many viruses.)	15 seconds.	Fast acting at proper light intensity level in water that is free of suspended particles and ultraviolet absorbing matter in solution.
Other Factors To Consider:				
EFFECT OF MINERALS IN WATER	Some chlorine is "used up" if iron or sulfur is present in water. If mineral content varies from time to time, dosage will need to be adjusted with simple chlorination to maintain proper chlorine residual. With super-chlorination, dosage is not readily affected.		Heating may cause mineral deposits to form thus slowing heat movement.	Minerals gradually coat lamp sleeve surfaces and reduce efficiency.
EFFECT OF HIGH WATER ALKALINITY	Purifying action slowed.	Purifying action slowed.	Not affected.	May tend to coat lamp sleeve(s).
EFFECT OF SUSPENDED PARTICLES IN WATER (Such as contained in pond water)	Water should be filtered to remove particles. Otherwise, it is difficult to maintain proper amount of chlorine residual, and the particles may protect some bacteria from the killing action of the chlorine.		Slows heat movement. May foul heat exchanger.	Greatly reduces effectiveness. Particles may protect some bacteria from killing action of light. Water must be effectively filtered first to remove all particles.
EFFECT OF INCOMING WATER TEMPERATURE	Increase in temperature speeds disinfecting action.	Lower temperatures slow disinfecting action.	Purification is not affected.	Most efficient at 100° F. water temperature. Less effective as temperature lowers.
RESIDUAL EFFECT (Ability after treatment to keep water disinfected)	With chlorine residual of 0.2 ppm or more, protection continues for several hours after treatment.	3 ppm or more residual provides excellent protection for many hours after treatment.	No protection after leaving pasteurizer.	No protection after leaving ultraviolet unit.
EFFECT ON WATER TASTE	May have some chlorine taste but is still palatable.	Not palatable for some humans until dechlorinated. Activated carbon filter is used at kitchen faucet to remove all chlorine taste for drinking-water purposes. Water is palatable to livestock and poultry.	Taste not affected.	Taste not affected.
PROTECTIVE MEANS USED TO ASSURE PROPER OPERATION	Color check with test kit enables user to determine amount of residual chlorine present. Water should be checked weekly.	Odor of chlorine is noticeable in super-chlorinated water before dechlorination.	Solenoid (electric) valve shuts off water supply when heating element burns out. It also returns water to heater if inadequately heated.	Equipped with solenoid (electric) valve to shut off water supply when lamp(s) dims or burns out, or electric service is interrupted.
CAPACITY	Available for any capacity water system.	Available for any capacity water system.	20 gal. per hour (Size presently available).	Various size units available for any capacity water system.
ADVANTAGES IN ADDITION TO DISINFECTION	Can be used to remove iron, sulfur, and certain tastes and odors. Kills iron and sulfur bacteria.		None.	None.

Figure 3-6
Analyzing and Measuring Water-Conditioning Problems

SYMPTOMS	PROBABLE CAUSE	MEASUREMENT
HARDNESS • Sticky curd forms when soap is added to water. Causes well-recognized ring in bathtub. • The harder the water, the more soap required to form suds. • Glassware appears streaked and murky. • Hard, scaly deposits form inside of metal pipes. • Your skin roughens from washing.	Calcium and magnesium in the water (may be in the form of bicarbonates, sulfates, or chlorides). Iron also contributes to hardness. (See next group of symptoms—Red Water.)	Test kit: Standard soap solution is added to two oz. of water one drop at a time. Solution is shaken until lasting suds form. Number of drops are approximately equal to grains per gallon of hardness. (One grain is equal to 17.1 ppm.) 0 – 3 drops (approx. 50 ppm) — Soft water 4 – 6 drops (50–100 ppm) — Moderately hard 7 – 12 drops (100–200 ppm) — Hard 13 – 18 drops (approx. 200 - 300 ppm) — Very hard 19 or more drops (over 300 ppm) — Extremely hard
RED WATER **Dissolved Iron** • Red stains appear on clothes and porcelain plumbing fixtures, even if as little as 0.3 ppm is present. • Causes corrosion of steel pipes. • Water has metallic taste. • Freshly drawn water sometimes appears clear at first. After exposure to air, rust particles form and settle to bottom of container. **Iron Bacteria** • Red slime develops in toilet tanks.	Iron (sometimes including manganese) Caused by dissolving action of water as it passes through underground iron deposits, or contacts iron and steel surfaces. Caused by living organisms (bacteria) that act on iron already in the water. Often associated with acid or other corrosive conditions.	Test kit: • Standard acid solution is added to water sample to dissolve iron that has settled out. • Color solution(s) is added. • Resulting pink is matched with a standard color chart, which is usually rated in ppm. • Correction is usually recommended if test shows more than .3 ppm of iron. For iron bacteria check, remove toilet tank cover and check for slippery, jelly-like coating on surfaces.
BROWNISH-BLACK WATER • Fixtures stain brownish black. • Fabrics stain black. • Coffee and tea have bitter taste.	• Manganese is present usually along with iron. • Manganese bacteria	• Test for iron in solution also measures manganese in solution, when present. Manganese bacteria cause slippery coating similar to iron except of darker color.
ACIDITY • "Eats away" copper and steel parts on pump, piping, tank, and fixtures. • If copper or brass are being "eaten," water may leave green stains on plumbing fixtures under a dripping faucet. • If water contains iron, iron-removal methods are less effective.	Water contains carbon dioxide picked up from air, or from decaying vegetable matter, which combines with water to form a weak acid. In rare instances, water may contain mineral acid such as sulfuric, nitric, or hydrochloric acids.	Test kit: • Chemical indicator is added to water sample and resulting color compared with a standard color chart to determine degree of acidity. • Measurement may be either in ppm or by "pH." If the latter, any number less than pH 7 indicates an acid condition. The smaller the number, the more acid present. If pH is less than 6, it is usually best to correct acidity.
"ROTTEN EGG" ODOR AND FLAVOR • "Eats away" iron, steel, and copper parts of pumps, piping and fixtures. • If sulfur and iron are both present in water, finely divided black particles may develop, which is commonly called "black water." Silverware turns black. • Not satisfactory for cooking.	• Hydrogen-sulfide gas • Sulfate-reducing bacteria • Sulfur bacteria	• Dealers handling water-treating equipment will usually determine the amount of sulfur present from an on-the-spot sample. • Correction is needed if test shows more than 1 ppm of sulfur.
OTHER OFF FLAVORS • Water may taste bitter, brackish, oily, salty, or have a chlorine odor or taste.	• Extremely high mineral content • Presence of organic matter • Excess chlorine • Water passage through areas containing salty or oily waste, etc.	Some off-taste problems are associated with the other water-quality problems listed in this table. There is no one specific test to use for other off tastes.
TURBIDITY • Water with a dirty or muddy appearance.	• Silt • Sediment • Small organisms • Organic matter	Turbidity is generally measured in "turbidity units" based on the percent of light transmitted through the water sample. If measured in parts per million, turbidity may vary from less than 1 to as much as 4,000 ppm. More than 10 ppm is considered objectionable. Health departments and manufacturers of filtering equipment make such tests since special laboratory equipment is required.

conditions (see Fig. 3–6) prohibits a generalization of what water needs treatment and what does not. For example, the presence of off flavors in the water is of little consequence when the water is used in gardening, dishwashing, showers, or the toilet. On the other hand, if the water is hard, soap won't produce suds, which is inconvenient for dishwashing, bathing, and washing clothes. However, if dissolved iron is partially responsible for the hard water, it will still precipitate out and streak clothing, but with dishwashing or bathing, its effects are not bothersome and may, in the case of gardening, actually be considered beneficial (plants need iron, too). So the list of specific needs for treated water depends very much on the specific condition.

Certain combinations of conditions can complicate the selection of the proper treatment method. For instance, simple chlorination will not effectively kill bacteria in water that contains dissolved iron (see Fig. 3–5). For this reason, the iron must be filtered out *prior* to the chlorine disinfecting treatment or, if this is impractical, the system must employ another disinfecting method that is not affected by the presence of dissolved iron. So though *each* condition has an effective treatment, ignorance of the interaction of two or more conditions in the water can lead to ineffectual treatment results. This is no place for rank amateurs.

Water Treatment Through Distillation

Distillation has often been used as a means of disinfecting or conditioning water. In a still built for this purpose, the source water is heated and evaporated. Either way, the water vapor then condenses when it contacts the cool collector surface and is drawn off as pure water. The sustained high temperature of the still kills most bacteria; those that don't die immediately are left behind along with the minerals, elements, and other contaminants. With good design, proper care in operation (to ensure that the condensed water does not contact the source water), and periodic removal of the residue in the still's pan, this is an effective water-treatment method.

In the past, distillation has been ignored as a water treatment method because of the energy requirement and the prohibitive size of the equipment needed to cope with the volume of water needing treatment. However, as the pinpoint technique limits the treatment requirement to a small percentage of the total water usage, it also increases the probability that distillation can handle that level of treatment. Given the strides made in the development of low-cost distillers utilizing solar energy as the heat source (see "References"), the amount of energy needed for water treatment can be minimized or altogether eliminated!

Fig. 3–7 A solar still is a cost-effective means of water treatment.

Final Comments

If you leave the decisions related to water treatment to "experts," be aware of the disadvantages in doing this. An expert associated with the manufacture and sale of water-treatment equipment has a conflict of interest, and may sell you a treatment system to combat a condition that would not have adverse effects if left as is. The best you may hope for in this circumstance is that the system won't also be several times the size it really needs to be.

Water treatment is big business. One of the hardest-pushed industries is water softening. What they *don't* tell you is that soft water leaches cadmium and lead from the galvanizing in steel pipes, the solder in copper pipes, and the stabilizers and joint cement in plastic pipes. Even in trace amounts, these metals are two of the deadliest substances humans can ingest. And still, onward marches the water-softening industry. However, just knowing the effect soft water can have on pipes or your health is of some benefit. If your water is only mildly hard, leave it alone; there are soaps that are effective in hard-water conditions. If the water is really too hard, soften it only somewhat. And if any type of water-softening equipment is installed, locate it as close to the usage point as possible to minimize the amount of pipe the soft water contacts.

It is beyond the scope of this book to deal extensively with water treatment principles, methods and equipment. To do so would also be an unnecessary duplication of some really good material that is available on the subject. Hopefully, you will not need to treat the water in your system. However, if a test sample indicates that you do, I refer you to one single reference on the subject: *Planning for an Individual Water System* (see "References"). It will help you diagnose and treat the wide variety of conditions affecting water purity. This is necessary reading for anyone who plans to use treatment or to select and install treatment equipment. It is, as well, recommended reading for the individual who will have someone else do it. Why? Several treatment methods exist for each condition; selecting the one that fits your system is best done by you, and not someone unfamiliar with it. Additionally, this will give you an idea of what you really need; some of this equipment can be expensive, and having this information beforehand gives you a check of a company's estimate of the equipment you need. It's nice to know that you're *not* getting ripped off as well as important to know when you *are*.

MULTIPLE USE OF WATER

High-capacity water sources are not always abundant. Even if they are, they're often contaminated enough to require some form of treatment. And with the rising cost of utility-supplied electricity and of the devices to convert on-site energy sources (wind, water, methane, etc.) into a useful form, processing a lot of water is an expensive proposition. Conservation makes sense, but after the elimination of wasteful habits or inefficient usage, a sizable amount of water is still required to carry out daily functions—drinking, cooking, washing dishes and clothes, bathing, brushing teeth, shaving, flushing toilets, irrigating flowers, lawns, orchards, and food-producing gardens. So what else can one do to minimize the amount of water that is processed daily? How about using it several times?

The multiple use of water goes by a number of names: "gray water," "recycled water," "reused water." By whatever name, it defines a circle. Most water systems are circular. Water is extracted from the ground, processed into a rate of flow and pressure that is useful in the household, then returned to the ground via the septic tank. Sewer lines, such as those found in the city, violate this principle, resulting in a linear process that does not return water to the ground except through the earth's hydrological cycle. However, the various farm uses of water also tend to be linear, with freshly processed water on the input side and dirty, used water on the output side. (See Fig. 3–8.)

One-time usage of water is very American. By convention, when water is used, it's thereafter "dirty," and the uppermost thought in the minds of most people is to flush it away. This *is* valid for toilet water—it is extremely dangerous for humans to reuse it without first treating it—but no other usage of water requires such extensive treatment before reuse is possible. With some applications, *no* treatment is dictated for direct or immediate reuse.

This should not surprise anyone; the absurdity of using grade AAA (pure) water in the toilet—*the* most glaring example of poor water use today—has undoubtedly registered in the minds of many people. People who have to make do with limited water supplies in droughts or other emergencies

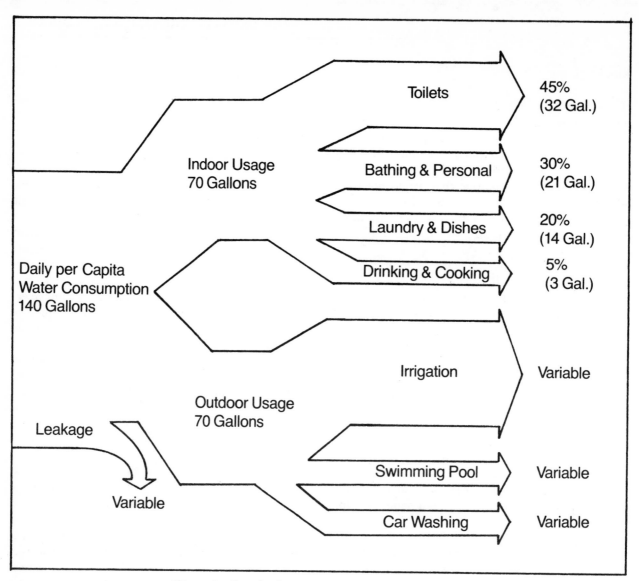

Fig. 3–8   Standard per capita water consumption.

have discovered no ill effect in using dishwater and shower (or bath) water on their gardens or plants; in fact, the produce seems to thrive on the used water. It should—food particles and some types of soaps are welcome nutrients to a food-producing garden.

Before we can adequately address the reuse of water, it's important to know how and where residential water is presently used. Time to break out the old pencil and paper and make a list of each water use in your household. Or, if you consider yourself "average" you might identify with the figures given in Fig. 3–8. This drawing is taken from the first chapter in *Residential Water Re-Use* by Murray Milne, and his summation of the drawing is enlightening:

"The flow chart shows that, as a rough rule of thumb, toilets use half of all indoor water while outdoor water represents about half of all residential consumption, and so toilets plus irrigation account for about two-thirds of all consumption."

In light of this information, the possibilities for water reuse seem suddenly infinite. However, before you run amuck, note a few realities.

1. Group all your water needs into "shades" of purity. Don't worry about accuracy; as you gain more information you can adjust the groupings accordingly. By doing this *before* you learn more, you'll discover the strength of your intuition in this matter. Do it now! When you're finished, drinking

and cooking water should be at the top of the list and toilet water should be at the bottom.

2. Reuse should match capacities. Channeling water left over from drinking and cooking (don't forget that some is consumed) for use in a toilet is well-intentioned but not efficient; drinking and cooking water amount to only 5 percent of indoor consumption of water, and the toilet takes a whopping 45 percent. Somehow, the toilet must acquire water from another source. Should you make up the difference with the same grade of water that feeds the tap in the kitchen sink? No! That water is too good for the toilet. That's a personal decision, of course, but there's another reason why you shouldn't do this. And that is—

3. *Never mix* "shades" of water. Connecting a water supply line to the inlet of both the kitchen sink and the toilet *and* routing the kitchen sink's drain to the toilet also is dangerous. What's to prevent the "used" water from cycling back to the faucet of the kitchen sink?

4. The resourceful designer will see a means of abiding by three of these points by grouping bathing and personal water, laundry and dishes, *and* drinking and cooking water together and channeling the combined (approximate) 55 percent usage into the toilet. That sounds good. Unfortunately, it's *not correct*. While only black water (any water carrying fecal material) requires extensive treatment, only water from brushing teeth, shaving, and spillage of drinking water requires *no* treatment if it's to be used in the toilet. And even if this capacity matched the water requirement for the toilet, there'd be a practical difficulty in channeling this water to the toilet since the kitchen sink is also used for dishwashing and the bathroom sink is also used for brushing teeth and face cleansing; waste water from both of these sinks, along with water from laundry, bathing, and the kitchen's garbage grinder, would first need minor treatment (usually filtering or settling).

If water from any of these functions were used *immediately* in the toilet and flushed away, there'd be no problem. However, loaded as this water is with suspended food particles, soap, and bacteria, the toilet's holding tank would soon be a teeming primordial soup. Given the current arrangement of the standard toilet—the holding tank situated behind the toilet bowl—this is a scary situation; in using the toilet, you'd never see the tank lid inching its way up!

At this point, the gray-water system might seem overwhelmingly complex and beyond useful consideration. However, long-term study, experimentation, and usage of water-recycling systems has clearly established what water can be reused where, directly, and where contraindicated, what minimum treatment is required. This information, coupled with the practical need to minimize the plumbing, points toward a system that cuts per capita consumption in half without sacrificing any usage requirements (see Fig. 3–10).

The gray-water system is an intriguing concept to the fledgling water-system designer who is confronted with the cost of developing a water source, equipping it with water-processing and, possibly, water-purification or conditioning equipment, and shelling out small but cumulative sums each month for the energy needed to keep it all going. Using *half* the water, then, should carry across the board, slicing the energy bills in half and reducing the size and hence the cost of water pumping, pressurizing, and treatment equipment. But so far all of this is just a bunch of words on paper. Besides, if this is so hot an idea, why isn't it being done everywhere?

That's a good question. The answer comes in three parts.

1. Gray-water systems lend themselves to new construction; retrofits are usually complicated by poor access to the existing plumbing and drains. In addition, in new dwellings the implementation of a water reuse system often influences the initial layout; by planning ahead you can avoid the cost of pumps to transport used water to holding tanks and other purposes. With a little forethought, it's possible to arrange household functions so that this water can use gravity to flow about. In the existing residence, however, there's little probability that things will work out as neatly.

2. Economics plays a big part in gray-water installations. Since the big water crunch hasn't hit yet (to some, that it ever will is pure speculation) implementing gray-water usage is left to conservationists and those in desperate need. Right off, there's little chance that any of these folks will use the commercial equipment that's available for this purpose; they will choose instead to fabricate or adapt equipment to this purpose. In the process, the system often loses any semblance of "automatic" functioning. For example, low-cost sand filters may be constructed in 30-gallon drums.

Figure 3-9
Examples of On-Site Reuse

Reuse

Original Source	Toilet[a]	Irrigation	Sprinkler[c]	Kitchen sink grinder	Carwash	Laundry[c]	Pool	Shower/tub	Bathroom sink	Dishwasher	Drinking	Cooking	Fire fighting	Rainwater	Groundwater
Toilet	2	2	2												2[f]
Irrigation*[b]		1	1										1		0
Sprinkler		1	1										1		0
Kitchen sink grinder	1	0	1												
Carwash*		0°			1										
Laundry[d]	1	0°	1°			0									
Pool							2						0		
Shower/tub	1	0°	1°			1		0							
Bathroom sink[e]	0	0°	1°												
Dishwasher	1	0°	1°	0											
Drinking* (spillage)	0	0	1	0				0				0			
Cooking	1	0	1	0						0	0	0			
Fire fighting													0	0	
Rainwater	0	0	0	0	0	0	0	0	0	0	1	1	1		0
Groundwater	0	0	0	0	0	0	0	0	0	0	1	1	1		

Legend

0 Reusable directly (without treatment)
1 Reusable with settling and/or filtering
  (primary treatment)
2 Reusable with settling, filtering, and
  chemical treatment usually chlorination
  (secondary treatment)

Notes

* Very difficult to collect
° Special soaps required
a Small valves & underwater moving parts
  may cause clogging problem
b Large orifice: unpressurized open hose or
  channel
c Small orifice: pressurized
d Assumes no diapers with fecal matter
e Shaving and brushing teeth
f Septic tank and leach field

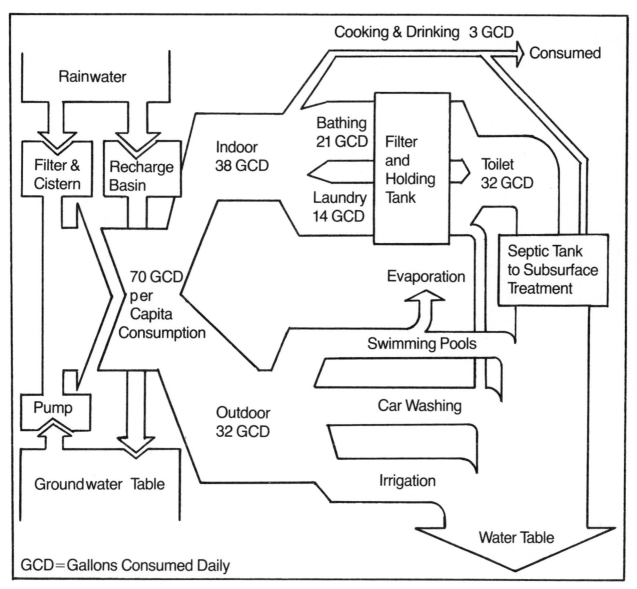

Fig. 3-10 This reuse system reduces water demand by 50 percent.

However, each filter must be regularly serviced; this involves cleaning or replacement of the sand, gravel, or whatever. This is not a problem, but faithfully remembering to do it *is*. A sand filter is a perfectly safe way of treating contaminated (used) water—but if overtaxed or left uncleaned, it actually becomes a *source* of contamination. Understanding human nature and oneself, then, can cause a person to shy away from implementing a system that counts too heavily on the user to keep it working safely.

3. For the most part, gray-water systems are illegal. The stigma attached to water reuse is reflected and, alas, perpetuated by the building, plumbing, and sanitation codes that govern the construction of new residences in the U.S.A. Some of these codes prohibit outright or so severely confuse, restrict, or red-tape *any* deviation from the connection to a sewage line (in the city) or septic tank (in the country) that the individual must surely feel that any attempt will be for naught. Nevertheless, countless gray-water systems exist inside the United States, while outside of it, the one-use water system is the *exception*.

What's the honest person to do? The codes were originally established to protect the homeowner. To some extent, some of them no longer serve that function. You can protest them, as others have done, some successfully, others not. Changes *are* happening; if you wait long enough, you can do it legally. If not, silently effect your own changes.

Final Comments

Just in case you hadn't noticed, I'd like to make one thing very clear. This section on gray water is meant as general information on what I believe to be a sound, practical, and cost-effective way to do more with less. However, this is intended only as an introduction; you cannot *safely* set up a gray-water system from the material presented here. If you're intrigued by the concept, obtain more information (see "References"). This will not only keep you out of trouble, it will enlighten you to the multitude of tried-and-proven setups, help you build the needed equipment, and introduce you to a lot of people utilizing water reuse in their daily lives. In short, you're likely to find precisely the right system for your own situation, retrofit or otherwise.

4

HARDWARE

A water system is a gathering of functions and, likewise, component parts. The hardware varies from system to system; some situations extract drastically different performances from the components selected to accommodate them. Does this make the job of hardware selection a difficult one? No—there is a finite amount of equipment that exists for water system use; by knowing, say, the type of system you'd use—demand or store—you will be a long way toward selecting your equipment. The rest is often just a matter of filling in the blanks or satisfying personal preferences.

Beware. In the midst of this process, it's easy to lose sight of one fact: *a system is no stronger than its smallest or weakest part*. So no matter how minimal the role, even minor parts must function as unerringly as a major component. It's true that selecting the correct parameters of a component like a pump or storage will take the lion's share of our attention as we strive to match it to our system and circumstances alike. But if taken for granted, a casual selection of other components —pipe and other accessories—can undo that labor. So while most of the hardware has been mentioned in previous chapters, this is where we add the rib-bons and bows, detailing essential parameters and critical aspects of their interplay with other parts.

PIPES

Once we've selected all of the major components in the water system—pumps, tanks, controls, etc.—we need only some way of tying it all together. To do that, we use pipes. There are three basic types of pipe readily available for use in water systems, and they're distinguished by the material from which they're made—galvanized steel, copper, or plastic. Ultimately one must select one of these types of pipe for a water system.

More often, however, all three types of pipe will be used in the water system. Why? Each has inherent characteristics that, in certain situations, become an advantage or disadvantage. So that you will understand which type of pipe will work best where, each type of pipe will be evaluated in the light of twelve factors: types, sizes, pipe smoothness, internal corrosion, external corrosion, deposits, temperature extremes, conductivity, ultraviolet resistance, ruggedness, weight, and cost.

After a factor-by-factor analysis, we'll take a look at other design or installation particulars, such as flow rates, pressure drop, layout, and fittings, that affect our selection of pipe.

Types

Galvanized steel pipe, copper pipe, and plastic pipe are available in 20-foot rigid lengths (the standard galvanized is 1 foot longer than the others). However, tubing, which is flexible enough to be wound in coils, is available in both soft copper and plastic, and in lengths ranging from 60 to 100 feet, depending on pipe diameter.

Several subcategories are notable. For example, two types of copper tubing are available: K (heavy-duty) and L (standard). The major difference is the wall thickness of the pipe; the thicker wall in the K type protects the tubing in crush (buried situations, under higher working pressures, and in a vacuum if the pipe is used as the tail pipe in push-pull pumping water extraction (see Fig. 2–25). Both of these types are standardly available in either soft (non-rigid) or hard (rigid) tempers; the hard-temper has a small percentage of nickel added to rigidize the pipe for use in installations necessitating long, unsupported spans.

Plastic pipe is normally PVC (polyvinyl chloride) whereas the softer, more flexible plastic tubing is identified as PE (polyethylene). A visual indicator completes the distinction: PVC is white or gray, and PE is black. In the PVC type, a list of "schedules" defines differences in wall thickness, working pressures, and other characteristics.

Sizes

Pipe of any type is available in various diameters; most small-scale water systems will require pipe sizes of ½, ¾, 1, 1¼, 1½, 2, 2½, and 3 inches. This is the *inside* diameter of the pipe. Along with total pipe length, working pressure, and desired flow rate (in gallons per minute), diameter is a crucial factor in the selection of pipe.

Unfortunately, this calculation is seldom performed. Instead, the selection of pipe size is generally based on other factors—primarily cost and questionable advice. As pipe length is determined solely by circumstance, and working pressure is inherent in the purchased pump, the inside diameter of the pipe is the key factor affecting the rate of

flow, often adversely. If it's satisfactory, either the owner is awfully lucky or the pump has been intentionally sized too large to accommodate inadequate pipe size. If this occurs, the owner has only traded pump dollars for pipe dollars.

Pipe Smoothness

The smoothness of the pipe's internal surface directly affects flow rate. The rougher the surface, the greater the resistance to flow. This immediately affects the water directly in contact with the interior surfaces; in any pipe, the water flowing through the center meets the least resistance. However, when higher pressures are used to force water through a pipe to compensate for this resistance, the effect of interior surface resistance becomes more pronounced; water in contact with the rough surfaces will be turbulated, and will spread this effect to water not in contact with the surfaces. As rates increase, so does the effect, further frustrating efforts to compensate for friction losses by establishing higher working pressures.

Internal Corrosion

Pipes have a life-span; unless you live dangerously, chances are they'll need replacing before you die. It's hard to get worked up on this issue; after all, who needs to be worrying about the day when the pipes need replacing when they're not even in the ground yet? Nevertheless, give it some thought; it is convenient to prolong the moment for as long as possible. If you plan to keep your place until you die, there's only one thing worse than having to replace the pipes sometime in the distant future, and that's having to do it *twice*.

Corrosion can occur from within or without. If we're looking at internal corrosion, we must give first honors to plastic pipe, a second-place award to copper, and the consolation prize to galvanized steel. The galvanized steel pipe is affected by extremes in the water's pH; either a strongly acid or strongly alkaline pH will rapidly corrode it.

External Corrosion

The exterior of any pipe is also exposed to corrosion. Water is the main culprit here, and as is the case with internal corrosion, its greatest effect occurs with galvanized steel; however, the galvanized coating is there to slow down the corrosion process, and it does. Copper is less susceptible than PVC pipe, but more apt to corrode. Both galvanized steel and copper pipe will last five times longer in relatively dry soils than when buried in earth that is saturated year-round.

Deposits

Both galvanized steel and copper pipes are susceptible to lime deposits from hard water, though the steel pipe may be protected from this and the corrosive effect of water with a strongly acid or alkaline pH by a coating of a phosphate material; if this is necessary, oversize the pipe to accommodate the thickness of the coating without sacrificing flow rates. Copper pipe is also particularly susceptible to deposits of matter suspended in the water, though no pipe is entirely free of some type of mineral deposit. Only plastic pipe is resistant to corrosion and deposits of any type.

Temperature Extremes

Temperature, particularly extremes of hot or cold, can affect pipes. PVC is far less resistant than either copper or galvanized steel pipe in this regard; extreme heat can melt, deform, or crystallize the plastic, making it brittle. However, if sufficient temperature is reached to boil water in the pipes, PVC might fare better than either galvanized steel or copper pipe; its ability to expand may permit it to survive pressure that will burst the others. Nevertheless, PVC is not recommended for use in hot-water lines (and the plumbing code prohibits it) since repeated exposure will make it brittle. In addition, water contamination from PVC rises to alarming levels at increased temperatures; it'd be okay for showers but horrible to drink.

By the way, the plastic pipe industry is presently involved in a struggle to change the codes to permit the use of plastic pipe for waterlines inside the house, particularly for hot-water lines. Original objections to the use of plastic pipe stemmed from contaminants released from the plastic, or the glue that joins it, when exposed to hot water. The industry claims to have made changes that have eliminated these dangers; since I'm not privy to

that proof, I can't judge these claims. However, all three types of pipe—galvanized steel, copper, and plastic—release contaminants (see "Eliminating the Source of Contamination," Chapter 3).

The other extreme, freezing, is toughest on galvanized steel, with copper a close second and PVC a distant third. PVC has the edge here with its ability to expand and contract. However, none of these pipes will withstand a hard freeze, so all will need proper burial below the frost line; check with a local plumbing shop to ascertain that depth in your area. If you bury a pipe at only the frost line or aboveground in unheated spaces, insulation is required. However, remember that insulation only slows down the transfer of heat; a sustained freeze will get to even insulated pipes. In this instance, the pipes may be wrapped with electrical heating tape, which can be plugged into the nearest outlet; a temperature-sensitive switch can turn on the juice whenever the pipes are just above the freezing point.

Conductivity

Pipes that conduct electricity are subject to an electrolytic action which can result in a form of corrosion. This occurs when a metal pipe, buried in dissimilar soils, comes in contact with dissimilar materials (metals or conductors), or is buried in the vicinity of an improperly grounded electrical circuit. The resultant flow of current is corrosive in nature and is most pronounced at the actual junction of dissimilar materials.

The remedies are straightforward. Trenches should be inspected for drastic changes in soil composition. Distinct junctures *perpendicular* to the length of the trench should be "diluted" by mixing the removed soils, part of which will form a bed for the installed pipe to rest on and the remainder of which will be used for fill. Soil differences in layers along the trench should be mixed in the same manner, or the pipe should be laid in one soil type and the refill carefully done with the same type. Wherever copper is joined with galvanized steel pipe, special copper-to-galvanized steel connectors should be used; they're designed to minimize the electrolytic action. Use correct procedures when grounding all electrical circuits.

No electrolytic action occurs wth PVC pipe; it's a nonconductor.

Ultraviolet Resistance

Exposure to sunlight has its effect on any type of pipe; the heating effect varies with the situation. However, an additional ingredient—ultraviolet radiation—is of concern. Copper and galvanized steel are not affected, but ultraviolet radiation breaks down any type of plastic, disintegrating the bonds of the polymers and turning the plastic brittle. There's enough ultraviolet in indirect rays to do the job, but direct sunlight is the real killer.

Type PE plastic tubing has virtually no protection against ultraviolet light and deteriorates rapidly; in a few years it won't hold water. PVC pipe is loaded with ultraviolet inhibitors; for this reason, it's said to be UV-resistant. However, this is a play on words, the same ploy used in describing wristwatches—there's a lot of difference between water "proof" and water "resistant!" So all PVC pipe should be buried in the ground or inside walls; in low-level indirect lighting under houses, it'll get by.

Ruggedness

There's no real "ruggedness" rating associated with pipe, but there should be. Long before it gets into the ground, it will be subjected to use and abuse, and possible damage. This may start before you buy it, so check it out; it's always hard to prove later that it was that way when you got it. Then, too, most vehicles aren't equipped to handle the 20-foot lengths of most pipe. The ride home with the pipe strapped onto the roof of a car or projecting from the back of a pickup truck can be rough indeed. After all that, there's the installation itself, where the pipe is usually expected to fit into trenches that really didn't turn out all that straight and into couplings that are a little too close or too far away. You should run pressurized water through all pipe prior to burying it to discover if it's survived it all.

Once buried, the pipe may be subjected to pressure that will crush it or push it against sharp objects that may penetrate the wall. If this doesn't happen, the pipe need only contend with overzealous bulldozer operators, fencepost drivers, hole diggers, sharp-teethed gophers, and ripper earthquakes.

Ideally we need a pipe that's resistant to bending but flexible enough to withstand transport and placement in curvy trenches, and that's punctureproof, crushproof, and gnawproof. Understandably, galvanized steel pipe is the toughest; its only drawback here is its rigidity, which makes it difficult to bend, over even long spans, to fit trenches. Copper pipe resists most of these abuses but can't survive flagrant abuse; it curves within limits but will collapse if pushed too far; it's gnawproof but easily penetrated by sharp rocks and crushed under some conditions; the thick-wall (type K) copper pipe should be used for burial and the standard (type L) reserved for in-wall or under-house usage. Long, unsupported spans dictate tempered copper.

Plastic pipe is the most vulnerable to these conditions. Type PE is *very* easy to lay in trenches but is easily penetrated and crushed, and is the sort of material gophers dream about. PVC fares better, although the heavy-duty (200, 80, or 40 schedules should be used. It's rigid but flexible, crush-resistant but fairly easy to puncture; obviously, the thicker the wall (the higher the schedule), the higher the puncture resistance.

Weight

Diameter for diameter, foot for foot, plastic pipe is light, copper pipe is close to light, and galvanized pipe is downright heavy.

The weight of the pipe is usually not a factor in selection, except for certain occasions. For example, if you live in the boonies and have to walk it in, you'll love plastic pipe, manage with copper, and call your friends in for handling the galvanized steel pipe. Per foot, it won't seem like much, but don't forget that 20-foot length. The pipe may be cut in half to make it more manageable, but this decision must be made prior to taking it to the site, since the cut ends, in the case of galvanized pipe, must be threaded. This will cost extra, but the company you purchase it from will normally have the machinery to do this quickly. Doing it on your own necessitates the purchase of a costly cutter (which handles only one size of pipe) and a lot of hard work; if you don't figure to do this for a living, get it done elsewhere or use another type of pipe. Given the cost of couplers, it seems better to invite friends over for a pipe-hauling and -laying party when it's time.

Cost

The smallest size of pipe used in a water system is usually ½ inch in diameter, and the largest normally 2 inches. As of this writing, plastic pipe is the cheapest overall pipe for the diameter, only competitive with copper pipe in the ½- and ¾-inch sizes and thereafter very inexpensive. Copper quickly becomes prohibitively expensive for sizes larger than ¾ inch, about that point even surpassing galvanized steel in price. Galvanized steel cannot compete with plastic at any point, but it fares better than copper at sizes larger than ¾ inch (see Fig. 4–1).

The cost of pipe is usually the first thing that people will look at, but I've placed it at the end because that's where it really belongs. The cost of pipe makes people buy too little of it, the cheapest type, and the smallest size. In the end, these people get what they pay for, not realizing that *pipe is the most important component in the water system*. A larger size of pipe will handle future increased water needs. A larger size of pipe reduces pipe friction and therefore pressure losses, minimizing the pump size required to deliver water at satisfactory rates and pressures. Of course it costs more; understandably, then, one doesn't want to buy a pipe that's larger than necessary.

Other system components may be more expensive to purchase, maintain, and repair, but they've got one thing going for them: they're accessible. Pipe isn't, so after the purchase, connection, and burial, that's it. Digging up pipe is hard work, which seems even harder when it's unnecessary. Some "bargain-priced" pipe would be wonderful if we didn't have to bury it—but we do.

Pipe prices vary considerably, so don't be afraid to shop around. If possible, get it all at one shot and ask for a discount for quantity. Ask for a bid. Show the bid from one place to another; someone may go lower to beat out a competitor. Transport it yourself to chop the cost of delivery. Do whatever you need to do, but *don't buy cheap pipe,* or pipe that is too small or otherwise not right for your situation. Remember, the bitterness of poor quality is remembered long after the sweetness of low cost is forgotten!

Pipe and System Design

Sizing the pipe for the water system and planning the layout is a process. It's also fun; think of it as a

Figure 4-1
Pipe Costs

Pipe Size (in inches)	Galvanized	Price Index*			
		Copper		Plastic	
		Type M	Type L	PE	PVC
1/2	23	18	23	2	4
3/4	28	28	37	3	6
1	39	41	53	4	9
1-1/4	51	60	71	7	11
1-1/2	61	81	91	9	12
2	82	125	138	15	16

*represents comparative values. For mid-1981, low-quantity prices, multiply indicated index number by 7¢ to get the cost per foot. Example: 1-inch, type L copper pipe would cost $3.71 per foot (53 multiplied by 7¢).

big puzzle that's uniquely your own. Solving it will require a little time, some forethought, a modicum of patience, a smidgen of imagination, a few sharp pencils, and some paper. Four other major ingredients are required.

Water Needs

I'm supplying a table (see Fig. 4–2) that lists approximate daily water consumption tallies, and also a table (see Fig. 2–9) of average rates. However, since your situation is unique, your water consumption is unique. If you believe yourself to be average (whatever that means anymore), select the appropriate gallons of consumption per person, multiply by the number of persons in your household, and total those figures. It's permissible to represent children as fractions with the possible exception of any that have an irritating habit of flushing the toilet repeatedly—that will really throw off your daily water needs.

Computing water usage is not meant to embarrass you or give you a case of the guilts; however conspicuous your consumption of water, it's privileged information. Besides, this process determines the size of your pipes, and they're *buried*. Your secret will be safe.

Figure 4-2
Average Water Consumption

FUNCTION	GALLONS
Bathtub, each filling	30
Shower, each time used	30-60
Lavatory, each time used	2
Flush Toilet, each filling	6
Sink, per day	20
Laundry Tub, each filling	20
3/4" Hose Nozzle, per hour	300
Dishwasher, per load	3
Automatic Washer, per cycle	17
Members of Family, each per day	25-50
Chickens, per 100, per day	4-9

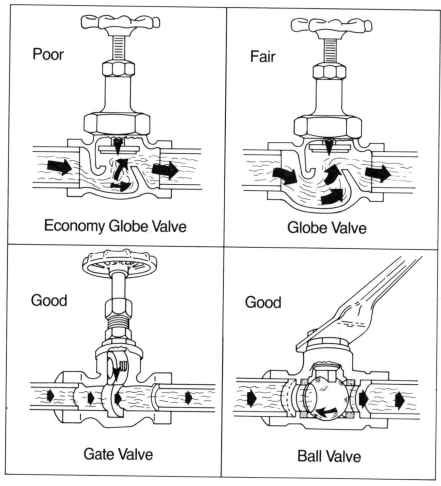

Fig. 4–3 Some types of valve are restrictive to water flow.

Flow Rates

Once the uses are stated, the figures must be translated into flow rates. The *amount* of water used sizes storage; the *rate* at which it's needed selects valves (see Fig. 4-3) and sizes pipes. For example, a ½-inch pipe and a 2-inch pipe will both easily transfer 500 gallons per day. However, for a pipe length of 300 feet, it would take the ½-inch pipe sixteen times as long as the 2-inch pipe to do it; that could be an hour compared with a few minutes!

How did I know that? Easy—I looked at a chart. That's all you'll have to do, too; I've supplied it for you. There's one for each of the three types—galvanized steel, copper, and plastic—for pipe sizes between ¾ inch and 4 inches in diameter (see Figs. 4-4, 4-5, and 4-6).

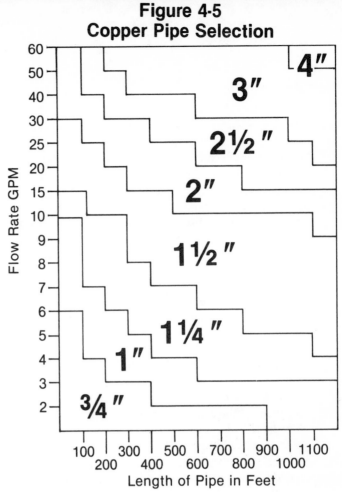

**Figure 4-5
Copper Pipe Selection**

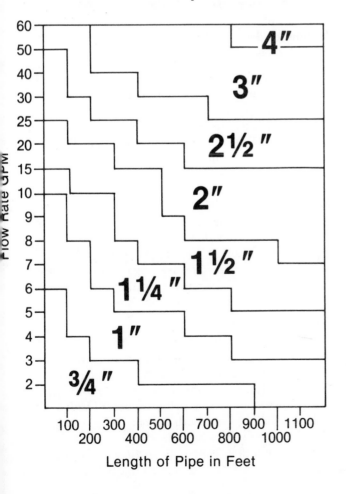

**Figure 4-4
Galvanized Steel Pipe Selection**

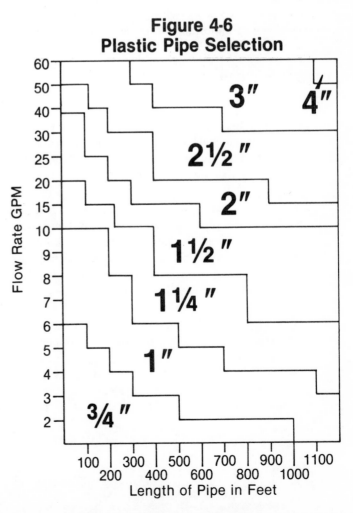

**Figure 4-6
Plastic Pipe Selection**

Distances

To use the flow charts effectively, you need real distance values; the next requirement, then, is that you take a walk and do some measuring. In a supply system you must measure the distance between the water source and the storage site, then the distance between storage and the usage site. In a demand system, you need only measure the distance between source and usage site. It helps to think like buried pipe; by comparison, it's *easy* to walk over boulders, wade streams, and pass over the large roots of trees!

If there are several options for siting storage or where the house will be, fine. If you can hold to a uniform stride, you can omit the tape measure. However, dividing the number of steps taken over a known distance is more accurate than measuring a hypothetical stride. After this check, the stride will suffice for measuring long runs.

Inside the house (or where the house will be), measure off the relative distances against the building plan or blueprint, or use a tape measure. Don't eyeball it! All those little water fittings, such as shower, lavatory, toilet, kitchen sink, washing machine, and dishwasher, add up to high rates of flow that quickly approach the capacity of a given size of pipe. Vertical distance—up and down and over doors, windows, wiring, fixtures, framing and such—is also important. Be generous without being lavish.

Minimizing Pressure Drop

Pressure is important in water systems; even if the actual numbers may seem abstract, without pressure water can't get from the source (or storage) to the usage point—or if it does, it exits faucets in an irritatingly slow way.

Gravity and other factors can rob us of pressure (see "Water Pressurizing," Chapter 2). Some is also lost in the pipes that connect the system parts together. However, in most instances accounting for pipe losses is compensated for by *increasing* the system's working pressure. The immediate effect is a larger-than-necessary pump, and the long-term effect is higher energy bills.

For a given length of pipe of a certain diameter and type with a given number of connectors (elbows, valves, and couplings), a given rate of flow (in gallons per minute) will produce a certain pressure drop. In low-pressure systems the effect of pressure drop is more serious than it is in high-

pressure systems. For example, if the working pressure is over 60 psi, a loss of 6 psi in the pipes connecting the source to the usage site represents only a 10 percent loss; that's scarcely noticeable. The same 6 psi loss in a 30 psi system, however, amounts to a 20 percent loss, which is substantial. In a 13 psi system like my own, it would be disastrous; losing half your pressure by turning on a faucet is no joke.

Pressure drop cannot be altogether eliminated. However, there are a number of ways to minimize the pressure drop in a water line; in your own system you may wish to juggle one or more of them to balance system considerations against the limitations of your pocketbook. But what factor can be adjusted the least for the most benefit?

As you might suspect, it's situational. However, there are eight basic ways to accomplish the deed:

1. Use a type of pipe with smooth interior surfaces. Galvanized pipe has extremely rough interior walls compared with either copper or plastic, both of which have equally smooth walls. After a period of use, however, plastic pipe wins out over copper because of its resistance to corrosion and the buildup of deposits that roughen the interior walls of the copper.

2. Increase the pipe size. Even if the same wall roughness exists, an increased diameter means that a smaller proportion of the water flowing through the pipe will *not* be exposed to the wall surfaces. Fortunately, this is not a direct proportion. That is, to halve the resistance, we do not need to double the diameter of the pipe. In fact, *four* times the cross-sectional area is available from a pipe with *twice* the diameter (see Fig. 4–7).

However, note that, as the price of copper zooms skyward, the smoothness advantage of copper pipe is quickly lost to the rough-walled galvanized pipe for larger diameters. It's possible to purchase a large-diameter galvanized pipe that boasts lower effective resistance than does the smaller-diameter copper pipe of equivalent cost.

3. Select a pipe that is resistant to corrosion or the formation of internal deposits. Admittedly, this is a question of aging and the type and content of the water flowing in the pipes. Galvanized pipe will corrode in extreme pH conditions (high-acid or high-alkaline), and both copper and galvanized pipe are susceptible to lime deposits from hard water; in addition, copper is particularly vulnerable to deposits from suspended particles. Plastic

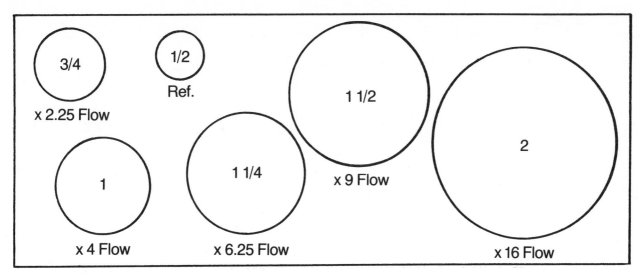

Fig. 4–7 Small changes in pipe diameter yield large changes in flow rates.

pipe, on the other hand, is extremely resistant to the effects of pH, hard water, or suspended materials.

4. Use a lower working water pressure, which reduces the resistance of the pipe walls. Of course, the rate of flow will also decrease at lower pressure, so this method of decreasing resistance is often pooh-poohed. However, we don't always *need* high rates of flow, particularly if the flow rate will never increase beyond a calculated amount. Too, low rate of flow is useful in systems designed to use conservative amounts of energy in the water extraction and transport process (see Fig. 2–10). Larger pipe sizes are recommended wherever financially possible, but low pumping rates can make use of smaller pipe sizes in long runs. This technique, however, should *never* be applied where water is directly transported from source to usage (in the demand system) or from storage to usage (in the store system); experience proves that for these sections of pipeline, usage inevitably increases. Any system can suffer growth pains, but there's little reason to penalize it from the outset by undersizing its pipes.

5. Use a higher working water pressure in the system. I know, I know—this contradicts what I listed under number 4 above. Or does it? Higher pressure aggravates the effect of pipe resistance but, of course, higher pressure losses have less effect with a higher overall pressure. Nevertheless, higher system pressure is recommended as a remedy only in an existing system that is suffering from a poor design or has outgrown its original one.

6. Reduce the length of pipe runs. A straight line is defined as the shortest distance between two points. If that's the way you've run your pipe, there's *nothing* you can do to reduce the effective resistance of the pipe, short of moving the two points closer together. If one's a well and the other's a house, that should be interesting to see! However, the terrain is not always so cooperative in planning or installing pipe runs; the shortest distance may be effectively blocked with rocks, trees, and other obstacles. To connect a pipe, then, may require rerouting to circumvent such barriers. Whatever happens, it doesn't make sense to aggravate the situation by carelessly planning a meandering pipe layout. This is usually done in the guise of the so-called perimeter gambit (see Fig. 4–8) which assures water access everywhere, now and in the future.

7. Establish feeders. Dig up most pipe systems and you'll be surprised at the uniformity of pipe size throughout. Efficient water systems, however, employ varying pipe sizes (see Fig. 4–9). Think of it as rivers running backward. Taps are placed as needed, either in the big pipe for high rate-of-flow needs, such as fire fighting, or in the smaller ones for smaller needs. They build pipe reducer fittings for just this reason, to connect big pipes into smaller pipes.

8. Use the proper fittings. Pipe is connected to other lengths of pipe through a variety of fittings. Simple *couplers* are used in straight sections; the more complex *union* is used if neither pipe can be rotated. For corners, *elbows* are used; they come in 45-degree and 90-degree configurations. *Straight*

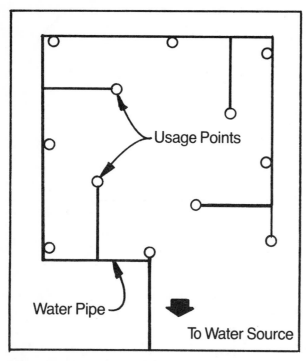

Fig. 4–8 A perimeter pipe layout supplies poor pressure and flow rates.

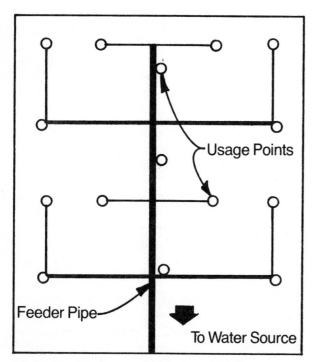

Fig. 4–9 A centralized feeder pipe layout supplies even pressure and flow rates.

tees (or T-fittings) are used whenever a pipe must "split" into two pipes; a *reducing tee* will handle splits where one of the pipes is smaller than the other two. *Reducers* are couplers that mate two different sizes of pipe. Finally, there's the *valve,* an adjustable fitting that controls water flow.

There's no way that we can avoid the use of fittings of varying types and combinations. However, each fitting represents a resistance to the flow of water; for instance, at standard flow rates the losses experienced in some types of valves can be equivalent to the loss in several hundred feet of pipe of the same size! In some systems, this is not significant; in others, it is. Not surprisingly, low-resistance valves (gate or ball types) cost two to five times as much as a high-resistance, economy globe type.

We'd go broke fast if we stocked the household with the best valves we could buy, but I've seen some people do it and at the same time lose the game by installing 90-degree elbows throughout the system. A better way to handle corners, where possible, is to use two 45-degree elbows (with a short nipple between) at a turn point. This changes an "intersection" into a simple "curve"; what works for cars on the highway works for water in pipes.

If they were available for all of the types of pipe, Y-fittings would be less resistive to water flow than T-fittings. However, since they aren't, the only strategy that works here is to restrict the use of tees to larger pipe sizes, reducing to smaller-size pipe *after* all of the branching is accomplished.

Installation Notes

If there are no other objections, PVC pipe seems to be the best option for most water systems (in essence, all outside and underground needs). Its smoothness and resistance to corrosion and the formation of deposits assures minimal resistance to water flow from the time of installation to far into the future. Schedule 40 should give gophers a tough chew, take care of the possibility of crushing, and take all but a direct hit with a pickax. In addition, it's fast to work with, it conforms to unusual trench shapes, and is easier to repair when mauled by a bulldozer or anything else.

At the house, the large-size PVC is reduced to ½- or ¾-inch size and is thereafter copper. This practice stems from the requirement of copper pipe for hot water lines; that the cold water lines are also copper keeps everything orderly, I suppose. It definitely saves on those plastic-to-galvanized and galvanized-to-copper fittings.

A similar practice is observed with free-standing faucets. It's not unusual to want a faucet in some area the pipe layout may cross; this acknowledges future building sites, gardens, orchards, or fire-fighting capabilities. However, with no convenient building to which one might secure the fittings, the standard practice is to use a section of galvanized pipe—one end screwed into a plastic tee inserted in-line in the PVC buried several feet in the ground, and the other end supporting the needed faucet.

Quite frankly, I'm puzzled by the origin of this ritual. If I'm to believe the things I've heard, the galvanized pipe is supposed to resist freeze, handle exposure to weather, and take punishment. But run one of these things over with your car and you'll see just how tough they are. Hopefully, the threads will strip themselves out of the tee rather than maul the PVC main. And the fact is that galvanized steel can't take even a mild freeze, whereas the plastic pipe can. Weatherability? True, the old PVC wasn't ultraviolet-resistant—but the new stuff supposedly is; besides, if the aboveground PVC is wrapped in insulation (as so many galvanized pipes are), there *is* no UV problem.

These stand-ups *do* need protection, and a sturdy little mount (see Fig. 4-10) will take care of visibility (most people only run down what they can't see), aesthetics (neither galvanized nor PVC pipe looks all that great), insulation, and a means of protecting the pipe *and* its insulation from the elements. Galvanized pipe may be removed altogether from this application; with the new thermoplastic faucets, nobody's stuck with dealing with PVC-to-galvanized connectors anymore.

A map of the pipe layout for the entire system should be extensively detailed at the time of installation. This should include pipe sizes and types used, and distances of trenches to various objects of a permanent nature. The fear you may have that the trench depression will *never* go away is baseless; when you *need* to know where the pipes are, there's virtually no trace of it. So the map is helpful for later additions, modifications, or repairs of the system. However, it's worthless to go through this process, then lose the map afterward. So tuck it away in a good place. Or, better yet, make a copy of it, tuck the original away in a good spot, and post the other with a suitable clear plastic or glass overlay on the wall of the pump house or some other appropriate place.

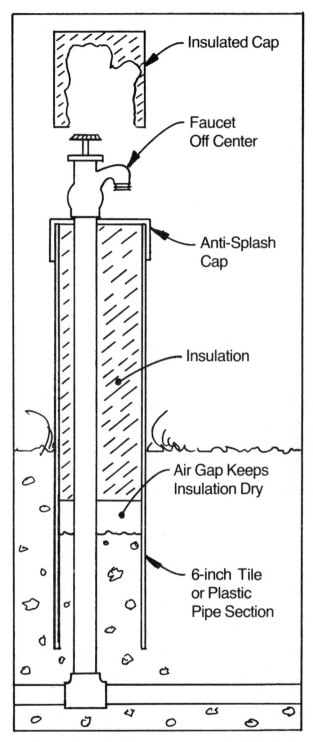

Fig. 4-10   A well-designed pipe stand will protect water outlets from mild freezes and mechanical damage.

The only means of protecting the pipe against damage by bulldozers, fencepost drivers, and hole diggers is to know exactly where the pipes are. Remembering to check is the tough part here; however, it's usually not much of a problem once you've had to dig out and replace a section of holed or ripped pipe. If you've got a gopher problem, use thick-wall PVC, galvanized pipe, or get a cat. No pipe is earthquake-proof, though it might be lucky enough to escape damage even in the most violent one; you can only stock spares, take your chances, and stay out of California. Little can be done about carelessness; don't support it in others, or, if you're the problem, either mend your ways or make lots of money to support the habit.

TANKS

Tanks are one of the best ways of storing water. The relatively high cost of storage by this means (compared with ponds or reservoirs) is often justified in light of convenience, better protection against contamination, effective shielding from sunlight, and the ease of determining the precise amount of water that's stored.

Tanks come in all shapes, sizes, and materials. Four basic materials are used in tanks: wood, metal, plastic and concrete.

Wood Tanks

One of the oldest materials used for tanks is wood (see photo). Typically these tanks are round-sided, flat-bottomed, with a top that's open, flat, or sometimes fluted to shed precipitation, airborne dust, and other debris.

Not just any ole wood will do for water tanks. Typically, successful ones are fabricated from redwood, mahogany, or white oak, because these woods, after an initial leaching of acids and resins, offer a sterile environment when in contact with water. Water in contact with other woods will warp or rot them, leach undesirable chemicals and resins into the water, or promote the growth of bacteria and algae in the water supply.

Just as redwood or oak swells in the presence of water, it shrinks in its absence. Therefore any portion of the wood in a tank that is not *covered* with water will, after a few days, dry out and lose its water-sealing function. In view of this, tanks constructed of either oak or redwood should be kept

Fig. 4–11   Wood is an aesthetically pleasing material for storing water.

filled or, if that's not possible, either sprayed with water several times a day or excused from verbal abuse when they do leak!

Other woods are used in the construction of tanks. However, they must be treated so that, in effect, the water does not come into direct contact with the wood itself. Varnishes, resins, fiberglass, tar or other coatings will be necessary. Or the water may actually be enclosed in some type of plastic or rubber bladder inserted in the tank. If the water is to be used for household purposes such as drinking, cooking, dishwashing, bathing, and washing clothes, the coating or bladder material should be carefully selected; taste is often the main consideration, but care should be taken to avoid the injection of undesirable or dangerous substances into the water. FDA-approved epoxy paints or resins do exist.

Metal Tanks

Water storage tanks may also be made of metal. This is usually sheet steel, and even very large tanks may have surprisingly thin walls. Since steel exposed to water rusts, it must somehow be protected; paint, tar, and galvanizing are three common coatings.

Steel tanks are characterized by one of three techniques used to secure the metal sheets together in tank construction. They may be welded, bolted, or soldered.

Welded

Welded tanks are used for smaller capacities than bolted tanks. Thicker steel is arced to the desired shape and welded to similar sheets. The component parts of the tank are welded together into a rigid tank. This type of tank may be easily manufactured in a shop and transported to the usage site (see Fig. 2–14). The limiting factor on size for this type is the carrying capacity of the transport system used to ferry the tank from the shop to the site. Of course, the shaped steel sheets could be transported as is along with the welding equipment to put it all together on-site.

Bolted

Another possibility is to use a steel tank designed to be bolted together; this eliminates the need for any on-site welding while solving the transport problem for thick-wall tanks of immense proportions. Tar or another petroleum-base sealant is sandwiched between the bolted sheets during assembly to prevent water loss (see Fig. 4–12).

Soldered

If the potential for on-site construction exists, a third option is to use very thin sheets of galvanized steel for the tank. Because of the thinness of the material, welding cannot be employed; instead, solder is used to seal the joints. The solder is a good sealant against water leakage but, alas, it's not strong enough to withstand the "shear"—the forces that tend to separate the joined sheets—

Fig. 4–12 Bolted and caulked tanks are built on-site.

when the tank is filled with water. For this reason, bolts or screws are also used to secure the sheets.

The thinness of steel or tin in galvanized sheet tanks is sometimes a disadvantage. In coastal areas, for example, the effects of the salt-laden air are all too evident in anything that passes for metal.

While welded or bolted steel tanks may be transported about, the thin galvanized tin or steel tank usually can't survive transportation from one place to another or rough handling in any form. Out of necessity, then, they are constructed on-site. This makes their resale value quite low, since they cannot be easily transferred from the original site to another. At the very least, the soldered joints will probably break and one small tank may sport several dozen leaks when first filled. However, a far more serious threat exists: the thin walls will, because of their design, handle tons of water—but empty, they have the potential for total collapse. To circumvent their relative fragility, internal wood cross bracing is often added if removal and transfer to another location is imminent. Even at that, some resoldering may be required.

Fig. 4–13 Plastic tanks are a quick means of establishing water storage.

Plastic Tanks

The high price of steel has prompted the production of plastic tanks in the 400- to 2,000-gallon range for water storage. Usually pale yellow and cylindrical, they have molded fittings for the inlet and outlet, and an access hatch in the top (see Fig. 4–13).

In the 400-gallon-size tank, I have found a fiberglass type; I haven't seen tanks of any larger size made from this material. However, a plastic type of coating may be used as a water sealant in a wood tank.

Concrete Tanks

Concrete is material used in the construction of water-storage tanks. The basic setup is a poured slab for the base of the tank and poured, formed walls. Since this is similar to constructing a building's foundation, the resulting tank is square- or rectangular-sided. Or if a round tank is preferred, a slip form constructed in the shape of an arc can circumvent the many difficulties in producing a contoured form. A rebar (a reinforcing bar used in standard concrete construction) is needed for ei-

ther type to oppose the water's weight and pressure when the tank is filled. On the other hand, a larger square or rectangular tank, even with an internal rebar, will need additional external bracing to maintain structural integrity in use.

An offshoot of concrete tanks is one using masonry or concrete block. Unless one or two ends of the block are ground to the required angle for making a round tank, the final tank will be either square- or rectangular-sided. Standard masonry or concrete block wall construction is employed in the first half of the tank's construction. However, two additional requirements must be met. One is that the completed sides must be sealed to hold the water; this may involve either brushing on a tarlike substance or any waterproofing (not merely water-resisting) material, or reinforcing with some kind of lathing. And two, the finished tank walls must be supported externally against the pressure of the water.

External support for a tank of any material may take one of three forms: band, buttress, or burial.

A band is a strong, continuous material that encircles the tank; it is demonstrated in banded wood barrels. The operating principle of banding is simple. Pressure is identical in all directions; therefore,

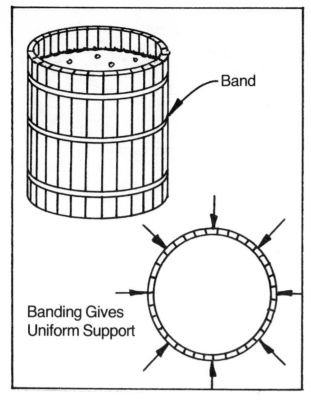

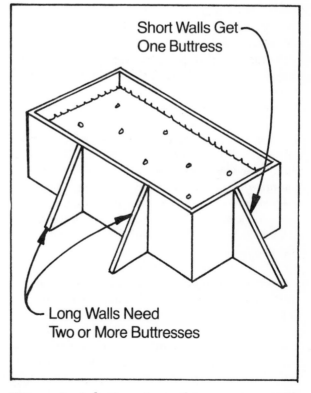

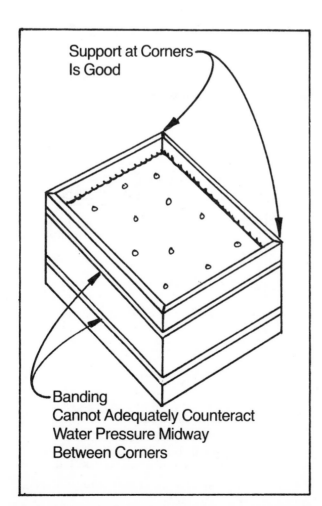

Band

Banding Gives
Uniform Support

Fig. 4–14 Banding is a simple means of supplying tank support.

the outward pressure at any point is opposed by the band's inward pressure on the tank wall directly opposite that side of the tank. Obviously the band material is under heavy tension and must be strong enough not to shear.

Bands work on circular tanks only. Square or rectangular tanks may also be banded, but the only points where the bands are really working (see Fig. 4–15) is at the corners. The outward pressure at any point between the corners works perpendicularly to the tensioned band and is, therefore, not as effective. The weakest point is the midpoint between the tank's corners; the walls would bulge outward at these points.

One solution to this problem involves buttressing, which takes two forms. One is an external, angled support (see Fig. 4–16). Accordingly, if one buttress is used, it should be placed at the midpoint between the corners of the tank on each side. Long tanks will require several buttresses on each side.

A second buttress solution is to use an arced

Support at Corners
Is Good

Banding
Cannot Adequately Counteract
Water Pressure Midway
Between Corners

Fig. 4–15 Banding doesn't work as well with square or rectangular tanks.

Short Walls Get
One Buttress

Long Walls Need
Two or More Buttresses

Fig. 4–16 A buttress is another way to provide tank side support.

section of material along each side and to band it as you would a perfectly round tank (see Fig. 4-17). Either a square- or rectangular-sided tank will be best supported if the selected arc describes a full circle, but satisfactory support is also assured with non-circular arcs (see Fig. 4-18); correspondingly larger band tensioning will be needed as the arced buttresses become more shallow. In theory, triangular-sided buttresses will produce the same effect, but their use assumes that the banding material will be able to "flow" easily around the sharp edges when the tensioning occurs.

Concrete, masonry, and concrete block tanks may also be supported by burial. There are two ways to do this. One is to dig the hole and insert a ready-built tank. The other is to dig the hole and build the tank in it. Either way, the tank's walls will be firmly supported by the packed earth surrounding the tank, and water pressure will be thwarted in its effort to push the tank walls outward.

This is no problem with concrete block or masonry construction, but a poured-concrete wall will require forms. Putting them in is easy, but extracting the exterior portion of the form (facing the pit's walls) afterward may not be. Nevertheless, it should be removed, as the wood could swell enough during the wetter season to crack the concrete wall.

Because of this problem, there's a temptation simply to "form up" the inside surface of the tank and use the pit's wall in place of the exterior form. The penalty for such laziness is the cost of all that extra concrete; due to the gross imprecision of a backhoe in digging the pit, nearly twice as much concrete will be needed. Also, concrete is *heavy*. A cubic yard weighs four tons, and it'll really compress that earth, particularly when it's stacked up for four to eight feet. As if that's not reason enough not to do this, concrete doesn't cure against dirt as nicely as it does against forms, which means that it won't be as strong.

Cisterns or reservoirs built into a slope may have a good percentage of the complete tank showing and, therefore, unsupported. Banding or buttressing will not be required if some of the leftover dirt is shoved up against the wall; the result is a "bermed" wall. Since this technique will work, no tank need be completely buried. While retaining the best aspects of a buried tank, a partially buried tank saves on cost, time, and materials and solves the problem of what to do with all that "extra" dirt displaced by the tank.

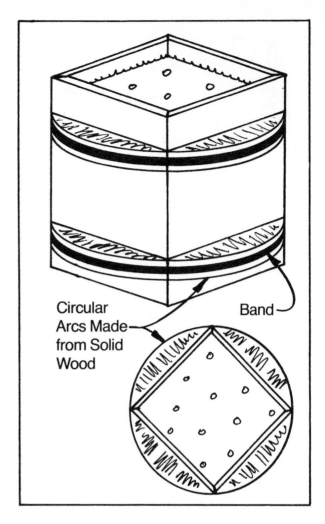

Fig. 4-17 Banding circular wood arcs to square tanks provides uniform support.

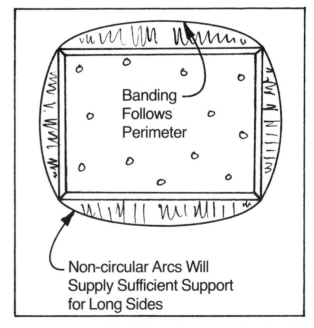

Fig. 4-18 Non-circular wood arcs may be banded to larger rectangular tanks.

Bottom Support of Tanks

Irrespective of the type of tank used, it must have adequate support from below. Water hits the scale at 8.33 pounds per gallon. A thousand gallons, then, weighs over 8,330 pounds or over 4 tons. A 4,000-gallon tank holds a whopping 16 tons, and that excludes the weight of the tank. The point? *Never place a tank on fill.* If a tall and slim tank is desired over one that's short and squat, the problem becomes more acute; an analysis of the soil density may be needed to assure that it will not settle.

Wood tanks placed on bare earth will rot. Steel tanks (even galvanized) placed on bare earth will rust. How fast is anyone's guess, and it doesn't really matter. Don't do it! Large tanks are usually set on a bed of gravel over leveled earth. This takes care of the rust or rot problem—precipitation and condensation are drained away. This also lends a self-leveling feature; otherwise, when the water is added the bottom will be deformed or punctured by the smallest object.

Wood and steel tanks may also get some help from treated wood beams; old railroad ties spaced evenly over leveled ground will do the job. A raised platform also helps to lessen the probability of rot or rust in wet climes. If, on the other hand, it's desirable to use gravity flow and/or pressurization, but a higher elevation than the usage site is not available, the platform may be extended upward the needed distance to accomplish either or both. Obviously, this has a limiting effect on the type of tank used; a tank that can be constructed piece by piece on the tower will be preferable to one that must be raised to the top. Another drawback is that tank size is restricted; the tower, including footings, tower legs, and cross bracing, must be sized to evenly support the tank's bottom area, its weight, and the weight of the water it can hold. Add in the extra problems of wind pressure on both tower and tank and any propensity for the ground to move through settling or earth tremors, and both the logistics and expenses are formidable. Nevertheless, tower raising can be a lot of fun (see Fig. 4–19)—and once it's up, you can always turn it into a house! (See Fig. 4–20.)

Fig. 4–19 Towers for large tanks must be strong to handle the water's weight.

Fig. 4–20 A water tower is a good start on a tower house.

Tank Coatings

Redwood, mahogany, and white oak tanks have a built-in coating that prevents leakage, the formation of organic growths, and deterioration of the wood itself from rot. Water loss is prevented because it is the nature of these specific woods to swell and seal the tank. Newly constructed tanks, then, will leak like the proverbial sieve. For this reason, before the first filling, water is sprayed about the interior, wetting the wood uniformly to initiate the swelling and avoid the otherwise lengthy process of filling the tank. Another idiosyncrasy of these specific woods is that most of the harmful resins are leached from the wood during the initial period of use and will thereafter remain inert.

The scarcity and high demand for these woods make them prohibitively expensive for large tanks.

However, other woods—pine, fir, oak—may suffice. But, while these substitutes do give the nice wood appearance and provide the necessary structural support, they do not exhibit the self-sealing and preserving qualities of redwood. Moreover, once the resins are leached from the wood, fungus growth will occur.

For these reasons, the inside of tanks constructed of other types of wood must be sealed. Sealers and paint will counteract many of these problems, but preventing leakage is the tough one. So, a hard, completely watertight coating is called for, and that narrows the possibilities to some kind of epoxy or resin. Fiberglass is the usual choice because it may be used in conjunction with fiberglass cloth to make a tightly bonded, impenetrable finish.

In the presence of water, steel rusts. So, irrespective of the type of steel tank—whether soldered, welded, or bolted—a first requirement of a coating is to keep the water away from the metal; a waterproof paint or tarlike sealant is the primary choice. Pick one that prevents the growth of algae. Be wary—select a coating that meets your own standards in what you're willing to put into your water in the way of chemicals, trace minerals, and elements.

Provided that the solder or weld joints are good ones, steel tanks don't need leakage protection. The application of *any* type of paint or epoxy over these surfaces if they're even slightly encrusted with rust, dirt, or oil is cosmetic only. Don't do it! Wire-brush or sand off the rust, wet-mop the dust, and use something akin to alcohol or lacquer thinner to remove any trace of oil or grease prior to the application of a primer. Avoid the use of any rust-inhibiting primers not specifically approved for potable water. Fortunately, red lead primer is no longer available, but even zinc chromate primer would not be a good addition to drinking water; these are strictly weatherizing primers, for external use only. Apply the epoxy paint or other good water-base paint in one or two coats. Redo as required; access to the tank will assure sufficient warning when a recoating is indicated.

Galvanized sheeting that is soldered for waterproofing should also receive a coating of some type. It's not usually done—the solder takes care of leaks, and the galvanizing takes care of the rust protection. However, long-term exposure of both solder and galvanizing to water, particularly soft water, can be dangerous; the water tends to leach lead from the solder (solder is lead and tin in various mixes, usually fifty-fifty), and both lead and cadmium from the galvanized coating (see "Water Quality," Chapter 3). If you decide to cover the galvanizing with a coating that reduces this risk, choose it carefully; many types of paint or epoxy will not adhere to galvanizing, and fewer still will meet potable water standards.

Concrete tanks will need a coating to prevent the escape of water and the formation of organic growths. A standard coating technique is that used for swimming pools: a mudlike, cement-rich plaster applied over the cured concrete, inside or out. An alternative is to use one of the newer concrete sealants such as cement paint or bituminous mastic. Both ways are expensive; with the former, it's the specialized labor in applying the coating; with the latter, it's the sealant itself that's expensive.

PUMPS

There are four types of pumps that may be used in a water system to extract water from a source and deliver it to storage or immediate use: the piston pump, the centrifugal pump, the hydraulic ram, and the air-lift pump.

Piston Pump

The piston pump, also known as the positive-displacement pump, sees wide uses in water systems. Working on the reciprocating principle (that is, an up-and-down movement), a piston moving inside a cylinder (see Fig. 4–21) draws water through an intake check valve on one part of a stroke and pushes it out through an outlet check valve on the second part of the stroke. Irrespective of the outlet or inlet water pressures, the same amount of water is pumped during each stroke; hence the term "positive displacement." This no-nonsense action also enables the unit to pump air efficiently—the air compressor and tire pump are both piston pumps. With this feature, the piston pump can suck water up from as far as 25 feet below the pump (see "Induction," Chapter 2).

There are two common configurations of the piston pump in water systems. In the first setup, the pump mechanism and its power unit, the motor or engine that drives it, sit atop a shallow well with a tail pipe reaching down below the water level. As long as this distance is not greater than 25 feet (see "Water Extraction," Chapter 2), the pump's

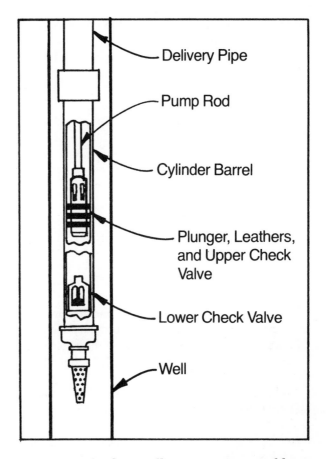

Fig. 4–21 The deep-well piston pump assembly.

Delivery Pipe

Pump Rod

Cylinder Barrel

Plunger, Leathers, and Upper Check Valve

Lower Check Valve

Well

action will suck water up to the pump and then push it onward to usage or storage.

The second configuration handles well depths where the water level is more than 25 feet below the ground. Here the power unit operates a converter—a device that translates the rotary motion of the power unit into the reciprocating motion needed in the pump mechanism—at the wellhead (ground level). Through a section of rigid rod, usually referred to as "sucker rod," this power is transferred to the piston pump mechanism situated deep in the well; the deeper the well, the longer the sucker rod. Since the water must be pumped to the surface through a pipe anyway, the sucker rod is designed to operate the piston pump from *inside* the delivery pipe (see Fig. 4–21 and "The Gold System," Chapter 6), sharing this space with the upward-moving water.

This arrangement *seems* hokey, but in **reality** it's very simple and straightforward. Also, it has a built-in feature having to do with servicing the piston pump. An aboveground positioning of well pumps is always preferable, for the convenience it affords in servicing the equipment; however, this specific arrangement allows the removal of the *entire* pump mechanism, including valves and leathers—the only section of the pump mechanism that is subject to wear—up through the pipe for servicing without hassling with the pipe and cylinder itself. This is a nice bonus; all that 2-inch (inside diameter, or I.D.) galvanized pipe is *heavy*, and removing it would add many hours and considerably more equipment to an otherwise fast and easy overhaul.

If the cylinder diameter is increased beyond 1⅞ inch to increase the pumping rate, a pipe size larger than 2 inches I.D. is required if the option of removing the wearable portions of the pump up through the pipe is to be retained. In practice, it seldom is; the cost of the larger diameter pipe usually wins out over the beauty of the feature. Accordingly, larger-size cylinders threaded for the 2-inch pipe are available. Whatever the choice, the size of the sucker rod remains the same, irrespective of cylinder size.

A second benefit stems from the piston pump's ability to pump air and therefore suck water: with the addition of a tail pipe, the pump's reach for water is extended to 15 to 20 feet, saving that much expensive sucker rod and galvanized pipe. In addition, maximum use of the well's depth is assured; *no* type of pump can be placed close to the bottom of a well without sucking in a lot of sediment and doing itself irreparable harm. However, the bottom of the tail pipe *can* sit just above the bottom of the well while the pump itself is safe 15 to 25 feet above it.

If connected to an electric motor or gasoline engine, a pressure switch, and a pressure tank, the deep-well piston pump will function in a demand system, supplying water as it's needed. However, the maximum number of strokes (in this sense, the stroke is one cycle consisting of one up-and-down movement of the piston in the cylinder) that this type of pump can withstand is limited to 30–45 per minute. In consequence, a system that uses a 6-inch stroke (total distance of movement) and a 3-inch cylinder (the biggest available) can supply only up to 7.7 gallons per minute (see Fig. 4–22); this is a low rate compared with other pump types such as the submersible centrifugal pump, and will barely cover most household needs. In the shallow well, the piston pump fares much better (see Fig. 4–23).

For this reason, the deep-well piston pump is utilized primarily in the store type of water system where its only job is to pump water to storage; transporting and pressurizing water for usage is left to another means. Accordingly, the pump mechanism may be operated in four different ways: by hand (via the pump standard—see Fig. 6–4), by a gasoline engine (driving a pumping jack—see Fig. 6–8), by an electric motor (driving a pumping jack—see Fig. 6–9), and by a water-pumping wind machine (connected directly to the sucker rod—see Fig. 6–5). Frequently two or more of these pumping methods are combined, since the equipment is designed to accommodate multiple sources.

Centrifugal Pump

The centrifugal pump works on the same principle as a rock on a string that you swing around your body. The rock wants to travel in a direct line, but the string prevents it from doing this. If, instead, you held a bottle with one end of a long section of rubber tubing secured through its cap and whipped the hose around in a tight circle, the water in the bottle would travel down the tubing. That's centrifugal pumping.

The centrifugal pump built for a water system uses impellers instead of tubing and is much more compact; coupled to a high-speed electric motor, it is capable of delivering water at a very high rate (see Fig. 4–24).

However, a single set of impellers in a centrifugal pump can pump against only so much pressure (head); naturally, the pumping rate drops off as the pumping head increases. This limitation is alleviated in design by stacking individual impeller sections on top of one another, each with an outlet connected to the inlet of the stage above it and its own inlet derived from the outlet of the stage below. Standard centrifugal submersibles are available with as few as seven stages and as many as forty-five stages, depending on the final in-well depth, total pumping head, pumping rate, and delivery pressure.

Note the difference in pumping rates compared with the deep-well piston pump (see Fig. 4–22) for equivalent motor horsepower, pumping head, and pressure delivery. For example, a ⅓-HP motor attached to a 2½-inch piston pump can, with a 6-inch stroke and 42 strokes per minute, deliver water into a 100-foot head at 5.4 gpm and (about) 5 psi of pressure. A centrifugal pump rated for the

Figure 4-22
Deep-Well Piston Pump Ratings

Discharge Rate*		Cylinder Size (I.D.) in Inches	Electric Motor Size		
			1/3 HP	1/2 HP	3/4 HP
GPH	GPM		Maximum Lift in Feet		
146	2.4	1-11/16	228	336	513
157	2.6	1-3/4	212	318	477
180	3.0	1-7/8	186	277	416
205	3.4	2	162	244	366
260	4.3	2-1/4	128	192	289
321	5.4	2-1/2	104	156	234
389	6.5	2-3/4	85	128	192
463	7.7	3	72	108	162

*Assumes 6-inch stroke and 42 strokes per minute.

Figure 4-23
Shallow-Well Pump Ratings

Discharge Rate*		Cylinder Size (I.D.) in Inches	Electric Motor Size		
			1/3 HP	1/2 HP	3/4 HP
GPH	GPM		Maximum Lift in Feet		
540	9.0	1-1/4	90	140	200
720	12.0	1-1/2	75	115	165
980	16.3	2	55	80	130
1140	19.0	2-1/2	30	45	95
1360	22.6	3	10	20	50

*Assumes up to 25 feet of suction on intake, 20 psi at delivery point.

Figure 4-24
Centrifugal Pump Ratings

Electric Motor Size	No. of Stages in Pump	Total Pumping Head									
		20	40	60	80	100	120	140	160	180	200
		Discharge Rate* in GPH/GPM									
1/3 HP	10	745/ 12.4	690/ 11.5	620/ 10.3	535/ 8.9	430/ 7.2	285/ 4.8	65/ 1.1	—	—	—
1/2 HP	13	820/ 13.7	775/ 12.9	735/ 12.3	690/ 11.5	635/ 10.6	580/ 9.7	505/ 8.4	415/ 6.9	300/ 5	125/ 2.1
3/4 HP	18	870/ 14.5	845/ 14.0	820/ 13.7	795/ 13.3	760/ 12.7	730/ 12.2	700/ 11.7	665/ 11.1	630/ 10.5	585/ 9.8

*Assumes 30 psi at delivery point.

same horsepower delivers a little more than 7 gpm into the same 100-foot head at 30 psi of pressure. Compensating for the difference in pressure (25 psi and .433 psi/foot), the centrifugal pump, at 5 psi service pressure, only "sees" a 40-foot head (see "The Lift Pump," Chapter 2, for the relationship between head and the pressure it produces); consequently it will deliver approximately 11.5 gpm to the same point where only 5.4 gpm arrives from the piston pump. That's more than *double* the piston pump's capacity.

With such a difference in performance, why then isn't the piston pump retired to dusty shelves alongside other antiques? Simple—the centrifugal pump can't pump air, and therefore must be submerged. The water level in a well drops as the water is pumped from it; this is called "draw-down." At the high rates the centrifugal pump will extract water, it must be located deep enough in the well so that the point of greatest drawdown will not fall below its inlet.

This is no particular problem for the pump mechanism, but it does raise a few engineering nightmares for the power unit. Since both operate in a rotary fashion, coupling the two units together over a distance of more than a few feet is difficult; at the kind of rpm the pump works best, there's also a real problem with balance.

There are several solutions to this problem. In shallow wells, the pumps are mounted over the wellhead and are equipped with an injector mechanism that pumps a high-velocity stream of water upward through a tail pipe; well water is caught up in the flow and rises to the pump, where the centrifugal pump takes over. In this instance, the

Figure 4-25
Jet Pump Ratings

Electric Motor Size	Suction Lift in Feet	Discharge Rate*	
		GPH	GPM
1/3 HP	5	560	9.3
	10	470	7.8
	15	400	6.6
	20	340	5.6
	25	290	4.8
1/2 HP	5	855	14.3
	10	750	12.5
	15	660	11.0
	20	570	9.5
	25	455	7.6

*Assumes 1-1/4 inch suction pipe and a pumping head of 5 feet (above the pump) at 20 psi.

jet pump can exceed the performance of a piston pump of equal specifications if the water level is only a few feet below the pump (see chart), but it falls off rapidly as the distance approaches the suction limit of the piston pump.

A better solution joins the pump to the motor in a single, watertight housing as in the photo; this is the highly acclaimed submersible centrifugal pump. By simply attaching a 1-inch plastic pipe (type PE—see "Pipes," this chapter), the pump may be lowered by its delivery pipe and the protruding electrical wires to any desired depth. Pretty simple!

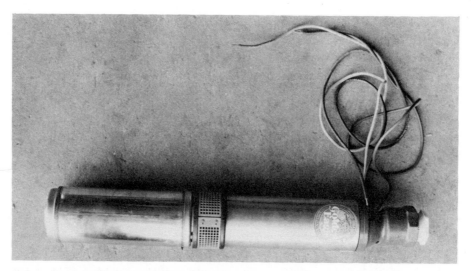

Fig. 4–26 A centrifugal pump designed for complete submersion.

Fig. 4–27 A hydraulic ram is simple in theory and construction.

Hydraulic Ram

While different in appearance and operation from other waterwheels or turbines, the hydraulic ram is a water-powered device (see Fig. 4–27). It has one function: to pump water.

The ram uses the energy of moving water to pump a small portion of that water to a higher point (see Fig. 4–28). It starts when we let water flow through a drive pipe into the ram and suddenly shut it off. Water, once moving, doesn't like stopping so abruptly, so it piles up. And because it's virtually incompressible, it builds up pressure. If we put a check valve in the chamber, the pressure will pop it open, moving a small amount of water into the vertical pipe beyond. Once the penned water has spent its pressure, the check valve closes and the flow automatically resumes. Preset adjustments again shut off the flow, and the pressured water acts again on the check valve. The water in the pipe behind the check valve climbs higher and higher with each cycle. You can attach extra sections of pipe until the suddenly blocked water does not create a pressure sufficient to overcome the weight of the water in the delivery pipe and deliver any more water through the check valve. That's the limit of the ram, and it can be increased beyond that point only with a larger inflow of water (larger diameter of drive pipe) or a higher pressure of incoming water (greater initial drive head).

Theoretically, the ram pumps $\frac{1}{10}$ of the water 10 times as high, $\frac{1}{5}$ of it 5 times as high, and so on. As we might suspect, in practice the results are much lower because of friction in the working parts such as valves and inlet and delivery pipes. Nevertheless, the results are impressive and beneficial if you want to fill a reservoir or get water to your homesite on the hill from the stream in the canyon below. If you have gross amounts of water in the stream or river, you can use the hydraulic ram to pump water to an elevation and then let it drop into a water turbine that's back down the hill, thereby producing electricity. Sort of roundabout, but undeniably practical under the right conditions.

The hydraulic ram is manufactured worldwide, and the units are simple and easy to maintain and operate; they are, however, quite expensive. Owing to its simplicity, a multitude of do-it-yourself ram designs exist for the owner-builder or person with a few shop connections (see "References").

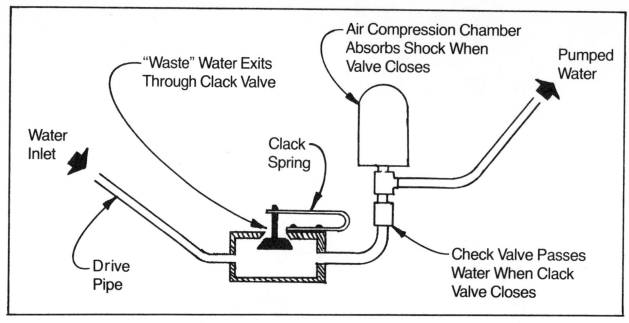

Fig. 4–28 A hydraulic ram's vital parts.

Air-Lift Pump

A novel approach to water pumping is the air-lift system. Basically this involves a compressor that compresses air, forces it down a tube into the well, and "injects" it into a delivery pipe in much the same way that a jet pump works. The combined effect of the stream of high-pressure air and the lighter water (it's full of air bubbles) causes the water to rise. The uniqueness of this approach is its ability to use low-producing energy sources (particularly the wind) and the "offset" capability (which means that the compressor may be located at some distance from the well; see "Offset Systems," Chapter 6).

Limitations exist, however. The air-lift idea requires submersion of the ejector to a depth below the source's water level representing not less than one third of the total lift required (measured from the ejector). So if the storage tank is located 30 feet above the wellhead, and the water level in the well is 30 feet below the surface, the air-lift pump must be situated at least 30 feet below the water level—more, if possible. In addition, the pump's maximum capacity is 5 gpm. However, for a wind-pumped installation (see the Bowjon Water Pump, in "References"), 5 gpm represents a high-wind, low-head, non-pressurized (storage only) extraction rate. Nevertheless, where these conditions exist it would be cost-competitive with other wind-powered, water-pumping machines.

Pump Evaluation

The two most popular pumps are the deep-well piston pump (hereafter the piston pump) and the submersible centrifugal pump (hereafter the submersible pump) and we will focus on these two. This is not meant as a slur against either the hydraulic ram or the air-lift pump; each has its place. However, the hydraulic ram needs running water which, over the length of your property, must drop in elevation 10 to 15 feet to be useful. The air-lift pump, on the other hand, has potential in shallow-well applications, but its output in deep-well situations parallels the lowest outputs available from the piston pump.

Well size, pumping capacity and head, the power unit, the rate of energy use, and usage rates versus pumping rates are all factors in the selection of a pump.

Well Size

A submersible pump is not made for well sizes below 4 inches in diameter, whereas the piston pump can be utilized in well sizes as low as 2 inches.

Pumping Capacity and Head

The pumping capacity (rate of flow) of the submersible pump decreases rapidly with drawdown, particularly if the water approaches the level of the pump's intake; effectively, the pumping head is increasing (since it's measured from the level of water in the well—see Fig. 2-28). This situation may be accommodated in three ways. First, the well can be dug deeper to reduce the effect of drawdown; this also increases in-well storage (see "Water Storage," Chapter 2). Second, a submersible pump with more "stages" and a higher horse-power rating may be selected for the job. And third, a higher-capacity well—one that won't experience much drawdown—can be dug. In terms of both energy and money, all three are expensive solutions.

A piston pump's efficiency, on the other hand, is not affected by drawdown; positive displacement always assures the delivery of the same amount of water. So if the pumping head increases because of normal drawdown, the only effect it can have is slightly to increase the load on the aboveground power unit.

Positioning in the Well

The submersible pump must at all times be submerged, and a tail pipe will not work with this type of pump. This necessitates a deeper well, both to maintain the pump's clearance above the bottom of the well and to assure that the drawdown will not uncover it.

A piston pump, at the slower pumping rate, causes less drawdown, can pump water from as much as 25 feet below the pump level (using the tail pipe), and requires less clearance above the bottom of the well.

The Power Unit

The power unit of the submersible pump is limited to an electric motor (ever try to run a gas engine underwater?) that is built for 220-volt, 60-cycle A.C., single-phase. For motor sizes above 1½ HP, the local utility company would need to string a special three-phase line.

The piston pump can utilize a number of "power" units—muscle power, wind power, gasoline-engine power, and electrical power; if an electric motor is used, it can be wired for high or low voltage, A.C. or D.C. Additionally, if the pumping equipment cannot be positioned directly over the well, an offset system may be installed (see "Offset Systems," Chapter 6).

Pumping versus Usage Rates

In the "demand" system, the water pump must be closely matched to the rate at which water is used. At the very least, the pump must have a capacity equal to the *largest* single rate of use. The toilet and faucets and the kitchen and bathroom sinks use water at a 5-gpm rate. A 15-gpm rate is standard for washing machine, dishwasher, and shower. Outside faucets equipped with a hose for water sprinkling or light irrigation will need 15–20 gpm. Large gardens or orchards will need water at a minimum capacity of 20–40 gpm. Fire fighting needs the highest rates; while the flow rate needed to halt the spread of fire in grass is only 10 gpm, a minimum 20-gpm rate is needed to save small structures—and this figure may soar upward to 1,000 gpm for a fire well under way in a large structure!

Most of us could not afford to install and operate a pump that delivered water at a 1,000-gpm rate even if the well could supply it. But even if the pump is needed only to supply water for the highest single *normal* usage, a conservative estimate of this rate would be 20 gpm.

Don't rush out to buy one of this capacity, though! Even if the largest usage rate is 20 gpm, this represents a single usage and assumes that under no circumstances will water be used for two different applications simultaneously. Now, are you going to wait for the dishwasher to finish before you take your evening shower? Are you going to wait to flush the toilet until the garden watering is done? No, of course not.

The pump in a demand system must handle simultaneous usage of water; you must analyze your own habits (or those of your family) to arrive at the figure. The range is pretty broad, extending upward to the absurd where everything is used all at once. Once you've found an answer, it's decision time. Are you really going to install a pump of that size? If you do nothing else, you *must,* or one day you'll find yourself all soapy under a trickle!

So, what can be done? Let's look at the situation. First, we know that the pump *must* have a minimum capacity equal to the maximum single-use rate needed. If that's 20 gpm, it means that we also can use water simultaneously for two or more other applications whose *combined* rates do not exceed this figure.

Second, schedule high-rate water use throughout the day to avoid concurrent use. Schedule showers for early morning or early evening, the laundry for midday, the dishwasher after showers in the morning, and its button is pushed again by the last person to go to bed at night. Accidents will occur. However, the habit of checking the available pressure beforehand will catch them. Or, before the washer goes on, make it a policy to see if a shower is imminent or someone is doing some garden watering.

The store system's pump capacity is not affected by usage rates, singularly or in combination; instead, it is concerned only with equaling the total quantity of water that is used daily. However, storage must be sized to handle this amount of water, pipes must be sized for the use rates, and the energy source must be selected so that, at whatever rate, the pump will replenish the water. Fortunately, though the water is at times used at high rates the pump has a twenty-four-hour period in which to restock the water in storage for the next day (see Fig. 2–10).

Energy versus Pumping Rates

It could be argued that for deeper wells, the submersible pump is capable of handling the needs of a "store" system, whereas the piston pump cannot function in the "demand" system. This is a clever observation, but it's marred by the excessive amount of energy required to do a job quickly when there's normally lots of time to do it slowly. Nevertheless, it brings up an interesting point: There are times when it would be nice to have *both* pumping rates.

Conclusions

The inherent advantages and disadvantages of the submersible pump and the piston pump are as distinct as the differences between the deep-well systems they commonly serve—that is, the "demand" system and the "store" system, respectively. In a nutshell, we could say that the piston pump works best in situations where only low energy levels are available, high pressure (head) exists, and low flow rates are acceptable. Conversely, the submersible pump shines in situations where high flow rates are required, low head exists, and energy availability is not an issue. For shallow wells, these differences lessen since the piston pump *can* approach the highest pumping rate required for the household without suffering the submersible

pump's wildly varying pump rates for the same water drawdown.

Combinations: The Side-by-Side and Piggyback Systems

If you're building backup capability into the system anyway, there's really no reason to view the situation as strictly either/or, demand versus store, piston pump versus submersible pump. Why not a combination?

There are two basic ways that the submersible pump and the piston pump may be merged into one system combining the best features of both pumps (and systems) and effectively neutralizing

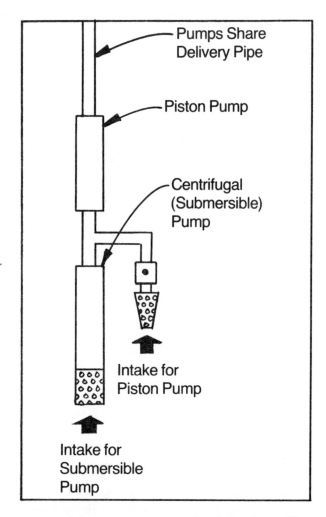

Fig. 4–29 Two pumps may be "piggybacked" to increase system versatility.

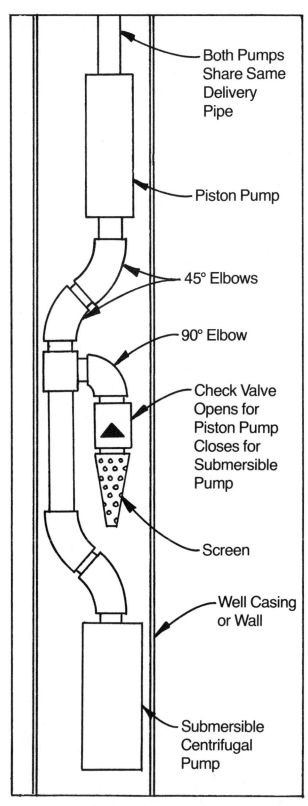

Both Pumps Share Same Delivery Pipe

Piston Pump

45° Elbows

90° Elbow

Check Valve Opens for Piston Pump Closes for Submersible Pump

Screen

Well Casing or Wall

Submersible Centrifugal Pump

Fig. 4–30 Limited space in a 6-inch drilled well forces the use of extra plumbing to fit the piggyback arrangement of pumps.

the disadvantages of each. One is the side-by-side system; I call it the "Silver System," and it's fully described in Chapter 6.

The other combination is frequently called the "piggyback" arrangement because the submersible pump is joined with the piston pump (see Fig. 4–29) to feed the same delivery pipe to the surface. While no harm would come of operating both pump mechanisms simultaneously (and, I might add, no gain either), normally only one or the other pump would be operated at a time. When the piston pump is operational, it draws water through the check valve as it would through a tail pipe; when the submersible pump is operated, it draws water through its own strainer (located under the submersible) and pumps it through the piston pump and up the delivery pipe.

Controls similar in type and function to those used in the Silver System will permit the piggyback arrangement to act alternately as a demand or a store system; in reality, it is both. However, the use of this system presupposes that the owner/operator is utilizing a non-utility energy source as the power unit for the piston pump; for this reason, water pumped to storage from the submersible pump must be limited or the piston pump will have no place to put water when it is functioning.

The piggyback arrangement is not an unknown technique; it is illustrated in a number of pump manuals circulated by manufacturers. However, in practice the actual connections between the two pumps *cannot* be made as shown for a 6-inch well size. Instead, a number of 45-degree pipe elbows are needed to offset the interconnecting pipe to accommodate the room taken up by the check valve (see Fig. 4–30). It is possible to use flexible pipe between the two to surmount this obstacle, but it's not recommended; a submersible pump, on start-up or shutdown, exhibits a vicious little jerk—about a quarter turn—due to motor torque. Therefore a short section of interconnecting plastic pipe will fatigue in short order and break; when this happens, water will be pumped everywhere *but* up the delivery pipe.

ACCESSORIES

The demand and store water systems have component parts, most of which have already been discussed. However, two things are noteworthy.

One is that the components used in one system are as different from the other system's parts as the systems themselves are different; therefore, very few parts are interchangeable. And, second, these are the *basic* parts of a system—water purification or conditioning equipment is an additive item. It is conceivable that either system might sport fewer components than those listed here; however, if so, it will be at the expense of automatic functioning or a respectable life-span.

A bare-bones demand system (see Fig. 4–31) has a submersible pump, plastic delivery pipe, electrical wires, a torque arrester, a pressure switch, pressure tank, pressure gauge, an in-well detector, a screen, check valve, and well seal.

The basic store system (see Fig. 6–1) is composed of a piston pump and cylinder, galvanized steel delivery pipe, a stuffing box or pump standard, a pumping jack, a gas engine or an electrical motor, an (optional) wind machine, a well seal, a screen, a check valve, and an in-tank sensor.

Just to be sure that you have a complete idea of the parts involved in each system, they're listed here in alphabetical order. If they've been discussed elsewhere, I'll refer you there; if not, they're detailed here or in the Glossary.

Centrifugal (Submersible) Pump (demand system)

See "Water Extraction," Chapter 2, and "The Centrifugal Pump," this chapter.

Check Valve (store and demand systems)

It takes energy to extract water. Therefore it's a waste when water we've pumped slowly runs back down to the source. And this can happen.

In a store system, the brand-new piston pump can prevent this from happening—its own leathers will stop reverse flow. But in time, wear will allow water to get by, particularly in a system with a high pumping head. If the delivery pipe terminates in the top of a storage tank (see Fig. 2–15), only the water in the delivery pipe will be "lost"; however, if the inlet and outlet are shared at the bottom of the storage tank (see Fig. 2–16), you could lose a whole tankful of water.

Even a submersible pump's innards wear. Since a demand system doesn't store water, the only loss is system pressure; however, even though no water

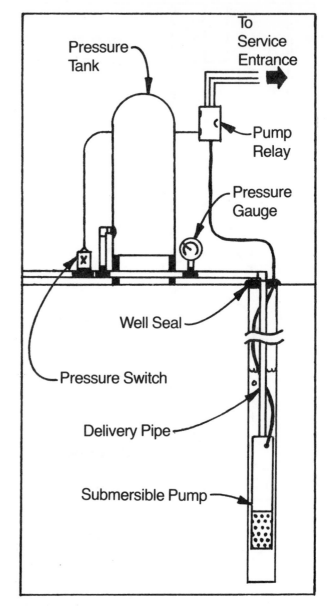

Fig. 4–31 Standard components of the demand type of system.

is being used in the system, the pressure switch will periodically activate the pump to reestablish the system pressure.

So both the demand and store system can make use of the check valve, a device that permits the flow of water in only one direction (see photo). Inserted in-line above the wellhead, the check valve prevents reverse flow. In the demand system, the check valve can be of the spring type (the cheaper version), but in the store system only the gravity type of check valve should be used. A

Fig. 4–32   An in-line check valve will prevent the reverse flow of water.

cleanout plug in the check-valve housing permits easy annual cleaning of the valve seat, as required.

Delivery Pipe (demand and store systems)

In the demand system, the in-well delivery pipe (which transports the pumped water) is usually 1-inch, type PE (black) plastic pipe (see "Pipes," this chapter). If the submersible pump is used in the piggyback configuration, plastic pipe is not used. For a discussion of the delivery pipe in the store system, see "Pipes," this chapter, and "Delivery Pipe" under "The Gold System," Chapter 6.

Electrical Wires, Pump (demand system)

Only code-approved electrical wiring and connectors (used if well depth is greater than stocked lengths) that are specially formulated for water submersion are used with submersible pumps. Wires are strapped to the side of the delivery pipe to avoid fouling and to keep the wires from chafing against the well wall or casing.

Level Sensor, In-Well (demand system)

If the water source is ever pumped dry, and you don't catch it right away, the submersible pump may burn out trying to pump air. An automatic means of both sensing this condition and stopping the pump when it occurs is the in-well level sensor. By lowering two probes into the well—one positioned just above the pump, the other some distance above it—the magnetic relay into which they connect will stop the motor when water reaches the lower sensor, and restart power only after the well has refilled with the water to the level of the upper sensor (see Fig. 4–33).

Level Sensor, Tank (store system)

See "Monitoring Storage," Chapter 2, and "The Waterwatch," Chapter 6.

Piston Pump (store system)

See "Water Extraction," Chapter 2; "Piston Pump," this chapter; and "Deep-Well Piston Pump, under "The Gold System," Chapter 6.

Pressure Gauge (demand system)

A pressure gauge (see Fig. 2–5) may be added to the plumbing in the vicinity of the pressure switch. At this location, of course, it cannot be used for monitoring the system's operation (unless you fre-

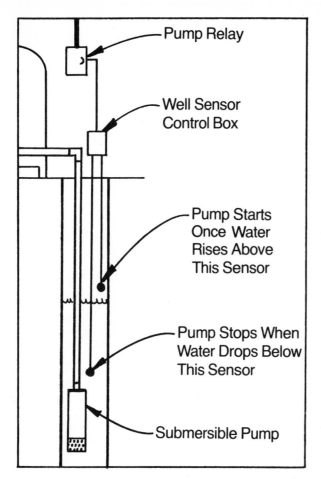

Fig. 4–33 An in-well level sensor will protect the pump during excessive drawdown.

quent the pumphouse)—it's there for two other purposes. Initially, when the system is installed, the gauge assists in the adjustment of the pressure switch to the correct range of operation. Later, the pressure gauge is a good visual indicator if there's some malfunction, letting you know at a glance what is working and what is not.

Pressure Switch (demand system)

Ever wonder how the water system automatically turns on when you open a faucet? In a demand system, a pressure-sensitive switch detects the lowered pressure, closes its contacts, and energizes the pump relay, starting the submersible motor. When usage stops, the water pressure builds to a preadjusted value, the pressure switch's contacts open, the pump's power relay is de-energized, and the submersible pump stops.

The pressure switch doesn't open and close at one specified pressure; rather, it closes at some low pressure and opens at some higher pressure (see

Fig. 6–21). Typical values are 30–50, 35–55, 40–60, etc. The range is adjustable, but the *difference* between the upper and lower open-and-close points is not; it's a built-in specification. Therefore if you want a smaller or larger difference you must buy a different pressure switch.

Pressure Tank (demand system)

Water is not compressible. A water system that uses only a pressure switch will suffer from "water hammer"—knocks like hammering as the pump switches on and off in its attempt to sustain system pressure; this also causes sputtering at a faucet when it's first turned on and uneven flow when the faucet is in use.

The remedy is the pressure tank, which is nothing more than an air chamber. Unlike water, air *is* compressible; inserted in-line, the pressure tank absorbs water hammer and assures an even flow to the faucets at any rate of use below the pump's capacity. The pressure tank is often considered a storage tank—it is possible to get some water from the system without having the pump start up —but this is merely a byproduct of the pressure tank's functioning. Indeed, even a 42-gallon pressure tank is not capable of supplying more than 6.5 gallons of water before the pump restarts. (See Fig. 4–34).

Since air mixes so readily with water, a recurring problem with older-style tanks was their propensity toward waterlogging; periodically, air had to be pumped in to replace that lost to absorption. This was done manually or, with suitable controls, it could be automated. Newer-style tanks use floating separators, minimizing the surface area and hence the interaction between water and air. Some tanks even confine the air to a bladder suspended in the tank.

Pump Standard (store system)

See "Stuffing Box versus Pump Standard" under "The Gold System," Chapter 6.

Pumping Jack (store system)

See "Pumping Jack" under "The Gold System," Chapter 6.

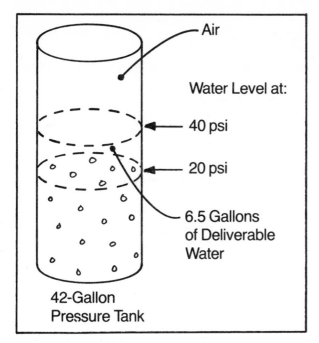

Air

Water Level at:

40 psi

20 psi

6.5 Gallons of Deliverable Water

42-Gallon Pressure Tank

Fig. 4-34 Only a small portion of a pressure tank's capacity is available for delivery.

Screen (demand and store systems)

A fine-mesh screen is attached to the intake (lower end) of the submersible pump to filter out anything that would clog or pit the pump's impellers or, heaven forbid, deliver some unmentionables into the water system. The screen is built in; if your well water is afflicted with particularly fine sediment, you may want to have the dealer install an extra-fine mesh screen, too.

While the submersible pump may function two to fifteen years in the well without servicing, the screen will not fare as well. Dealers often avoid mentioning this, but I'm not so inhibited: the thing clogs up. So if pumping performance diminishes in time, the first thing that should be checked is the screen. Unfortunately, the entire assembly—delivery pipe, wires, and pump—must be pulled for this five-second check and, if clogged, five-minute cleanup job.

There are two alternatives for lazy folks. One is to pretend that it isn't happening, suffer the poor performance, and pay the increased electricity bills. The popularity of this technique is illustrated in the very low average life—approximately four years—attributed to submersible pumps.

The remaining alternative is to leave the screen off, cutting it out of its framework. True, there's nothing to get clogged, but even if you could stomach what's coming up your water lines, this isn't even a stopgap measure; while your neighbor is

pulling his submersible out of the well for a screen cleanout, you're pulling yours out to replace the pump!

In the store system, the piston pump doesn't come equipped with a screen; it's sold as an accessory. Why? With a piston pump assembly you can use a tail pipe (see Fig. 2-25); if you do, you'll want the screen on the bottom end of it. So they don't affix them solidly to the bottom of the cylinder.

While all piston pump installations should use a screen, many do not. Two reasons are given. One is that much of the sediment filtered out by a screen is, in fact, stirred up at the high pumping rates characteristic of submersible pumps; at lower pumping rates like those exhibited by the piston pump assembly, there's not as much need for the screen. Another consideration is that in those systems where the pipe and cylinder have been sized so the pump innards may be removed up through the delivery pipe (see "Delivery Pipe" under "The Gold System," Chapter 6), it's ever so much easier to replace the leathers more often than it is to lift out the entire assembly to clean a screen. For the given conditions, I agree; consequently, my own installation does without a screen. However, if you're faced with a similar decision, weigh the options carefully.

Storage, Water (store system)

See "Water Storage," Chapter 2; "Tanks," this chapter; and "Installation Notes" under "The Gold System," Chapter 6.

Submersible (Centrifugal) Pump

See "Centrifugal (Submersible) Pump," this chapter.

Torque Arrester (demand system)

Mounted on the delivery pipe just above the centrifugal pump, the torque arrester is a flexible gadget that makes contact with the well or casing wall, resisting the "twist" of the pump assembly on start-up due to motor torque.

Well Seal (demand and store systems)

All wellheads need a sanitary seal (see "Eliminating the Source of Contamination," Chapter 3); this seal is always watertight and sometimes airtight.

In the demand system, the well seal is a pancaked rubber seal with holes bored through it; you buy the one that will fit the diameter of your well and pass the size of delivery pipe and electrical wires for your pump. Once these have been routed through, the seal is set on the wellhead casing and, upon tightening, it expands against the well casing and contracts around the wires to affect an impenetrable seal.

In a store system, the well seal is positioned over the wellhead casing before the pump standard or stuffing box is set atop it, expanding when either is bolted down to the concrete well pad.

Wind Machine, Water-Pumping (supply system)

See "Wind Power," Chapter 1, and "Water-Pumping Wind Machine" under "The Gold System," Chapter 6.

Part II

SHAPING

Now that you've gotten a general feel for the nature of water systems, it's time to roll up your sleeves and get your hands dirty. There are two ways to proceed. One is quickly to eliminate anything that will not work for your unique situation; this will clear the bench of a lot of clutter and will get things down to a manageable size. The other approach is to slap together a rough draft of a system utilizing whatever techniques or materials you prefer. Maybe you should try it both ways; if you end up at the same place coming from two different directions, you know you're on the right track.

This section is designed to help you shape your own system. Don't force this process; refer back to Part I frequently. Make a model of the system on paper; it's a lot easier (and cheaper!) to do a little erasing than to dig an extra trench or buy a bigger pump.

If you have trouble scheduling your day, much less designing a water system, check out the "special systems" chapter, where there are step-by-step solutions to a few common situations. However, there's nothing sacrosanct about these solutions; they may be modified to fit your own situation.

5

IMPLEMENTATION

So far, it's been only words and concepts—essential to system design, but nevertheless abstract. This is the point where you take the information, add personal preferences, and apply it to your own situation. You're not ready to buy any equipment, though—too much hinges on the outcome of any effort to develop the water source. Therefore, that's what we'll do now—site the source, develop it, and measure its capacity. Let's get started!

SITING THE WATER SOURCE

The specific site has much to do with detection—it may be obvious or not so obvious, or be chosen on the basis of other criteria.

Walking the Land

You'll be lucky indeed to be able simply to point at the water source you'd like to use. The presence of the ocean, a large lake, or a lazy river on or along the border of your property will fit such a circumstance. More likely, a water source that's much in evidence will be a stream, spring, or pond. Selec-

tion of any of these assumes that you have decided against rainfall collection as either a major or a minor source of water, and that you have a legal right to the water at your chosen source (see "Water and the Law," Chapter 1).

Even if there's no surface water, there may be water within a few feet of the surface. A marshy area, for instance, is a reliable indicator. But—is it wet year-round? A high clay content in the soil will prevent quick drainage of water from a hard rain; however, if it's still there after baking in a summer sun, it's a good indicator of a spring.

The presence of certain types of trees, poplars, is a good sign of water not far below the surface; with their shallow roots, if the water isn't there, they won't be either. The same goes for some types of bushes—for example, oleanders. Any relatively large growth of greenery is evidence of water, but there are limits to the conclusions one can draw from their presence. It helps to know about trees and bushes in general; not only do some plants stay green year-round but, other types of brush and trees as well need very little water to stay alive.

Stream beds, even when dry (see photograph), should be examined for traces of year-round water.

Fig. 5–1 A dry stream bed may be the overflow for an underground stream.

Small pools of water, however small or stale-looking, suggest water within a few feet of the surface; water that's been merely trapped will evaporate, whereas water that remains *must* be fed from some source.

Even if there is no visible water at all in a stream bed, it should be examined carefully. For example, an hour's digging should be sufficient to find out whether the water is really close to the surface. And not finding it doesn't mean it's not there—you may have picked a bad spot; if so, you really don't know one way or the other. On the other hand, if you do find water or a lot of dampness, you've got a potential water source. Many streams merely go underground when the rate of flow is insufficient to have it flowing both above and below ground level. However, don't assume that the underground portion of a stream necessarily sticks to the path of the stream bed, even though it usually does.

Detecting Non-Obvious Sources

If there are no apparent sources of water on a section of land—surface water, stream beds, or unusual clumps of greenery—the possible on-site water sources are reduced to shallow wells and deep wells. When this is the case, we must rely on other factors in order to estimate the probability of their existence.

Area's Water Reputation

One indicator that must never be discounted is the reputation of the area itself. High-producing wells on land bordering the property indicate a strong possibility of success with a similar installation on the land in question. While there are no guarantees, of course it's better to live in an area renowned for the availability of water than one that's not. Take care not to assume too much, however. If, for example, all of these strong water sources are deep wells, it's easy to assume that a deep well is necessary when, in fact, a shallow well might suffice. There's a *lot* of difference in the price.

Proximity to Good Wells

If both low- and high-producing wells dot the surrounding area, siting the well close to a high-producing well just over the property line has merit. As a matter of fact, we used this strategy on our own property; just over the property line are two wells that are artesian through three to seven months of the year—at a 20-gallon-per-minute rate, yet. It was a sweet temptation we were unable to resist. Unfortunately, we didn't hit the same aquifer; though our well was drilled a bit beyond the depth of either of the nearby wells, we got only 4½ gpm. In our desire to share in all of the water wealth, however, we failed to check on the quality of the water available from the two artesian wells; while not all that bad, ours is much clearer and sweeter-tasting. So—we get better water at a lesser rate. And insofar as we had no intention of using a high-capacity pump in our well, the lower capacity isn't really a disadvantage for us.

Well Drillers

Experienced well drillers in the immediate area are a potential source of good information; the older the firm, the better. After enough successes and failures, there's little doubt that anyone would get a *feel* for the presence of water just by looking at the lay of the land—contours, rock outcroppings, and other geological characteristics. The trick is to get them talking about the general area or, without committing yourself to having them do any work for you, get them out to your place for a look-see. Now, any reputable firm is going to come out to the place for precisely this reason before any work commences anyhow, but it'd be dishonest to bring them out on the pretext of having them do the job. While all too often we end up paying more for something than it's really worth, we should always be willing to pay for helpful information.

There are a number of major disadvantages in using well drillers as a source of information. One is that they're prejudiced toward the types of systems they can install. Consequently, if they're equipped to drill only deep wells, they may not point out any shallow-well possibilities they may detect. Another problem is that unless they specialize in alternative types of water systems, their main business is electric utility-oriented. Since they'll want to keep the bid on the job to a minimum, this automatically favors a site and installation that:

1. is close to an electric-utility tie-in (minimizing electrical wire runs),

2. is close to the house or other water usage sites (to minimize trenching, pipe materials, and pipe laying),

3. is a high-producing water source,

4. has a well that's deep enough to ensure high pumping rates, and,

5. is easily accessible for their drilling rig (see "The Deep Well," this chapter).

We'd all like a high-producing water source. Why do I list it as a *dis*advantage here? There are two reasons. One, the utility-powered submersible *needs* a high-producing well. So, in the stampede to match the well to the system, any source of water that is high enough to be satisfactory to your needs but is too low to handle the submersible itself may be ignored. There's no way around it; it's a net loss to you. And, two, if the well doesn't produce the needed quantity, the problem is kicked

on to number 4—the well is drilled deeper to supply more in-well water storage.

In short, there's a horrible conflict of interest involved that cannot easily be circumvented; it's going to happen any time you ask people to do something that is outside their area of expertise or line of work. Pushing them into it may not help; keeping them on track tends to pinprick egos, and it's as likely to get them mad as to get you any information. Experience is not always transferable or negotiable!

Dowsing

An excellent way to find water and determine its depth in the ground and the approximate flow rate in gpm is by dowsing, or water witching. Though the process is far from understood, the detection of water and interpretation of the results are accomplished through the use of a device such as a bent wire clothes hanger, forked tree branches, or pendulums, and the abilities (natural or developed) of the person wielding it. To the uninitiated, it's an eerie feeling to see someone calmly walking about, instrument in hand, scratching notes onto a pad, then announcing this or that potential water source.

Because so much ridicule has followed dowsing, as it has so many other unorthodox methods of doing things, it is only recently that evidence has been collected to substantiate many of the claims made for it. While electromagnetic waves are suspected of being involved, the significant role of the individual in the practice of dowsing understandably complicates the process of pinning it down. Incidentally, while "water witching" and "dowsing" are often considered equivalent terms, this is technically not so. Dowsing means "searching," and the subject of the search can be almost anything organic or nonorganic. Dowsing has been successful in finding minerals, oil, tunnels or passages, human beings, livestock, lost objects, pipes, wires, etc.

While there's no doubt that some folks seem to have a natural talent for dowsing, it's a technique that can be developed and honed to a fine degree of sensitivity. Willingness, practice, and faith are all powerful allies in this process. Why not try your hand at it on your own property? Pick up a book on the subject, make a simple device, and go for it! Pick a day when there's nobody else around; doing it feels ridiculous enough without the added com-

Fig. 5–2 Vanessa Hackleman tries her hand at dowsing for water at Finn's Wind Farm.

tempted to site our well to hit the same aquifer that blessed our neighbors with artesian wells. *Finding* water is only one part of the art; a competent dowser probably could have told us that the water we detected wasn't what we were looking for.

In our own area, the services of a professional dowser in finding water on a small piece of property—say, 10 acres—would cost fifty to seventy-five dollars. This is not a high price to pay for such valuable information—but while boasting a high reliability, dowsing is not a guarantee of finding the water, its depth, or capacity. There are dowsers who claim 100 percent reliability, but most of us can neither find them nor afford their services and must rely upon less-talented practitioners of the art. Nevertheless, considering how scanty the information gleaned from other indicators is by comparison, I'd at least use dowsing as a check—if not, in fact, the major indicator—of a water source.

Other Considerations

Finding water where it's not useful is not really much of a "find." If there are two or more possible sites, one must consider other factors in the selection of a site, such as the best energy site, best gravity potential, and best proximity to usage.

Energy Considerations

If alternative energy is under consideration, the best energy site should be first determined (see "Energy Sources," Chapter 1), then checked for its potential as a water source. However, this should *never* compromise a water source that is higher in elevation. Offset setups—where the highest water source is distant from, but connected to, the best energy site—will handle this problem (see "Offset Systems," Chapter 6); it's normally simpler and less costly to transfer energy than it is to transfer water.

Gravity Potential

Using gravity as a means of water transport or pressurizing greatly simplifies any water system (see "Gravity Flow" and "Gravity Pressurization," Chapter 2), rewarding *any* effort to find a water source at a high elevation—or, failing that, one that's higher than the best water-use site. The "start from the top and work down" principle,

plication of onlookers, and any embarrassment may prevent you from the fine-tuning needed as your eyes behold the rod's first flicker of movement.

If you're ready to admit that you've neither the confidence nor the time to search for a reliable water source on your own place, consider hiring a professional dowser. Even well drillers use dowsing; if some member of the well driller's crew is not a dowser, the firm is likely to have one on tap who, for a modest fee, will perform this service.

Admittedly, we did not use a professional dowser in the siting of our own well, but if we had it to do over again, we would. In this instance, it would have been wise to check our own findings. You see, my wife and I did the dowsing (see photo). Actually, this was our second try. Several years before, we had attempted dowsing as an alternative to the extensive digging that would have been required to find a missing septic tank in need of pumping. We were immediately successful; both of us got "readings" and, digging there, found it! However, only Vanessa got a reading as we at-

then, always applies when searching for water sources.

Access

A major factor in the selection of a water source site is access to it for any equipment and materials needed to develop it. Unless you're going to hand-dig your well or hire a helicopter to bring in the gear, sites for shallow wells will need access for a backhoe, and deep wells for a well-drilling rig. This is an unfortunate fact; if the land is cut by deep ravines, for instance, the cost of cutting in a road will greatly add to the cost of an otherwise ideal situation. The backhoe is not extensively inhibited, but the well-drilling rig is. Due to its size, weight, and ungainliness, it will need a level drilling site, as well as an access road with a minimum grade that is compacted enough to keep the rig from bogging down; in most cases, the landowner is liable if the rig gets stuck.

Distance

Naturally, it's desirable to locate the water source as close to the usage site as possible; at the very least, this minimizes plumbing and, where applicable, the length of electrical wires. But to accomplish this, most people would have to relocate the building site itself. It often happens that the distance between the two is very large, in part due to the dogmatic belief that the best building site is at the top of the hill and the best water site is at the bottom. Fortunately, neither is true. If the choice is between a close but lower source versus a distant but higher source, rarely will the shorter length of pipe or electrical wire for the former warrant the loss of system versatility and simplicity in the latter option. This can be proven more cost-effective even if no factors besides direct cash outlay are considered.

Development Contamination

The possibility of contamination is always present in the development of a water source; since this is most likely to occur at the point where the water leaves the ground, effort at preventing contamination is best concentrated at this point. No effort should be spared in the correct construction of a spring box (see photo on page 114) or the proper sealing of either shallow or deep wells. Clearing foliage and debris from the immediate vicinity of the water source will discourage creeping, crawling, burrowing, and flying critters. Since water runoff from rains can wash debris and other surface contaminants down onto a well or spring site, careful grading will prevent any pooling of this contaminating water or material.

Septic Systems

Obviously, any type of sewage-treatment system should be distant from the water source site. Sanitary codes specify minimum distances to separate the two, but because of the large number of factors involved, acquiring a permit for a septic system or a well will usually entail the prerequisite of an on-site visit by the local sanitation officer to look over the specific situation. Since septic systems are located "downhill" from the house, this is a factor further favoring the siting of the water source *above* the building site; if the possibility of water-source contamination cannot be wholly eliminated, one can, at the minimum, assure that the tap is *above* the point of contamination. When camping by a river or stream, you get your drinking water upstream from the campsite, and you bathe downstream from it. Make sense?

A primary reason in lining the top 20 to 30 feet of a well with a casing (see "The Deep Well," this chapter) is to eliminate the contamination of the well by either surface, subsurface, or septic water. Since the bottom of the septic tank is 10–12 feet deep, the soil around it or the leach lines will rarely be contaminated beyond a few feet. Nevertheless, it's possible inadvertently to site the septic tank in a good water site, which automatically increases the chances of contaminating water to shallow well depths, if not deeper, in the surrounding area. If the hole dug for a septic tank immediately fills with water, trouble may be brewing. If it's in the springtime, you can't say one way or another; a hole that fills with water after a long, dry summer, however, is very suspect.

People in the business of installing septic tanks aren't stupid; they know what this means. Unfortunately, nobody's going to pay them for being so observant; if they dissuade you from the task under way, they're out their own labor and effort to that point. So—it rests with you. Either declare the septic tank site unsuitable and lay out the cash to do it elsewhere (hoping all the while there's no recurrence of what just happened) or take your chances with subsurface contamination.

Incidentally, this is a case for dowsing the property in the immediate vicinity of the building site; get the dowser to map out *any* indications of water. Then, when you're ready to site the septic tank you can put it smack-dab in the middle of any area that showed no trace of subsurface water.

Not all sanitation officers will be receptive to this kind of evidence, but it's certainly worth trying. Poor judgment on the part of a sanitation official is difficult to prove because of the variance in conditions that might lead to the contamination of a water source, particularly by the installation of the prescribed septic systems. Ultimately, you bear the responsibility for the cost and difficulty in treating polluted water and living with it from that point onward. It makes sense, then, to be aware of how you can get hurt; just hoping for the best isn't always going to work. If you won't stand up for your rights, who will? Even this won't always guarantee success, but it sure beats doing nothing.

Final Thoughts

Finding water is not a matter of punching a hole in the ground—just ask anyone who's paid the price for a dry hole. It's unfortunate that some people have had this experience even after having doggedly considered many, if not all, of the factors presented here. However, these are exceptional situations; a far more common circumstance occurs when a landowner naïvely points to the place where it's convenient to site the well or when it's left entirely up to the well driller to pick the site. In consideration of the inherent top-heaviness, weight, and bulk of his rig, he often elects to choose a site immediately adjacent to what may be the only road on the property. It's an absurd situation when the owner just wants it "done as cheap and fast as possible." In this scenario, I find it surprising that any water is found at all.

Our own well constituted the first development of our land. Even at that, we were comfortably camped nearby and didn't feel particularly pressured by the situation of living on our own land and not having any water. However, avoid this situation at all cost. Need can get things accomplished, but desperation severely compromises the situation. And while no well driller wants to drill a

dry hole on anyone's land (it *is* harmful to their reputation), unless they guarantee water (a minimum gpm—see "The Deep Well," this chapter), you foot the bill either way. So if you're low on water, establish an alternate water source (filling a drum each time you go to town or visit a neighbor?) so your thirstiness does not bypass good judgment. The entire water system doesn't have to be designed prior to drilling a well, but you can count on a more complicated, energy-intensive, and costly system for every one of these factors that is compromised or ignored.

DEVELOPING THE WATER SOURCE

A spring is developed in a different manner from a well; the final appearance of each should be proof enough of that. However, there are more similarities than differences. Since the drilled well constitutes the most extensive development, I'll focus on that water source, although I've included some installation notes at the end of the section on some of the other sources. Don't let that stop you from obtaining all the literature you can on the development of the specific water source you intend to use —spring, pond, shallow well, rainwater collection, etc. (see "References")—before proceeding with these installations. Your primary objective should be to do it right the first time, and that published material is designed to steer you clear of the many pitfalls that await the unwary, as well as providing time- and money-saving tricks of the trade.

The Deep Well

The process of drilling a well is not simply a matter of making a phone call, having someone show up, and punching a hole in the ground. It's easy for people who haven't had it done to think that's all there is to it. And, on reflection, I'm sure that some people who *have* gone through the experience will describe it in such simplistic terms. However, after reading this section you'll agree that this person simply let everybody else make all the decisions. A close examination of the system that resulted will frequently verify this statement—nowhere else could one get so little for so much money.

The procedure for drilling a well is divided into three parts: predrill, drill, and postdrill.

Predrill

Predrill involves decisions *after* the water source is sited. Basically, predrill includes selecting the driller, fixing the price, and preparing the site.

SELECTING THE DRILLER

For the most part, this section assumes that you will not drill the well yourself. You *could,* of course. There are numerous advertisements in a variety of magazines that list all the advantages of drilling your own well. You'd even find a number of people with a lot of experience in this area who'd agree that the idea has merit. However, there are alternative means of doing the same job that are cheaper, faster, and easier.

Four things make the job difficult for the inexperienced person. One is that the experience cannot be fully communicated; there's just too much detail. Two, every situation is somewhat different; what works for one doesn't necessarily work for another. Three, the novice usually gets only half the cake; knowing what *not* to do is sometimes just as important as knowing what *to* do. And, four, the experienced person doesn't always have experience in the alternative itself, and until he does, its merits and shortcomings are really unknown.

Also, if equipment is leased and you're unsuccessful in drilling a well, you're out the money. On the other hand, if you have to buy the equipment and it doesn't work, you're out even more money. And you still need a well. The claim that you can have a well and the equipment that drills it cheaper than or for the same price as getting a professional well driller to do it sounds good. However, unless you plan to gain a livelihood from it, you have no need for the equipment once it's done its job. A frequent claim is the high resale value; if that's true, you should have no difficulty in finding one used, right? Try it! I can say nothing about the reliability, quality, or success of using the advertised equipment—I've never seen one up close, and have heard no feedback, positive or otherwise, about its operation. I am, however, very concerned with some of the claims made in the advertisement of this equipment. In the end, it still comes off as just "punching a hole in the ground," and I *have* seen the misery and misfortune that that attitude brings.

Whatever the situation, shop around for a professional well driller. In some areas there may be

Fig. 5–3 A hard-rock, deep-well drilling rig at work.

no choice; most hard-rock drilling rigs (6-inch bore capability) are the size of small locomotives (see photo), and they're difficult to move about. Therefore driving them any distance means extra expense. It's not necessarily *that* much extra—you'd gladly fork it out if you could get a better all-around deal—but check it out. Of major concern is the reputation of the company itself, and you might be lucky to have the best closest at hand.

Since people who have wells drilled are frequently questioned by new neighbors as to why they selected the well driller they did, they usually have some pat answers prepared. (After all, do you really expect they'll say they picked the first name in the Yellow Pages?) Few people are willing to admit their own poor judgment. Glowing reports of the well driller who put in their system over the other "shysters" in the same business should be double-checked. Then, too, someone who's supercritical of the well driller would probably have a similar experience with *any* well driller.

Asking the well-drilling company itself for the names of customers who've received an installation similar in nature to your own and checking with those folks may be the best strategy.

While you're at it, check out similar systems. If you're planning a hybrid system (see "Special Systems," Chapter 6), there's little sense in looking at a system based on a utility-powered submersible. Additionally, the cost of well drilling may depend very much on what system you will ultimately install.

FIXING THE WELL-DRILLING PRICE

The cost of drilling a well is standardly fixed at a per-foot price—for example, ten dollars per foot of depth; I call this the CDF, or "Cost per Drilled Foot." Most well drillers are asked to do an entire system, from supplying the equipment (pumps, pressure tank, controls) to digging and installing the plumbing to connecting the electricity. To do the job quickly, they stock the related hardware. Also for this reason, most companies offer two CDF rates. One is the "drill-the-well-and-leave" rate. The other lower CDF rate is offered if you go for a package deal of drilled well *and* the equipment. It may also, but does not always, include installation. When you ask for quotes, make sure you understand which rate includes what.

At present, the "standard" well installation involves a utility-powered submersible pump. Accordingly, that type of system gets the lowest CDF. In all fairness, if you bought the equipment elsewhere and hired someone to install it, you probably couldn't beat the deal. If you want someone other than yourself to install the system, you might as well have the same place do it all; at least it will save you a lot of running around. However, a spot check of comparative prices is still a good thing; the system price isn't *always* the cheapest.

Any company will order whatever you specify and, if you wish, install it for you if you'll buy the equipment through them. However, if it's not the specialty of the house, the odds don't favor any kind of a good deal. So, if you plan to supply the labor by installing the equipment yourself, and only want to hire a company to drill the well, don't be lured by the lower CDF rate into buying the equipment through them. The difference between the "well only" CDF and the "well and hardware" CDF is usually not more than a dollar or so. The difference in the drilling of, say, a 150-foot well is then a mere 150 dollars but the markup on the

non-specialty, special-order equipment can be several multiples of this amount. Again, check prices—don't just assume that a package deal will be cheaper.

When asking prices, always ensure that you and the person to whom you're speaking are talking about the same thing. For instance, well drillers don't have the same capabilities, nor do they drill the same-size holes. In our area, most of the rigs drill a 6-inch-diameter well; however, the reason for one lower quote became clear when it turned out to be for a 4-inch hole. The company cannot be faulted—they assumed we knew it was 4 inches, and we assumed they were quoting for 6 inches.

Additional fees may be charged for drilling a well. The best solution is to get a quote in writing for the job even if they quote a specific CDF, just to be certain there are no additional charges. In one area a "move-in" fee for equipment may be added as a standard procedure, or if the distance to your place is more than the company permits free of charge.

Another major expense in drilling the well is the cost of the casing. This is one or more sections of a steel (case iron) pipe inserted in the well at the start of drilling. To accommodate this, the first bit of drilling involves an oversize drill bit, which is taken as deep as the casing may extend. Once the bit is withdrawn, the casing is forced downward, effectively sheathing the hole in steel to that depth. This distance varies with the area, the type of terrain, and the whim of well drillers. Once the casing is installed, a bit that will fit inside the well casing is then used to drill the well to its final depth.

The casing serves a number of functions. One is that it protects the well from collapse during the drilling and any time after, it shores up the sides of the drilled hole, particularly where the layers of earth are simply loose soil, clay, or another soft material. The casing is usually ended once bedrock is reached. In those areas of the country where bedrock does not lie within a few hundred feet of the surface, the entire well may be cased.

Water doesn't simply enter the drilled well through the bottommost point, although many people think it does. Since, in fact, most of the water comes in from the sides, a well that is cased to its bottom will use perforated casing below 40 feet; while shoring the well walls, this will still let the water pass. However, the topmost section of well casing in *all* wells is not perforated. That's because a second, very important feature of the well casing is to help prevent contamination of the well by water on or near the surface: water from any source above 40 feet simply can't enter the well. This is particularly important when the well is not that far from a septic tank. Understandably, this doesn't mean a well can't be contaminated, but this procedure certainly minimizes the risk to acceptable levels.

Getting the well cased to the depth of the bedrock is good insurance in earthquake country, as the slightest shift in the strata can sheer off a well, or at least cause it to collapse either partially or completely. However, there's little sense in trying to exploit this feature by casing the well down through the bedrock. In either instance, if the earthquake is severe enough it will scarcely notice the resistance of a steel casing with a wall thickness of $\frac{1}{4}$ inch if it's in the process of swallowing buildings, splitting the ground, or shoving half the state into the ocean.

The cost of the casing varies; it's standardly priced by the foot. At the time of this writing, the price in our area is $3.25 per foot. While you're at it, you might as well find out what minimum length of casing will be required; this may be set by the county sanitation department. If they're familiar with the area, they may be able to give a relative probability of the need for additional casing. Don't expect a firm answer on this, but if it's an unknown, you'll want to consider the worst case for your own situation in the price limit you'll establish prior to drilling. That subject is soon discussed.

SITE PREPARATION

The site selected for the well may require preparation for the drilling. For some, this may only involve staking out a path from the nearest road for the drilling rig. What will you want to do? Remove rocks larger than a baseball. Remove shrubs, tall grass, dead trees. Note the position of ravines, ruts, holes that must be bypassed. Check the slope of the ground; well-drilling rigs are usually top-heavy and cannot take a side tilt of more than a few degrees without the threat of rolling. If the ground isn't level, ask the company how much of a tilt the truck can take. Check the soil for compaction. Even though most of these rigs have wide tires, they are *heavy*, and if yours sinks to its hubcaps you might be liable (in dollars) for getting it unstuck. And believe me, no dinky little tow truck is going to do the job.

Particular attention should be given to trees between the road and the well-drilling site. Note any low-hanging limbs that might impede the truck's passage. Again, the company can tell you to the inch what the overhead clearance of their rig is (they need this information for passage under bridges), and you can easily find out beforehand whether there's going to be a problem. If there is, either reroute, or cut off the offending branches. Of course, it's always best not to have to cut any branches for such a one-time, in-and-out affair as having a well drilled, but it's not always avoidable. Don't wait to do the dastardly deed. A cut-and-seal approach to tree trimming is preferable to the chop-and-slice effect you'll get with the truck idling a few feet away on well-drilling day. Or the inevitable ripping that can savage a tree (worse than any cutting) if the truck bulls its way through the foliage. Not everybody's concerned about this sort of thing, but it's unnecessary cruelty to trees, in any case.

The drilling rig must sit level before the drilling commences; this assures the straightest bore. The truck comes equipped with pads that may be lowered to assist in leveling, but they can adjust for only a few degrees of slope. Consequently the well site must be fairly level. If there's a question about this, ask. Since most companies will look at the site prior to driving a rig up to it, they'll indicate a problem if there is one. Unless you're lacking things to do and you have a strong back, this is a bulldozer job.

A leveled site, natural or bought with hard-earned dollars, may not be the only place a bulldozer is needed; wherever the rig cannot go it alone—because of loose soil, too much side slope, too sharp a grade, or whatever—the bulldozer must cut the path. If this expense was expected, fine; proceed. If it wasn't, include it in the well-drilling cost estimates or use it as a factor in assessing overall water system development.

It can be tough to know what's a problem and what's not. Fortunately, there's some help available —the company itself. It's rare indeed for a well-drilling rig just to show up for the job. Instead, the owner, foreman, or drill operator will visit the site prior to D-Day (Drill Day) to isolate potential problems. Being familiar with the rig itself, this person will experience little difficulty in "thinking like a dinosaur" and knowing how much room will be needed to maneuver the beast into place. Listen intently, ask questions, suggest alternatives and ask for them whenever there's something you don't want to do. Understand that this person's job is to

assess the trouble getting to and from the site, lining up for the bore, and dealing with any threats to the rig itself; some of these folks don't even like to get the paint scratched on their trucks. It's your job to let him do *his* job without causing unacceptable damage to the terrain, trees, and your pocketbook.

Though I've never heard of a drive-up-and-drill outfit, I suppose one might be lurking in the Yellow Pages. If it's not standard procedure but you think you may have a troublesome site, ask for a visit. I can't imagine they'd charge you for it; if they did, I'd think about taking my business elsewhere.

PRICE LIMIT

Because of the high cost of well drilling, most outfits that drill a well, particularly if it's a drill-and-leave situation, want their money right after the job. This is not, in my opinion, an unreasonable request; admittedly, I'm amazed that any place can work on a credit system. Nevertheless, that kind of cash outlay can be tough, especially if it's in the wake of forking out a few thousand dollars as a down payment on the property. In truth, anybody can scrape together enough cash or bite into the emergency funds if there's a genuine need. But just how much are we talking about? Site preparation and any landscaping for access will be paid for prior to D-Day. If that leaves nothing left over, D-Day must be postponed. But the elusive figure in dollars and cents will still need to be pinned down.

So what we need is a price limit. In a nutshell, this is the amount of money you have or can scrape up in a hurry to pay all the bills. If you don't have a lot of money, drilling until you run out of it does make a certain kind of sense. On the other hand, if you do have a lot of money, you'll want to fix the price limit carefully; after a certain point, you may be merely throwing it away.

The price limit may be established by roughing the estimates of critical phases of the well drilling. For example, the cost of the casing may be easily computed; at so many dollars per foot and a required minimum depth, it's simple math. If there's a possibility it could go deeper, establish two figures—the minimum and a probable maximum. If all the wells in the area are cased through their entire depth and your research verifies that this *is* necessary, as unwelcome as the answer may be, its cost is easily computed.

The company supplies the information on the CDF (cost per drilled foot). Again, once the depth of the well is known, this is easily computed. Beforehand, unless you live in an area with a definite water table, it's pure guesswork how deep the well will be drilled. If you've had a dowser find the water on your land, that person should be able to tell you at what depth the water may be found. Dowser or not, check the immediate vicinity. How deep are the wells? Record both the depth and the capacity.

Now, establish "levels" (see Fig. 5–4). Level one should reflect the shallowest well of satisfactory production in identical terrain. Level two should represent the deepest well depth in the general area. And level three is the deepest that you will permit your own well to be drilled before trying elsewhere.

Traditionally, the depth for level three is greater than that of level two. But level three is really an arbitrary figure, and, for lack of other information, it seems wise that it be based on something rather than being picked out of a hat. So may I suggest that you consider the difficulty in pumping from a very deep well? It can take a lot of energy to lift water hundreds of feet, and too deep a well can both limit the kind of system that can be applied to this task and skyrocket the initial and operating costs on the remaining ones. Level three, then, can be a reflection of that thinking—which can often put its depth *between* the established figures for level one and level two. Multiply all three of these figures by the CDF to establish the minimum, the maximum, and the optimum drilled depth.

Juggling money reserves is the next step. You must have enough money to drill to level one, maybe to level two, and hopefully there will be enough if you have to go to level three. If you don't have enough, wait until you do. Some people have a knack for just scraping by on the cash they have, but it's difficult and consequently expensive to reset a drilling rig back over a hole to drill it deeper. That can happen to anyone, but if it didn't even reach the probable depth for water, that's just poor planning.

Assuming you've got enough money to buy into the game, all of these estimates should be applied to setting the SLR (Stop, Look, and Reevaluate") point. It should be based on the depth for level one or level three *or* a certain percentage of money already spent. If you make it 50 percent of what you're willing to spend, you have enough to do it all over again somewhere else. In any case, the

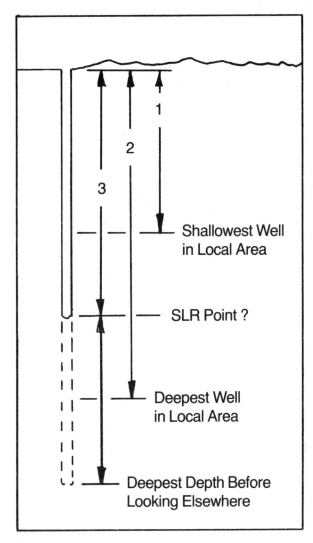

Fig. 5–4 Establish drilling limits if your funds are low.

SLR point may be thought of as a meditation point in the midst of all the confusion, noise, and progress (or lack of it). More on this later.

Drill Day

The well-drilling company can give you an estimate of how long it will take them to drill to a certain depth. It might be a matter of hours, half a day, a full day, or several days. Irrespective of the answer you get, well drillers exhibit a propensity to start early in the day. Find out when that might be and get the chores, breakfast, and other morning rituals out of the way; awaking to the sound of the approaching truck and scrambling into clothes to greet them is not the best way to start off the affair.

The person who's been out to the property may or may not accompany the drilling rig, so assume that you will have to show the driver where the site is. If there's no real road, be prepared to lead the driver and rig by the way you've plotted. If the space is tight, it might be better to get the driver to walk the route with you first; if he can't turn around at the site, he may want to back into it. If you haven't allowed enough room for the turns or sufficient overhead clearance, be prepared to deal with that—chain saw, ladders, and limb sealant (where required) should be at hand. Really high stuff can be cut as interference is experienced; it's not only safer to stand on the rig to do the job, but also easier to gauge precisely how much cutting is needed.

Well drillers are required to fill out some kind of a log; it varies from place to place. In it they indicate the depth at which they enter certain types of soil or rock. They discover this in two ways. One is the rate at which the drill bit descends. The other is by the type of "mud" that's discharged. Water is pumped into the hole to lubricate the cutting head and to float away the pulverized earth; there's enough pressure in this setup to wash the mixture up and out of the bored hole. By looking at this, the driller can tell what type of soil or rock the bit's chewing through.

The novelty of well drilling wears off after thirty to forty minutes. In no way should you feel as if you *should* stay there; unless the crew is quite gregarious, they'd just as soon you didn't. So once the fascination of the process wears off, get out of there; hovering can actually impede the process of drilling. However, before you go, don't forget to tell the driller when you want to be contacted. At the very least, indicate the SLR point whether water has been struck or not. Obviously, if a real gusher is struck you'll want to be informed of that; I call this the IAG ("It's A Gusher!") point. In any case, indicate where you may be found (if there are only a few people in the crew, they'll need every person) as things happen; a few honks on the horn will suffice.

Since well drilling can be hot and boring work, consider offering some refreshment—cool water, tea, or whatever. Leave the alcohol, in any form, to the last as celebration; the crew doesn't need the temptation, and it has no place when this kind of massive machinery is working. A good crew knows what it's like to drill a well; consequently, they'll bring their own lunch or liquids, so don't feel obligated. On the other hand, it's a nice gesture even if it's refused.

AT THE SLR (STOP, LOOK, AND REEVALUATE) POINT

Once the rig has drilled to your preset SLR, you've been informed, and you *don't* have the water you wanted, it's time to reevaluate the situation. Here are some criteria to go by:

1. Where are you with the money? Is this the halfway point? If it's not, are you being too stingy with your allowance for the well? None of us wants to spend any more than absolutely necessary, but don't forget the importance of water. On your own land, there is probably no other factor that is more important in the long run. Setting a limit is one thing, but under the right conditions you should be willing to pass that limit.

2. How much water do you need? Basically, nobody has any problems with artesian wells. Also, for the small landowner with water needs limited to the household, a garden, and a little livestock, there's never going to be any difficulty with 50, 40, 30, 20, or even 10 gpm. Some submersible-based systems may experience some difficulty with flows under 5 gpm, but systems using, say, a water-pumping wind machine seldom have trouble with flows as low as 3 gpm. Do you have any water now? Ask the well driller to do a test, measuring outflow (see "Capacity Measurement Techniques," this chapter). The accuracy of a short test leaves much to be desired, but some information is better than none.

3. If there's some water and you judge it to be enough, was it just hit? If it was, think about having them drill a little deeper. This allows for the propensity for water tables to drop with high usage; no matter how large the gpm test at this point, the water table could drop a few feet and you'd lose access to it. Both population density and the chance of drought are factors here.

Another reason to drill a bit deeper than the level at which water is struck is to accommodate the positioning of in-well equipment. No system needs this hardware stuffed right down at the bottom; the commotion as pumping commences is sure to stir up fine sediment, and this is tough on the pump's innards. Additionally, any system that uses an electrical submersible pump must have some in-well storage capability, particularly wherever the gpm rating of the well and the pump capacity ratings are similar. However, for any type of system that does not extract the water at a high rate, in-well storage is not a factor. Admittedly it may be to allow for a dropping of the water table; however, it's expensive storage and the money is better spent on storing the water topside.

4. Just as drilling a well is no guarantee of finding any water, drilling a well deeper (past the SLR or IAG point) is no guarantee of getting a higher gpm capacity. If the test of the first IAG is insufficient, drill till you hit another IAG or the SLR point. If it is sufficient, drill to allow for water table droppage, storage (if needed), and the additional depth needed to keep the equipment off the bottom of the well. If you hit another IAG, fine. If not, set a precise amount of extra money to gamble on hitting another IAG footage and *stick to it*. Afterward, anyone will wonder if just a *few* more feet would have made the well artesian; this token effort will help quench that feeling, give the well a fair shake, and not cost too much if your funds are limited.

The deeper the well is drilled, the tougher will be the extraction of the water. However, the difficulty of extraction is not determined by well depth or the depth at which water is reached. Rather, this is set by how far down the surface of the water is in the well. Once water has been struck, the actual level of the water normally rises above that point. For example, our well hit water at 130 feet, and the level immediately rose to within 40 feet of the surface and has stayed there. However, it would be wise to consider the possibility that it will not rise by much, and that's how far down the equipment must reach and the depth from which the water must be pumped. At the time of the well drilling, the presence of the equipment in the well prevents a determination of this depth; only after it is removed can this distance be measured (see "Finding the Water Level in the Well," this chapter).

Drilling a well deeper than really necessary carries one further hazard: punching the bottom out of the well. This is a rare occurrence, but well drillers will talk about losing the gpm rate they've gotten because the drill breaks through into an underground cavern or a layer of rock that literally drains the well of the water that was hit at a shallower depth. No matter how remote the possibility, it *could* happen. If there's nothing to lose (that is, if you have a totally unacceptable gpm yield), there's no real risk; keep drilling. If, however, there's sufficient water, wanting more may cost you what you have.

5. Everybody has a **bad day** once in a while. If

the driller reaches the SLR point and there's no water or only a little water, a tough decision follows. If there's any water at all, it'd probably be worth trying deeper. However, if the SLR is at a footage sufficiently below the level one footage and even close to the level two footage, this is pretty much "eeny, meeny, miney, mo" time.

If the well drillers are unconcerned, I'd probably go on for another 10 percent of the funds and establish that as the new SLR. If the well drillers admit that it's rare for the area, I'd be very tempted to tell them to pull the equipment and start over at the alternate site. It'll be one of the harder things you've done in your life, but—there's no getting around it—it's your decision. Most hard-rock rigs can go hundreds of feet beyond your own limits if you let them; it would be an unusual situation for one of the crew actually to suggest that you try elsewhere after going only the SLR distance. Unless they are adamantly *against* pulling out at such an early stage, it's entirely up to you to bring up the possibility or make the suggestion. As well-intentioned as the crew or foreman may be, you have no way of knowing whether advice is sound, intuitive, or just "I'm going to bring in this well" pigheadedness. Win or lose, they get your money. If they're willing to back their feeling with a "no deliver, no pay" deal for the extension beyond what's already drilled, it'd be worth trying; suggest it, and if they accept it, great! People usually have difficulty with gambling away their own money; gambling with other people's money is infinitely easier!

There's simply too little information available to suggest which is better—drilling one well to a certain depth or drilling two wells, each to half the depth of the one. Even if it were possible to collect data from every well ever drilled, this would only suggest a probability that slightly favored one or the other. That's not much help, actually; once committed, you will get it or you won't. But two other factors come into play, and they can be the deciding ones if all of the other evidence is inconclusive. One is how the site was selected in the first place. If it was dowsed, I'd go deeper; if it wasn't, I'd go to the second factor. That is, if the point has been reached where the well is at the second level —the footage of the deepest satisfactory-yield well in the immediate vicinity—I'd pull and start over.

Regardless of whether the second hole is successful, don't destroy the first one! There's little need in one's life for a 6-inch-diameter, 200-foot dry hole in the ground, but it's there, it *was* expensive, and you shouldn't fill it up or collapse it. If it's cased and the well-drilling crew says the casing can be salvaged for the second hole, I'd probably go for it. If it can't be, leave it in. Just as wells abruptly dry up, it's conceivable that it could "come in" later; don't hold your breath, but it *has* happened.

Postdrill

After all of that negativity, it's nice to contemplate the higher probability that all will go as planned and you'll get your water. At some point the drilling will stop. Now what happens?

THE BLOW TEST

A final pumping will be initiated to determine the well's capacity—that is, the gpm it will deliver. The accuracy of that "blow" test is determined by the length of time allowed for the test. Most tests should be conducted for *at least* an hour to give even a close approximation of the well capacity. In the end, you must adjust the figures to give a more representative test result or conduct your own pump test; more on this in "Capacity," this chapter.

EQUIPMENT REMOVAL

After the tests, the crew will remove all of the equipment that's in the well—the bit and all of the extensions—and clean up. The well casing will not be flush with the ground; rather, it will be sticking up between 6 inches to 2 feet aboveground. Unless they miscalculate, they will usually leave enough of a protrusion for you to pour a concrete pad 4 to 6 inches thick and still have the casing sticking up.

The crew will not leave the well casing open; this only invites dirt, rocks, and other items to be dropped therein by fun-loving children. In fact, the plop made as these objects hit the water is so unusual that the barrage could go on for hours. To prevent the accumulation of this debris, and to keep out the living creatures that will crawl, fly, or stumble into the well, a cap is installed. There's nothing fancy about this—some sort of flat metal piece is often welded to the top of the casing. Normally, it's just spot-welded at a few points around the rim, not welded solid. When it comes time to install the equipment, this and the excess casing are torched off.

If the company that drills the well is *not* going to install the equipment, you may or may not want them to install the cap. The cap *is* a good idea and, in the highest likelihood, you will need to torch off excess casing to install the equipment anyway. But there's another reason to have the plate tacked in only one spot. That way you can pry up the cap far enough for . . .

FINDING THE WATER LEVEL IN THE WELL

Sometime after the well is drilled and the well-drilling rig is gone, you should determine the level of the water standing in the well. This serves several functions. First, you can compute the pumping head (the distance the water must be lifted—see "Water Extraction," Chapter 2). Second, you can compute the in-well storage (see "In-Well Storage," Chapter 2); later readings will help discover the drawdown. Third, it helps establish how far down the in-well equipment will be positioned, how much pipe will be needed, and so forth. And fourth—how about just satisfying plain old curiosity?

Taking the reading right after the well-drilling rig has left normally gives too high a reading. After all, they've been pumping water into the well, and some of that is bound to be still there. However, don't deprive yourself of satisfying your curiosity if the urge is overwhelming; I know it gives a poor reading, and I did it! But come back a few days later and try again to log a more accurate reading.

THE TEST

When you're ready to perform the level test, securely fasten (and I do mean *securely*) a small, heavy object (the "water sounder") to a roll of stout string or monofilament (fishing line). The sounder will keep the line taut and make the appropriate sound when it strikes the water. I used a ½-inch, galvanized-pipe plumbing elbow, which also confirms the depth by collecting a bit of water which, when pulled up the slightest amount, drips and makes an equally unique sound. Use your imagination for something that can do the same job.

I do recommend that you use something that will sink if the line should break. If it floats, it could get sucked into or block the inlet of the in-well pumping equipment if the water is drawn down to that depth. On the other hand, if it sinks it ends up on the bottom of the well, out of harm's way. By the way, the elbow I used had pipe

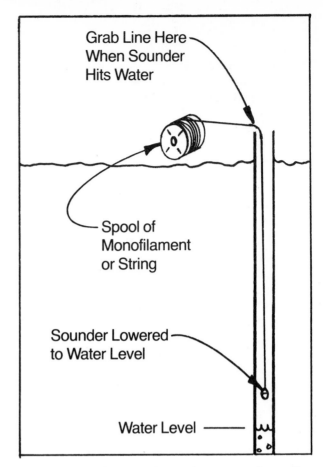

Fig. 5–5 Finding the level of water in the well is not a difficult process.

threads cut in it. The casing at the top of the well, too, has fairly sharp edges. Either can cut the string or monofilament, so be careful. Or use a chafing guard, okay?

Ready? Lower the sounder into the well, feeding it over the lip of the casing (see Fig. 5–5). Don't hold the spool directly over the well; you'd feel real silly losing both the sounder and the spool, too! Lower the sounder smoothly, letting out the line until you hear the plunk. Of course, the thing may rap against the side of the casing or the hard rock and make noise, but when it hits the water the sound is unique. This sound should be accompanied by a slackening in the tension of the string as the sounder momentarily floats, then sinks at a slow rate. Hold your thumb at the point on the string. Lift on the string just until you feel the tension increase sharply. At that point, or a few inches more, the sound of dripping water should be heard. Slide a thumb and finger down the line until they reach the lip of the casing and get a good hold on the string at that point. Now, get up and walk backward slowly. Slow down when you're certain the sounder is about to touch the end of the casing. Stop when it does, and mark the spot

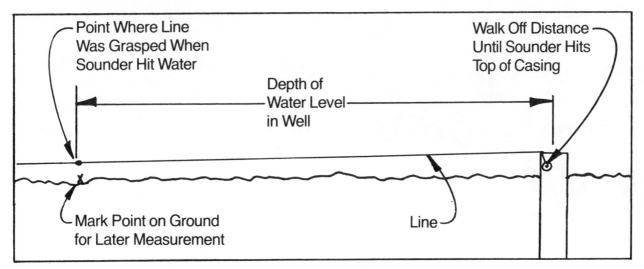

Fig. 5–6 Completing the water-level measurement.

where you're standing. Walk back to the well, lowering the line and allowing the sounder to slide back into it. When you're close to the well, wind the line onto the reel and ease the sounder over and out of the mouth of the casing. For a rough estimate, pace off the distance between the mark made on the ground and the well casing. Or use a tape measure if you want it to the nearest foot. Either way, this is the depth to the water standing in the well. Record it somewhere (along with the date) and *close up the casing*.

The Spring

A spring is developed when it is contained, cleared, and covered. Containment may be as simple as damming up the spring's outflow so that the only water that leaves the spring travels down your own channel or pipe to storage or use. Clearing the spring is a matter of ridding confined water of any immediate vegetation and aquatic life that would, after containment, likely end up in your drinking water; even when it doesn't, it can foul the water, particularly if anything dies and decays. Clearing and containment also include any attempt to increase the capacity of the spring, and that takes one or both of two forms: drilling or digging.

Drilling out a spring is not a complex procedure —often it's just horizontal drilling. But unless you have researched the matter thoroughly, get some professional help; you're just as likely to lose your spring altogether as to increase its capacity.

Digging, on the other hand, is almost always productive. At the very least, this increases the reservoir for the spring, but it often increases the capacity, too. Why? If the water comes from below

and you dig downward, it has less distance to go. Also, a little bit of clearing may decrease the number of obstacles that impede the spring water's flow. However, be careful; there is not much difference between drilling for more capacity and excessive digging. You can take the "bottom" out of the spring by inadvertently providing the water with another way to go.

Many old springs are "open." There's nothing inherently wrong with drinking water from a pool that's supporting other forms of life; if an occasional bug finds its way into your glass, that's okay since most are not bad-tasting and they *are* nutritious. However, this is no longer "the good old days," folks. With all of the airborne, landborne, and waterborne contaminants that abound nowadays (see "Susceptibility to Contamination," Chapter 1, and "Water Quality," Chapter 3), you're leaving your water supply wide open to a whole variety of pollutants at any time. Covering it is the least you can do. However, a loose-fitting cover is only handling a small percentage of the possible types of contamination; if you really want protection, you must seal the spring box.

Anyone who's ever poured a patio and seen a completed spring box may be tempted into developing his or her own spring. After all, what's so tough about a concrete box? You form up the sides, pour the concrete, remove the forms, and build a cover, right? Wrong!

A completed spring box looks simple (see Fig. 5–7), but if it's to be effective it must be built right. How do you do that? The best procedure is to follow a number of plans that exist for spring development (see "References"). Since the spring itself is often the "bottom" of the spring box, the

Fig. 5–7 A spring box supports fittings and protects against contamination.

sides must extend downward to fresh-cut earth (or rock) so that anything that wants to invade the finished box can't just go under it. The job is not difficult, but the fact that the available designs compensate for a whole range of factors—surface runoff, access, (for cleanout or inspection), overflow—will save you a lot of work in the long run.

The Pond or Stream

If a pond or stream is developed as the water source (note the comments on "Susceptibility to Contamination" and "Evaporation," Chapter 1) or as a means of water storage (limited by the same factors), one must consider how the water is to be extracted from the pond or stream. Several techniques apply (see "Water Extraction," Chapter 2).

A number of factors deserve comment. One, the screened inlet and pipe should be suspended in the water, or at least off the bottom. If you just drop it in, it will sink. How much water are you going to get if it buries itself in mud or moss? Two, one must consider the high-water mark; many an installation has been severely damaged by a flash flood or merely a normal, seasonally swollen water level. So provide for an overflow of dammed water (see Fig. 5–8) and some means of shutoff for the delivery pipe; a valve at the dam or one at the storage or usage site will do nicely. This setup also

Fig. 5–8 Pond or stream overflow must be diverted properly to avoid washing out the dam.

works for supplying water to a hydraulic ram (see Fig. 4–28). Neither requires the use of concrete—most dams are earthen—but the spillway (where the overflow exits the pond) should be fashioned from concrete or carefully placed rocks. Otherwise, the flow of water or the tail water will slice through and erode the dam's surface, costing you at least the stored water and perhaps the dam itself.

The Shallow Well

A shallow well may be dug by hand, drilled with a shallow well borer (see Fig. 1–5), or dug with a backhoe (see Fig. 5–9). Once water is hit, concrete rings are used to form the well wall or casing; the bottommost ring is perforated, and each ring is designed to "seat" on the one below it and, in turn, receive the one above it. After the rings are in, gravel is dumped around the outside of the hollow concrete cylinder (see Fig. 5–10), granting the water unencumbered access to the shell. The top 10 to 20 feet of the shallow well is then packed with earth, which is wetted and compacted to seal the well from surface or subsurface contamination.

A hatch may be added to the top of a shallow well; it may be formed of concrete, steel, or wood. Does it need to support a shallow well pump, or if an offset system is used (see "Offset Systems," Chapter 6), does it merely pass pipes? However it's done, the hatch must be seated high enough

aboveground (see Fig. 5–11) so that it will not be submerged or even washed over by runoff from rain. The access points must form a tight seal; a pretty wood hatch that will, in time, crack, warp, or shrink doesn't make it.

Fig. 5–10 Gravel is poured around the bottom of a shallow well to aid in water movement.

Fig. 5–11 A shallow well needs a tight-fitting cover.

Fig. 5–9 An inexpensive way to dig a shallow well is with a backhoe.

CAPACITY

Any water source has a capacity, irrespective of our knowing it. It may be too small to be considered significant, or so large as to defy our attempts to measure it by conventional standards. Nevertheless capacity exists, and it's useful to know what it is.

Time and again I've seen people go through the motions of meticulously measuring the capacity of their water source, and once a figure is obtained, not know what to do with the information. No doubt, such a person will have an answer for the standard question by friends—How much water did you get?—but that's about all. If it's high or what everybody else *says* is high, you proudly announce it. If it's not, you fume and sulk. But that's not what the information is really for.

Besides, measuring or calculating capacity and getting an answer that honestly represents water availability are not one and the same thing. If one takes into account *all* of the factors that affect capacity—use, evaporation, seasons, drought, increased population density on adjoining lands, etc. (see "Capacity Variance Factors," Chapter 1)—coupled with the discrepancies between measurements of capacity under varying conditions, this is still, at best, a guesstimate. Unfortunately, there *is* no precise formula into which one could plug all of the variables; the final "figure" then will be born more of intuition than the liquid-crystal figures of a calculator.

Does that bother you? If it does, think about it. Much larger stakes in money, effort, and time have been played out on much less "evidence." This can't be chalked up to luck, though; a careful assessment of what little is known usually beats the hasty decision. If you truly believe that it's unnecessary, don't even go through the motion of measuring capacity; if it's done haphazardly and results in a poor reading, think of all the worry it will cause you!

Capacity Units and Conversions

Capacity is expressed in terms of volume and time; for most household and farm needs, a unit of measure like gallons per minute (gpm) or gallons per hour (gph) is informative and handy. Other terms —such as time in seconds or days, and volume in pints, cubic feet, acre feet—are not as useful. Under certain circumstances, however, it may be necessary to use any one of them initially, converting, in the end, to a term that is easier for the mind to grasp (see Fig. 5–12). However, choosing the incorrect time frame will significantly reduce the accuracy of the measurement itself; a small flow measured for only a few seconds and converted upward to gpm or gph is subject to a higher degree of error than one measured for an hour and converted downward to one of these units.

Let's take an example. If we measure a flow of 1 gallon in 2.3 seconds, that converts to .435 gallons per second (1 gallon divided by 2.3 seconds). From there, we can convert to gallons per minute— 26 gpm (that's .435 multiplied by 60 seconds). Or we can convert to gallons per hour—1,565 gph (that's .435 multiplied by 60 seconds multiplied by 60 minutes, or 3,600 seconds).

Now, just suppose that our timing wasn't very hot and that the measurement was off $\frac{1}{10}$ of a second. Suppose it was really 2.4 seconds instead of 2.3 seconds. Does it matter? At one gallon per 2.4 seconds, that's .417 gallons per second and that converts to either 25 gpm or 1,500 gph. An error of $\frac{1}{10}$ of a second, then, corresponds to a 65-gallon difference in the yield in 1 hour!

On the other hand, if we measured this water capacity for one hour and got a 25-gallon reading in that time, we could convert this back to gallons per second and achieve a .417 figure. If we were a full minute over on the timing, then, our 25-gallon volume in 61 minutes would be equivalent to .410 gallons per second, which is a difference of only $\frac{7}{1000}$ of a gallon!

Choosing a long time frame is important, but measurements that take an hour are as ridiculous as readings taken in seconds are inaccurate; minute-long readings in the capture method, therefore, are good enough. Write down any figures that you do get—head math is good exercise, but it's easy to make a silly mistake. If the figure is staring at you from a sheet of paper, such an error is much less likely. Watch the computations, too; it's all too easy to go the wrong way, dividing when you should multiply.

Capacity Measurement Techniques

The technique used in capacity measurements is selected according to the specific water source to be tested. There are four basic ways to find capacity: volume, capture, pump, and data. One type of volume test is used on ponds and lakes, and an-

Figure 5-12
Measurement Conversion Tables

TO GET ➡ MULTIPLY ⬇	Gallons per Hour (GPH)	Gallons per Min. (GPM)	Cubic Feet per Min. (CFM)	Gallons per Second (GPS)	Cubic Feet per Second (CFS)
Gallons per Hour (GPH) by	1	0.017	0.0021	0.0003	0.00035
Gallons per Min. (GPM) by	60	1	0.135	0.017	0.00225
Cubic Feet per Min. (CFM) by	445	7.418	1	0.124	0.017
Gallons per Second (GPS) by	3,600	60	8.089	1	0.135
Cubic Feet per Second (CPS) by	26,700	445	60	7.418	1

other is applied for cisterns and reservoirs. Springs, streams, and rivers use the capture method, while a pump test is the best way to find the capacity of shallow and deep wells. Capacity for a rainfall system is "measured" from climatological data.

Ponds and Lakes

The capacity measurement of a lake or pond is usually complicated by its surface shape and varying depth. Nevertheless, a fairly accurate calculation can be made if two things are known: its approximate surface area and its greatest depth.

The surface area can be closely determined by simply marching off distances (on dry land, of course). If the lake is long and skinny, use the rectangular method (see Fig. 5–13); if these distances are converted to feet and the length and width are multiplied together, the product is the surface area. If the pond is more rounded, use the circular method (see Fig. 5–14); the approximated diameter in feet must then be halved (to get the radius) for use in the formula $A = \pi r^2$. Since π is

approximately 3.14, a pond 30 feet in diameter would have a surface area equal to 706 square feet (that's 3.14 times 15 times 15).

The greatest depth of the lake is needed for the next part of the calculation of capacity. If it's not known, borrow a raft, rowboat, or inner tube and, using a line and sinker, find the depth of the pond in a number of places out toward the center.

Next, multiply the measured depth by .4; this is an adjustment figure that supposedly represents the *average* depth of the pond. If the maximum depth has been established at 20 feet, the average depth would calculate to 8 feet (.4 multiplied by 20). The use of this factor assumes that the pond is uniformly contoured and that the maximum depth occurs at the center; adjust the depth reading for ponds with irregular bottom contour.

In the next stage of our computations, the surface area of the pond is multiplied by the average depth. Using the previous example—a pond with a 30-foot diameter—let's say we measure a 10-foot depth; this puts the average depth at 4 feet. Now we need only multiply the calculated 706 square feet of surface area by the calculated average

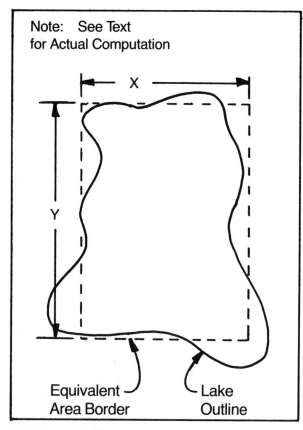

Fig. 5–13 Calculating lake or reservoir area by the rectangular method.

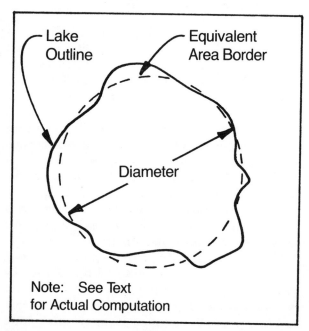

Fig. 5–14 Calculating lake or reservoir area by the circle method.

depth of 4 feet to compute 2,824 cubic feet of water in the pond.

There are 7.5 gallons in each cubic foot of water. Therefore the calculated capacity of the pond is 7.5 gallons multiplied by 2,824 cubic feet, or 21,180 gallons of water.

Measurements made when a pond is showing overflow will tend to reflect the largest capacity of the pond. Likewise, if the pond is at its lowest, this reflects its smallest capacity. However, if the level of water in the pond changes and you wish to find its current capacity, you must repeat the entire process; both the surface area and average depth will change.

Reservoirs and Cisterns

A different volume test is applied when measuring the capacity of cisterns and reservoirs. The surface area calculation will be the same, but the average depth calculation will probably be radically different. This is primarily due to the fact that artificially created reservoirs are much steeper-sided than a natural pond; consequently, the reservoirs tend to be deeper and the bottoms flatter. This is a design factor, and its object is to maximize pond volume while minimizing the surface area, and hence evaporation losses (see "Evaporation," Chapter 1). Cisterns, in particular, have flatter bottoms; a depth measurement then is both the maximum depth *and* the average depth.

If the reservoir or cistern has vertical sides, use conventional tables for length and width (or diameter) and depth to find the capacity (see Fig. 1–7). If the sides are uniformly angled to a flat bottom, the measured dimensions of length and width may be adjusted to compensate. If, for example, a pond has sides angled at 45 degrees and measures 24 feet long, 20 feet wide, and 10 feet deep, reducing both the length and width by 5 feet —24 feet to 19 feet and 20 feet to 15 feet—will supply a figure for the volume which is approximately equivalent to a tank with vertical sides of the same depth (see Fig. 5–15).

Rivers, Streams, and Springs

There are three ways to measure the capacity of a stream, river, or spring: capture, flow/section, and weir. Which one you use is determined by the approximate flow rate of the stream, how accurate you want the calculation to be, and how lazy you are. The capture method is best for water capacity

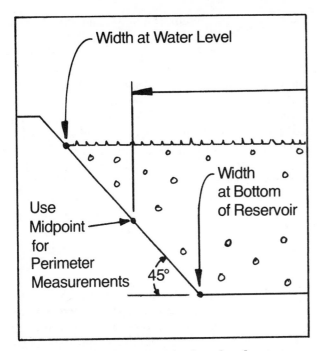

Fig. 5–15 Compensate for sloped sides in area and capacity calculations.

measurements; the flow/section and weir methods are routinely reserved for higher flow rates and waterpower calculations.

The capture method of finding capacity assumes that you are able to find a spot where the flow can be channeled into a container of known size, such as a 1-gallon jar or a 5-gallon bucket. If this is to be an accurate measurement, *all* of the flow must be captured. Timing the filling then gives us a rate that may be converted into gpm or gph. For example, if a 1-gallon bucket fills in 10 seconds, that's the same as 6 gpm or 360 gallons per hour. If the bucket fills in 5 seconds, you've got 12 gpm and 720 gph. If the 1-gallon bucket fills any faster than that, go to a 2- or 5-gallon bucket to increase the time frame for better accuracy. Repeat the tests until you get a series of identical and consecutive readings and write them down.

Shallow and Deep Wells

The toughest water capacity measurements involve wells, particularly deep ones. The problem is two-fold. First, the individual owner is not in possession of the right equipment for the testing; this is standardly left to the well driller. And since time *is* money, they don't get overly enthusiastic about

being accurate, or they don't use a large enough time frame to establish any kind of accuracy.

The second portion of the problem is the *kind* of test that is performed. Most well-drillers use a blow test to find well capacity; this is a notoriously inaccurate method. If it is used, whatever capacity figures are derived (you can discover them by looking at your copy of the well log or drilling report) should be divided by a factor of four. A 12-gpm well test by the blow method, then, is much more likely to be a 3-gpm well.

A more accurate measurement of well capacity is achieved from the pump test; well drillers equipped with this capability actually pump water from the well much in the same way a submersible (centrifugal) pump would. If the test is long enough, one can be assured that the water it is pumping is not merely water that filled the well prior to the pump test. In addition, this reveals the ability of the well to recover from a pump-down of the water from the rock, soil, clay, or whatever immediately adjoining the drilled hole.

The accuracy of the pump test is directly related to the length of time over which it is conducted; if it is tested for only five to ten minutes it is about as accurate as the blow test. A better time span is overnight pumping, but that's usually too much to expect without paying for it. Eight hours would be good, two hours okay, and one hour about the most you can expect.

DRAWDOWN

A very important part of both the blow test and the pump test is to determine drawdown—the "fall" in the level of standing water in the well during sustained pumping. At the very least, this information establishes the minimum depth that pumping equipment can be positioned in the well without the risk of having it suck air. Knowing the drawdown also helps to fix the maximum pumping head; this is always measured from the level of water in the well and *not* the depth of your own pumping equipment (see Fig. 2–28).

Unfortunately, it's impossible to measure drawdown during a blow test because of the presence of the drilling pipe and cutting bit in the well. Whether or not drawdown can be observed during a pump test by the well driller depends on the type of equipment used. Find this out; even if the well driller doesn't normally perform this measurement, *you* can if their equipment won't interfere.

CONDUCTING YOUR OWN WELL CAPACITY TESTS

There's nothing to prevent you from conducting a pump test of your own well's capacity. It's handy to know the well's capacity prior to installing a system since, in so many ways, knowing the capacity helps *select* the system. So, if you can, find (buy? rent? borrow?) a submersible pump, lower it into the well (don't forget the lengths of pipe and electrical wire you'll need), and pump away.

The primary requirement of this pump is that, for the depth from which you will be pumping (somewhere below the level of standing water in the well), it be able to pump water at the *maximum* rate you want. Remember, you can vary its pumping rate downward—a gate valve will regulate the flow—but nothing will vary it upward; too small a pump, then, only reveals the *minimum* capacity.

Since a high-capacity pump needs lots of electricity, it helps to have access to a utility line. However, if you live in the boonies you can rent a standby generator that can supply the needed power; don't forget to match the voltage as well as the wattage ratings.

Once the equipment—pump, power source, and pipe—is installed and you know that everything is functioning, establish the level of water in the well (see "Finding the Water Level in the Well," this chapter). Next, modify the sounder to include a fisherman's bobber so that you can detect the water level dropping in the well. Now, start the test. Since the whole idea is to find the sustainable rate of flow, let the pump go at full capacity. Time the flow into a container of known size, from 5 to 55 gallons, and convert the reading into a gpm figure. Watch the drawdown; if it drops rapidly and approaches the pump's position, you have a choice of lowering the pump farther in the well (keep it 10–20 feet off the bottom), stopping the test, or adjusting the pump's rate of flow until the drawdown slows or stops at a level above the pump's position.

Restricting the outflow of a submersible without some form of protection will hurt it. Therefore if the full flow rate of the pump is higher than the well's capacity—revealed by excessive drawdown—install an in-line pressure switch and pressure tank (see Fig. 4–3) and a valve on the outlet (near the bucket). By adjusting the valve, you can regulate the flow while the pressure switch and pressure tank protect the pump. The only alternative to this setup is to use a pump with lower capacity.

The pumping rate is affected by drawdown, since the pumping head is increasing, and by any adjustments to the valve; if either or both change and you want to know the new flow rate, you must measure again. When the pumping rate has been adjusted to where the drawdown stabilizes, just let it continue for as long as you're able or willing to stick around, or can afford the gasoline for the standby generator if you're using one, or can stand the noise and watching all that water run to waste. Write everything down; it's amazing how all the figures slip away afterward if you don't.

Rainfall

Capacity measurements may also be applied to rainfall, but the technique is wholly different from those used for volume, capture, or pump tests. Instantaneous readings of rainfall *are* possible; since rainfall is often channeled into a reservoir or cistern, the "capacity" of the last good rain could be determined by the volume method, noting the before and after water levels and making the necessary calculations.

A better measure of capacity in the design of rainfall collection systems is data from the closest climatological station; annual rainfall is commonly measured and recorded, and monthly as well as annual totals listed. Go back as many years as you can—you may find as much as fifty years' worth—to find the lowest annual yield, particularly in known drought years. This should give you some idea of the lowest capacity your own particular system will experience.

All of this data is given in inches of rainfall per year; that's not capacity. To find capacity, you must know two other pieces of information: the collection area and the water yield per square foot of the collection area.

The collection area is uniquely yours. If it's a rooftop, you must measure it. It can't be the precise area of roofing itself; a sharply angled roof will intercept much less water than one of equal area that's relatively flat. So the area is computed on the basis of its silhouette, as if the sun were shining directly overhead. Measure the horizontal distance from an outside wall to the edge of the roof (the overhang) and add this to the measurements of the building's foundation; multiplying the new length by the new width, you've got the collection area.

Water doesn't always fall perpendicularly; a good wind will slant it, and this can throw off your figure for collection area. Too, some water splashes off, and most systems "dump" the first bit of rainfall because it's washing off all the debris on the roof, which causes an approximate 25–30 percent reduction in the water yield (see Fig. 1–6). A rule of thumb for rainfall collection is a yield of $\frac{4}{10}$ of 1 gallon of water per square foot of collection area for each inch of rain that falls.

Rainfall changes with altitude; if your altitude differs enough from that of the climatological station, you might need to adjust the figures. The same goes for distance; the farther away the station, the less applicable its rainfall data are to your own place. Longtime residents may be of some help here; they can tell you in which direction the variance might be. Ask around, though; you'll find a large variance in the estimation of that variance! Incidentally, some folks practice meteorology as a hobby; if you are fortunate enough to have one of these people as a neighbor, any records from their own amateur weather station would be a real find.

Increasing Well Capacity

All too often a well will diminish in capacity over the years. When it reaches too low a value for even an efficient water system to handle, the owner faces a dilemma—drill a new well or attempt to increase the capacity of the troubled one?

A number of techniques exist whereby an old well can be "rejuvenated." None offers a guarantee of success, but if you have the time, a limited amount of money can yield an impressive result. Jetting and flushing, deepening, and dynamiting the well are three good possibilities.

Jetting and Flushing

Jetting is a technique using one of two means: air and water. If you use the air technique, there must be water in the well; if it's completely dry you must add water from another source. Then, with the well sealed by an airtight fitting, compressed air is let into the well; this forces the water back into the earth and rock immediately surrounding the drilled hole. Hopefully, the reverse flow of water will "back-flush" any matter that has clogged the fractures or porous soil in the first place. If water rushes back in, that's a good sign; at least you've regained the water that was in the well to begin

with. If you pump that out and more comes in, congratulations!

Jetting the well with high-pressure water also has a purging effect, water-blasting the surface area of the drilled hole and hopefully opening up the water cracks again. This also works wonders if the water normally enters via the bottom of the well; over the years, the pipe is easily plugged with the sediment that will naturally collect there. However, stirring it up won't help—you must rid the well of all that sediment; therefore a high-capacity pump is needed to pump the highly turbid water out of the well while everything's still in suspension. A normal submersible pump may be used, though it is a little rough on its innards to be handling such high-density water. However, that's a small sacrifice compared with the potential gain of a well that's productive once more.

Deepening

If a well has gone dry, its depth may be extended by a well-drilling rig that's repositioned over the hole. It's not always an easy task; the well site must be cleared of all interfering equipment such as the pump equipment, the well house, a tower and wind machine, and the rig must be precisely aligned to the present hole.

This is a good bet if you live in an area that exhibits a genuine water table which has merely dropped below the reach of your present well. In other areas, extending the well can be as risky as drilling a new one; considering the cost of the setup and the difficulty in removing existing equipment, it might be wiser to opt for the newly drilled well. Also, this may afford you the opportunity to site the new well in a better location than the old one. To help with the decision, enlist the help of a dowser (see "Dowsing," this chapter); a definite yes or no from this person will beat a flip of the coin any day.

Dynamiting

An old technique for increasing well capacity is to dynamite it. Sounds pretty violent, but a controlled blast can do wonders; between fragmenting the nearby earth or rock and severely jolting the surrounding area, there's a good possibility of increasing the water yield.

This won't help if the water table has dropped below the well's depth. And if you merely want to increase the well's capacity beyond a flow rate you only think is low, remember that you're gambling at high stakes; you may lose what you already have. The obvious threat in dynamiting is that the well will collapse; if it's dry anyway, that's no big loss. But if you're weighing the cost of jetting or extending the well against dynamiting, get some professional help. Dynamiting is a controlled art; just lighting a stick and dropping it down the hole is a waste of good dynamite and a well. If you don't believe me, you can ask one of my neighbors. When his well went dry many years back, he tried dynamiting it. That failed, but he got quite a show —the five or six lengths of 20-foot steel casing in the well (which he should have removed first) came rocketing up out of that hole like Minuteman missiles! Fortunately, none of them landed on anything important. Read and heed.

Living with Low Capacity

Once the measuring is done and the reading has been adjusted for all of those things that can influence capacity (see "Capacity Variance Factors," Chapter 1), you're left with an answer. Hopefully, it will be a good one and you can focus your attention elsewhere. However, it might *not* be a good one, and then you're left with some decisions.

A 10-gpm well is considered minimum for a demand system, and a 3½-gpm well is accepted as a minimum for a store system. For this reason, any water source producing less than a few gallons per minute is considered inadequate and is usually exempted from consideration for development and use. This is a ridiculous attitude. The only standard the water source *must* meet is the amount of water that's needed or used in any given 24-hour period. At present, for a small household with a small garden the average per capita water consumption is listed at 140 gallons per 24-hour period. Thus, an average family of four, using 560 gallons (4 times 140), will need a water source able to deliver 23.3 gph (560 gallons divided by 24 hours) or a piddling .38 gallons per minute (23.3 divided by 60 minutes).

Of course, this means that the water must be extracted from the source and transported to storage through the entire 24-hour period. Or, for fewer hours at a higher rate. That still totals to a lot of energy or an energy source that is very reliable.

This situation can be attacked from a number of angles. First, since the water source needs energy that is doled out in small amounts over a long period of time, use an energy source—wind, wood, methane—that does this. Second, decrease per capita usage. This is a three-pronged attack: One, employ conservation techniques. Two, use the water several times (see "Multiple Use of Water," Chapter 3); this maintains the same amount of water per application but reduces the overall intake. Third, consider the use of another water source, such as rainfall collection, that may be used in conjunction with the known low producer; two low-yield sources can add up to an inexpensive high-yield water system.

6

SPECIAL SYSTEMS

If you cornered a number of people who were involved, in one way or another, with an individual water system and experiencing some form of dilemma, the top three problems confronting them would probably be, one, developing a water system for a raw piece of land; two, converting an existing water system over to one that uses either alternative energy or alternate techniques of water processing; or, three, physically aligning the energy source with the water source.

For these hypothetical situations, I've provided appropriate solutions. Respectively, we have the Gold System, the Silver System, and several Offset Systems. As with *any* system, there's nothing sacrosanct about the details I supply; if the situation warrants it, by all means modify it.

To top off the chapter, I've added a section on building the Waterwatch, a simple, inexpensive, and reliable monitoring system for water levels; even if you possess neither the tools nor skills to do it yourself, you should have no difficulty in enlisting some local help to whip up this very useful circuit.

THE GOLD SYSTEM

The basic component of the store type of water system is the piston pump. In practice, it will pump water from many sources—ponds, springs, shallow and deep wells—but the most demanding situation is the deep well. Therefore, we will address that application directly; for other sources, simply subtract those factors that obviously apply only to the deep-well installation.

The Gold System (my own term) is built around the deep-well piston pump. Primary considerations in this setup are minimal use of energy, the application of low-yield energy sources, the variety of energy sources that may be applied, and accessibility to the pumping equipment for maintenance and repair. And, though only one energy source may be applied initially, this system boasts the ultimate in "add-on" capability—money permitting, other energy sources may be applied as the need arises to match increasing water usage or a changing energy picture.

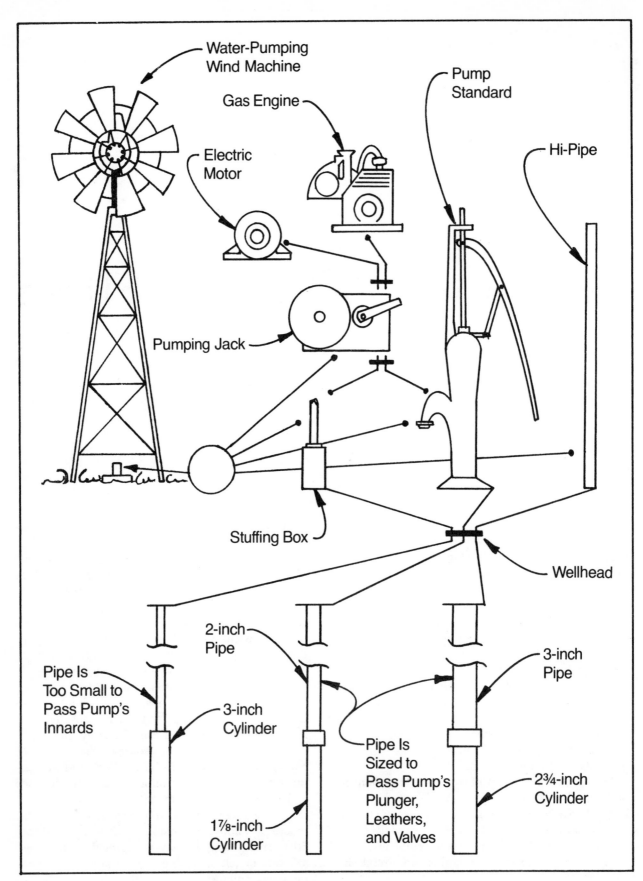

Fig. 6–1   Component options in the Gold System.

The Gold System is not of my own design; indeed, an illustration of it might be found in a manufacturer's manual showing the full breadth of options available for a water system based on wind power. In that context, however, the impression given is that the wind power aspect is the essential ingredient in the system and that everything else is merely an option. This is not true; if the wind isn't accessible, the system is still sound, easily able to utilize a number of other, equally good energy sources. The Gold System is not some newfangled idea based on this author's fantasy. Instead, it's an arrangement that has withstood the test of time and tough situations.

The Gold System is composed of a piston pump, the delivery pipe, the sucker rod, a stuffing box, pump standard or hi-pipe, a pumping jack, a motor or engine, and a wind plant in various combinations (see Fig. 6–1).

Deep-Well Piston Pump

The deep-well piston pump is composed of a plunger (the moving part—see Fig. 6–2) and a stationary cylinder; its operation has already been described (see "Piston Pump," Chapter 4). In the

Gold System, however, we must size it to the energy source that powers it, the desired gpm, and the pumping head. Through careful selection, we can vary the cylinder diameter, stroke (length of pumping motion), and number of strokes per minute (usually not to exceed an upper limit of 40) to fulfill the pumping needs (see Fig. 4–22).

Cylinders vary in size, ranging from 1¼ inch to 3½ inches inside diameter, and are made from iron, plastic, or brass. The all-brass cylinder and plunger assembly with the ball type of check valves offers the longest life, particularly in pumping highly turbid water. These cylinders come in different lengths to accommodate wind machines or pumping jacks, which can offer a longer stroke.

Delivery Pipe

A pipe is needed to position and support the piston pump in the well, house the sucker rod (which connects the drive mechanism to the piston pump itself), and transport the water to the surface. Since it must withstand water pressure, absorb the push-pull forces of the sucker rod, and guide the sucker rod with minimal resistance losses, the pipe should be rigid and strong. Two-inch (I.D.) galvanized steel pipe is the standard.

There's a unique feature in the 1⅞-inch cylinder and 2-inch delivery pipe combination: the pump innards, including the two check valves, the leathers, and the plunger assembly (the only portions of the pump that are subject to wear) may be removed up *through* the pipe for servicing and repair as required. However, if a larger size of cylinder (producing a higher pumping rate) is desired, without a corresponding increase in the size of the delivery pipe this feature is lost; when it comes time to service the piston pump, the *entire* assembly—cylinder, delivery pipe, sucker rod, and plunger—must be removed.

Faced with the higher cost of the larger pipe, it's easy for an owner to forgo this feature and size the cylinder so that the assembly cannot be removed up through the delivery pipe. A few years later, most regret this decision; a servicing job that normally requires only a few hours of work turns into a one to two-day nightmare of equipment and laborious effort in hauling out the delivery pipe, cylinder, sucker rod, and plunger assembly. And the same scene must be repeated every two to five years, too!

Fig. 6–2 The plunger supports the "leathers" and one of the two check valves in the deep-well piston pump.

The situation is not always unavoidable. The cumulative weight of pipe becomes a problem for wells over 200 feet in depth, and a delivery pipe *smaller* than 2 inches may be needed for wells double this depth. For wells up to 200 feet, the owner should seriously consider longer strokes and longer cylinders to increase pumping rates, rather than hasty increases in cylinder size.

Stuffing Box versus Pump Standard

At the top of the well, one of two pieces of hardware will be needed: the stuffing box (see Fig. 6–3) or the pump standard (see Fig. 6–4). They have similar functions, but the main difference between the two is that the pump standard has a lever attached for using muscle power to pump water from the well. This assumes that you have both the muscle and the inclination; however, for the added fifty dollars or so in price, it's not a bad deal. Besides, even if it's unlikely that it'll ever be used, the pump standard is an aesthetically pleasing piece of equipment.

Both the stuffing box and the pump standard perform several important functions. First, they hold the in-well equipment—delivery pipe and piston pump—in position and support their combined weight. Second, they have a watertight fitting through which the sucker rod passes and is able to move back and forth; this permits power transfer to the piston pump without spilling the pumped water. Third, the stuffing box and pump standard contain a number of fittings for attachment to the rest of the water system. And fourth, equipped with the correct type of gasket, both units provide a watertight seal over the well casing to prevent contamination by dirt, insects, and small animals.

Since the primary function of either the stuffing box or pump standard is to effect a watertight seal at the point where the sucker rod emerges from the delivery pipe, an alternative to using this hardware is the hi-pipe (my term). In essence, the hi-pipe is a delivery pipe that has been extended upward to some point *above* the level where the water is pumped (see Fig. 6–5); a T-fitting anywhere between the wellhead and that point allows the water to flow out of the delivery pipe and, a few feet higher, the sucker rod emerges. Where the sucker rod is used, however, no watertight fitting is required.

The hi-pipe technique is used extensively in systems using only a water-pumping wind machine;

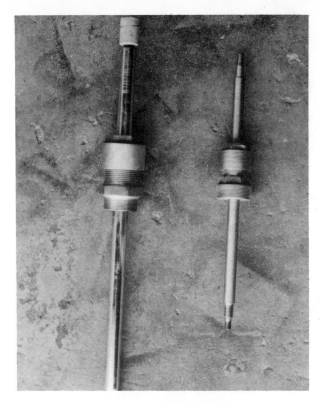

Fig. 6–3 Stuffing boxes.

Fig. 6–4 The pump standard.

Fig. 6–5 This water-pumping setup uses the hi-pipe.

the height of the tower permits an easy extension of the delivery pipe to some level above that to which the water is being pumped. The tank need not be directly alongside the tower; just as long as water storage is situated below the level of the wind machine itself, this technique can be used. However, if the delivery pipe does not extend all the way up the tower, it should be fitted with some type of cover; a watertight seal may not be required, but we'd still want to keep debris out of the well.

Sucker Rod

The piston pump in the well is linked with the stuffing box or pump standard at the wellhead via the sucker rod, or pump rod; moving up and down inside the delivery pipe, this transfers power from the energy source to the pump mechanism. The sucker rod is made up of sections of either wood or galvanized steel rod fitted with threaded ends so

that the required number of lengths may be screwed together.

Wood is the preferred sucker rod material for three reasons. First, it's bulkier, and so a closer fit to the inside diameter of the delivery pipe; this helps to guide the rod and, on the downward stroke, keep the rod from bending or flexing over long lengths. Second, since the power stroke occurs on the upward swing of the rod, the wood's buoyancy assists this motion; whereas, with the metal rod, the power source must overcome the accumulated weight of the rod too. And, third, wood rubbing against the steel delivery pipe is silent; with metal sucker rod, everyone gets to hear the repeated "clang" as the rod strikes the pipe wall during pumping operations.

The sucker rod ends just below the watertight fitting in the pump standard or stuffing box. There it is secured to the smooth rod that actually moves up and down through the seal. If a water-pumping wind machine is used in the system, sucker rod is also used to transfer its power to the pump standard or stuffing box, above the seal.

Pump rod and sucker rod are used interchangeably to describe the same thing. However, a rod that works between the wind machine and the pump standard will not necessarily work in the constant wet to which a rod connecting the pump standard and piston pump will be exposed. So, irrespective of the terminology, be certain that you and a supplier are talking about the same thing.

Pumping Jack

The pumping jack is a device that converts the rotary motion of a number of energy devices such as electric motors and gasoline engines into the reciprocating (up and down) motion needed to power the piston pump. Typically, the pumping jack is bolted to the stuffing box, the pump standard (see Fig. 6–6), or the concrete pad surrounding the wellhead (see Fig. 6–7). With long lever arms, it's designed for quick connection to, or release from, the sucker rod protruding from the stuffing box or pump standard. In the wind energy-based system, then, the pumping jack is connected during low- and no-wind conditions for water pumping as needed. In the Gold System, particularly if no wind system is feasible, the pumping jack may be the primary means of operating the piston pump.

The pumping jack is only a sophisticated conversion device; it is not an energy source. For this

Fig. 6–6 This pumping jack bolts to the pump standard.

Fig. 6–7 Some pumping jacks bolt to the concrete pad.

reason, a motor or engine must be attached. This is usually no problem; a bolt plate that will accommodate either a small engine (see Fig. 6–8) or an electric motor (see Fig. 6–9) is part of the assembly.

The pumping jack is designed to rotate in a specific direction—clockwise or counterclockwise—and the motor or engine you select may or may not turn in the same direction. If it does, fine. If it doesn't, there's a definite problem. With an electric motor the direction of rotation may be reversible; a local motor shop can do this in a few minutes. With a gas engine, forget it; they're not reversible. Of course, either a motor or engine could be mounted separately from the pumping jack, but it's a hassle to align the pulleys, maintain belt tension, and keep the respective assemblies from loosening up in operation. So—get a pumping jack that rotates in the same direction as your motor or engine or be prepared to buy a new one to match the pumping jack's rotation.

Better pumping jacks have their gears running in oil; this should provide quiet and trouble-free operation for a lifetime. Check your pumping jack frequently, replacing lost oil and occasionally draining the old and filling up with new. At a quart every few years, this won't dent anyone's pocketbook.

Electric Motor versus Gas Engine

Either an electric motor or a gas engine may be bolted to the pumping jack for water-pumping operation. Gas engines are considerably noisier, and they use expensive gasoline; if there's a choice, the electric motor is the preferred power source. However, this assumes that you have electricity, either utility-supplied or generated on-site; if you don't, the gas engine is the only alternative. Don't rule out the possibility of using both. If the pumping jack is normally powered by utility-supplied electricity, it's nice to have a small gas engine as backup during a blackout or other emergency.

Manufacturers' specifications clearly designate electric-motor horsepower for given conditions—the pumping head, pumping rates, cylinder size, etc. However, observe caution when using a gas engine with a pumping jack; without using an intermediate jackshaft, the smallest pulley that may be attached to the engine will overspeed the pumping jack (which operates at a maximum 40 strokes per minute) at optimum engine speeds. But at reduced

Fig. 6–8 Where there's no electricity, a gas engine will power the pumping jack.

Fig. 6–9 A pumping jack powered by an electric motor.

speeds, the available engine HP is a mere fraction of the engine's rating; it can be as low as $\frac{1}{10}$ the value! Hence, where a $\frac{1}{3}$ HP electric motor is specified, a 3–5 HP gasoline engine will be needed to deliver the same performance.

Water-Pumping Wind Machine

The deep-well piston pump is ideally suited for use with a wind machine of the type produced by the Aeromotor, Dempster, or Baker companies. Since these aeroturbines are designed for operation at low wind speed, there are few places where they cannot be used. The least that can be said about the aeroturbines themselves is that they have evolved over a long period of time (seventy-five to a hundred years) and that the present models are time-tested. For example, the last major design change in the Aeromotor wind machine was in 1933! Finding parts for either the new or older wind machines, however, is not a problem—a definite advantage over the change-the-model-each-year syndrome that affects other commercial equipment. This is good to know when buying a new wind machine and a lifesaver when restoring a used wind machine (if, in fact, any restoration is required).

New or used, the major expense in wind-pumped water systems is split between the wind machine itself and the tower; which one represents the higher cost depends largely on the circumstances. Unfortunately, the best spot for digging a well is rarely the best wind site. If this is the case, the tower must extend the wind machine high enough above surrounding obstacles such as trees and houses to reach undisturbed wind (see Fig. 6–10). This is not only an initial problem; since there's a tendency to site the well and wind machine near a house and also to plant shade trees in the same location, the problem may arise in later years. Many an old farmstead may be found today with the wind machine nestled deep in the trees which have, over the years, grown above it.

There are a number of remedies if the well site (old or new) is not the best wind site. The first is to use an offset system, siting the wind machine in the best wind spot and transferring its power to the well site (see "Offset Systems," this chapter). Another is to lop off the top of the tallest tree in the vicinity of the well and situate the wind machine atop it. This alternate "tower" technique is often used for electricity-generating wind ma-

Fig. 6-10 The tower must elevate the wind machine above the tallest trees.

which the blades come nearly alongside the tail, effectively shutting it down. A manually operated lever at the base of the tower effects the same result, side-facing the aeroturbine's blades to the wind and, in some machines, engaging a brake mechanism for positive stoppage. This is engaged for routine maintenance, when the storage tank is full and whenever extreme winds are forecast.

If wind energy is accessible, there are a number of ways to proceed. The first is simply to buy new equipment, letting the supplier size the wind machine and tower and having him install them. This is pretty painless and, not surprisingly, expensive. An alternative is to buy the equipment and install it yourself; this is particularly applicable if you're in the boonies and there's little chance that the supplier can get his baby crane in there. Don't let the size of the job intimidate you; learn everything you can on the subject (see "References") and get the necessary help or equipment.

A third alternative is to search for a used water-pumping wind machine and tower, buy them, transport them to your site, effect the necessary repairs or overhaul, and install them. In the years to come, the supply of used wind machines will diminish; already the cost of energy has forced many people to return to these reliable machines, and good "deals" on used ones are disappearing fast. Nevertheless, it's worth checking; in areas where they're abundant, these water pumpers can still be had for a fraction of the price of brand-new equipment.

If one has more time than money, there's always the option of building your own tower and wind machine. I don't recommend it for the wind machine; there are plenty of good designs around, but there's still too large a gap between reliability and experimentation. The tower is another matter; any competent carpenter should be able to put together a strong tower made of wood which, in materials, costs one third to one fourth the price of a tower of equal sturdiness and height made of steel. There's the brute-strength technique (see Fig. 6-11) and, for those of us who like a little grace in woodworking, one that uses the intrinsic strength of a gently curving arc (see Fig. 6-12).

In most instances, the tower is raised, concreted in place, and the wind plant lifted piece by piece to the top for assembly. An alternative technique is to form up the foundations first (see Fig. 6-13), pour the footings (see Fig. 6-14), attach two of the tower's legs to pivots, and raise the tower with the main body of the wind machine already se-

chines; while I know of none sporting a water-pumping wind machine, I can foresee no real difficulty in applying it. Both require branch clearing for some distance below the wind machine (to ease the play of wind on these surfaces), guying of the tree (to keep it from swaying), and allowing for expansion in the guyed wires (for tree growth). The water-pumping wind machine will, of course, require a pivot arm and weight device (see "Offset Systems," this chapter) for power transfer down the side of the tree, another at the base of the tree, and one more at the wellhead.

A water-pumping wind machine must have an automatic overspeed control for high wind speeds; a common one is called side facing (see Fig. 1-13). If the center of the aeroturbine shaft is offset from the machine's pivot point, the air pressure over the surface of rotating blades turns the assembly out of the wind and alongside the tail. The unit continues to operate, however, until some higher preset wind speed has been reached, after

Fig. 6–11   A sturdy wood tower will beat the cost of steel towers.

Fig. 6–12   This low-cost, 50-foot wood tower uses curved legs for increased strength.

cured; (see Fig. 6–15); the blade assembly may be affixed afterward (see Fig. 6–16). Those less inclined to putter about the top of the tower will tend toward attaching the completely assembled wind machine to the tower *prior* to raising; however, this is a dangerous policy. The tower and the gearbox of the water-pumping wind machine are stout components; by comparison, the blades are not. Therefore, if the tower is dropped a short distance, the experience is only embarrassing if the blades are not affixed; if they are, it's usually also very expensive.

Incidentally, don't deprive yourself of the experience of climbing a tower. Time and again I've encountered staunch resistance to doing this from people who think they simply can't. That may be true, but if you don't try it, you'll never know. People who do climb towers are not crazy—a little adventurous, maybe, but they know that safety is important. There are old tower climbers and there are bold tower climbers but there are no old, bold tower climbers!

Tactics

Any situation that meets the requirements of a store type of water system (see Chapter 2, "Water Processing") will find the Gold System a cost-effective and efficient setup, particularly when used with a low-yield energy source. Again, this type of system is still a viable alternative even if alternative sources of energy are not available in sufficient amounts; an electric motor powered from utility-supplied electricity driving a deep-well piston pump through a pumping-jack pump standard boasts a higher cost-benefit ratio than a submersible pump pumping into the same storage. Furthermore, if energy use, hardware, well capacity, system versatility, and usage are evaluated honestly, the two systems are even cost competitive; in this respect, only personal preferences will sway the decision one way or the other.

The hardware found in the two types of system, demand and store, is radically different (see "Accessories," Chapter 4). Therefore if an owner wishes to reap the benefits of a store system but a demand system is already installed, the changeover is both radical and expensive. A better alternative, then, is to use either the piggyback arrangement (see "The Piggyback System," Chapter 4) or tandem setup (see "The Silver System," this chapter).

If no equipment is installed in the well, one need

Fig. 6–13   Footings for the tower legs are formed and readied for the concrete.

Fig. 6–14   A free-standing tower is only as strong as its footings, so make a good pour.

Fig. 6–15 The tower and wind machine may be raised together.

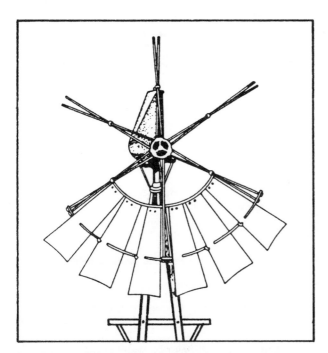

Fig. 6–16 The vanes (blades) of a water-pumping wind machine are attached after the raising.

only invest in the equipment basic to the Gold System. Cylinder size should be carefully selected; each size has a very definite upper limit of pumping capacity for a given pumping head. Pipe size is selected to retain or relinquish the ability of the in-well equipment's removal for ease of servicing. The pump standard wins out over the stuffing box if either the hand-operated feature is desired or if a pumping jack installation is planned; most types of pumping jack bolt neatly to a pump standard, but few bolt up to a stuffing box. If wind energy is available, the tower is sized to clear surrounding obstacles and the wind machine is sized to pumping rates, well depth, and local wind conditions (see Fig. 6–17); the lower the average wind speeds, the larger the wind machine. If electricity is available, the electric motor is used; if not, a gas engine will work the pumping jack.

Installation Notes

Complete instruction manuals are available from the manufacturers of water-pumping wind machines on the installation of tower, wind machine, and other hardware in the store type of water system; duplication here would be needless repetition of otherwise informative and detailed instruction. However, there's always *something* that doesn't get said that can save you work, time, or grief. Here are a few things that I wish I'd known beforehand:

1. Galvanized pipe comes in 21-foot sections; for a 2-inch diameter this is both heavy and, as you'll discover during an installation, awkward to insert into the well. No problem—take it down, get it cut in half, have them cut new threads, buy the additional couplers, and bring home the now 10½-foot-long pieces.

If you're like most folks, you'll proceed with the installation. However, when they cut the threads they use thread-cutting oil, and some of it stays inside the pipe. If you install them as is, you're going to taste that oil in your water for the next *six months*. In submersible pump installations, they dump some bleach into the well and pump it out to take care of such things. That's not a recommended procedure for piston pump installations; it'd take a *lot* of pumping to get rid of all that foul-tasting water even if you had the energy source to do it.

There is a solution (no pun intended). Make up a bleach, or ammonia-and-water solution, and pour it into each section of pipe *before* you install it in

Figure 6-17
Selecting the Water-Pumping Wind Machine

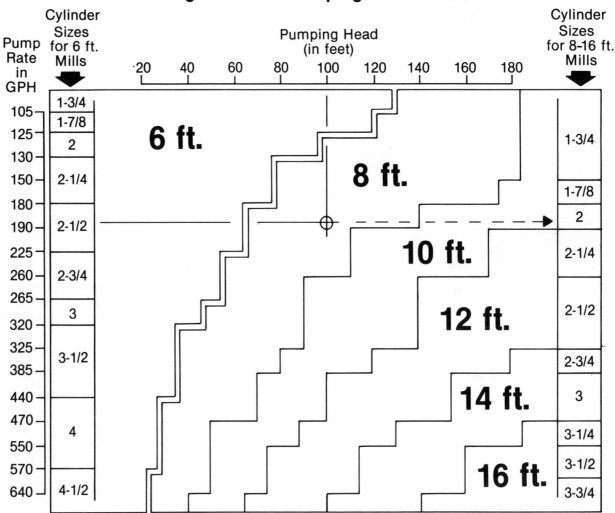

HOW TO USE THIS CHART — An Example
Assume:
  a) family of 4 consumes a total of 560 gallons of water per day (see Fig. 3-8).
  b) wind blows 3 hours per day.
  c) the pumping head is 100 feet (see Fig. 2-28).

Conclusions:
  a) the wind machine must pump water at the rate of 187 gallons per hour (divide 560 gallons needed per day by 3 hours of wind per day).
  b) note the intersection point on chart of pumping head and pumping rate.
  c) note that the wind machine size (blade diameter) is 8 feet.
  d) note that the cylinder size is 2 inches. (For 6-foot wind machines, read to the LEFT, under column marked "6-foot Mill"; for wind machines 8-16 feet in diameter, read to the RIGHT, under column marked "8-16 ft.Mills.")

CAUTION: This chart is presented here to give you some idea of the capabilities of a water-pumping wind machine and to show you how to use this type of chart (they can be confusing!). Obtain a current chart from the manufacturer for the specific wind machine you intend to use for the precise selection of the wind machine and cylinder size that best fit your own situation.

the well. If you're working alone, you'll need two 2-inch pipe caps (plugs) to contain it while you teeter-totter the pipe back and forth, sloshing the solution around. Do it to music to keep from getting bored; a good two or three minutes of this will be needed to remove most of the offensive substance. If you have help, you can forgo the pipe caps; with one of you at each end, a widespread palm will seal the pipe. Don't get chintzy; for every fifteen seconds of slosh, you cut back a month of icky taste.

2. Sequencing is important; if you plan to install a pumping jack for either an engine or an electric-motor backup system, install this part of the system first. Why? Two reasons. One, you'll want reliable water delivery. The mere presence of these options in the system (even if the primary source is wind) suggests that there will be times when you will need that backup; even a good wind area will experience occasional doldrums. The second reason is that most people who are ready to install some of the well equipment are still wallowing in the wake of paying for the well itself. If your money is limited, a tower, wind machine, and storage tank are pretty major expenses to tackle right away. A better idea is to install the pumping jack first. If electricity (utility, wind-electric, or standby generator) is available, an electric motor is used; if electricity isn't available, a gas engine may be installed. Both get you going right now. And even if you have no storage, you get water when you want and can turn it off when you don't.

The next item to add (as money becomes available) is the storage tank; this will save you from having to turn on the pump every time you want water. Additionally, it will allow you to use water at higher rates than that at which water is pumped directly from the well.

Eventually, if you plan a wind-pumping setup, the tower is purchased or made, installed, and the wind machine added.

There's an alarming tendency to reverse this process; it's understandable but, alas, rather stupid. Even if the money is available, you can't make effective use of wind-pumped water without storage. And there's no point in having storage if there's no water to put in it. Then, too, it may take weeks to correctly install a tower, wind machine, and storage tank and only a few hours to complete a pumping jack installation. So—get the water first, provide storage next, and then add an alternative means of pumping it.

3. I wholeheartedly recommend some kind of monitoring technique for the Gold System; without it, it's a constant battle to balance wind-pumped water against water uses and a lot of scurrying around to turn this or that on and off, or check the water level in storage. Even at that, you'll forget, and you find out the nasty way—when the faucet gives you a long sigh instead of fresh cold water— that something didn't get done. This gets old very fast, and in some circumstances can be dangerous (fire?), damaging (a thirsty garden?), or damned inconvenient (all sudsy in the middle of a shower?). The Waterwatch (see "The Waterwatch," this chapter) is one of the best monitoring devices I've seen, and its low cost puts it well within the reach of any system's budget. There are alternatives (see "Monitoring Storage," Chapter 2). Whatever the circumstance, choose one; it will spare you endless grief.

THE SILVER SYSTEM

Some friends of mine bought a place with a standard demand-type water system (see Fig. 4–31) using a submersible (centrifugal) pump, pressure tank, pressure switch, and other controls characteristic of this setup already installed.

After operating it for a number of years, the owners realized the availability of wind energy at their site and its potential as an alternative energy source for water pumping. Their present system was ill prepared to handle fire fighting (see "Fire Fighting," Chapter 2) and to operate during blackouts (see "Blackouts," Chapter 2); this coupled with increased water usage due to a newly installed garden and orchard, and the frustrated owners were ready to consider alternatives.

An extensive retrofit was designed—a water-pumping wind machine and tower, a piston pump, plumbing to handle two service pressures, etc. However, the owners were unwilling to commit themselves to a system with so many variables; for this reason, they decided instead to install the Silver System (my term) in discrete phases, evaluating the performance of each phase before proceeding with the next one.

Phase One

Using wind energy necessitated a storage tank; but while the property did elevate sufficiently to pro-

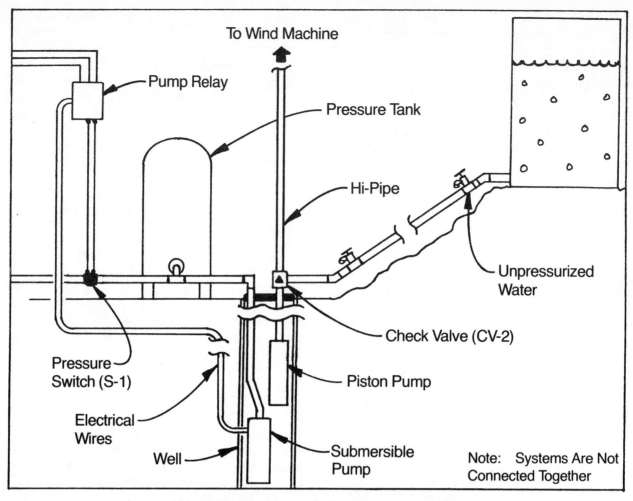

To Wind Machine

Pump Relay

Pressure Tank

Hi-Pipe

Unpressurized Water

Check Valve (CV-2)

Pressure Switch (S-1)

Piston Pump

Electrical Wires

Well

Submersible Pump

Note: Systems Are Not Connected Together

Fig. 6–18 Phase one of the Silver System illustrates two independent water systems sharing the same source.

vide gravity flow from a storage tank sited at the highest point, gravity pressurization was not possible. However, this was not considered a major handicap since all of the gardens and orchards were downhill from the ideal site for the tank.

A 2,000-gallon storage tank was purchased and sited. A 20-foot wood tower was built on top of the stone pump house and a water-pumping wind machine was purchased and set atop it. A deep-well piston pump was inserted into the well in addition to the existing submersible pump. However, instead of a piggyback system (see Fig. 4–29), a side-by-side mounting of the two pumps was chosen. In truth, the two pumps *cannot* sit side-by-side in a 6-inch-diameter well—there isn't sufficient clearance—so the piston pump was positioned slightly *above* the submersible pump. A chafing guard was attached to protect the submersible's 1-inch plastic delivery pipe; since this pump "twists" on start-up (due to motor torque), if the

pipe is in contact with the piston pump's cylinder, a hole might eventually be worn through the pipe.

A new wellhead was fashioned to accommodate the unorthodox side-by-side arrangement of these two pumping systems. An overflow pipe was added to handle the well's tendency to become artesian during a few months of the year; the overflow was routed to a nearby garden. A new anti-contamination seal was made to accommodate the 2-inch galvanized pipe for the piston pump and the 1-inch plastic pipe and electrical wires for the submersible pump. The hand-operated feature of the pump standard was waived for the convenience of the hi-pipe (see Fig. 6–5)—the tank was higher than the wellhead but lower than the level of the wind machine—and the necessary length of pump rod and pipe was routed up through the ceiling of the pump house to the wind machine perched overhead. A check valve (CV-2) was added to prevent flow back through the piston pump once the leathers

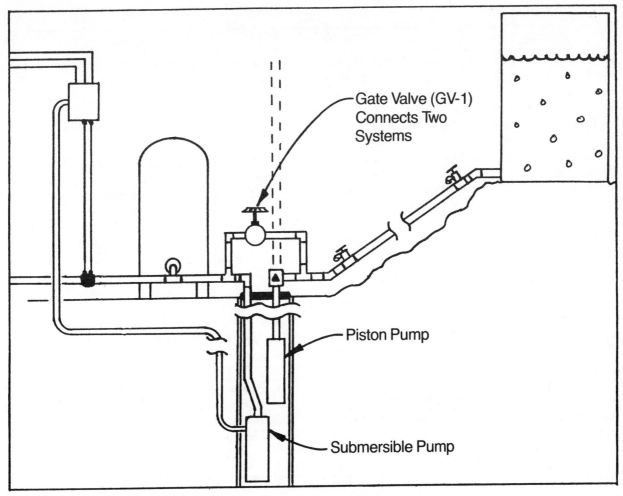

Fig. 6–19 Phase two of the Silver System connects the two services in a simple way.

became worn. Pipe was laid to the storage tank 150 feet away, and both the inlet and outlet of the tank were merged at the tank's bottom (see Fig. 2–17); spigots were added along the dual-purpose pipe for simple gravity flow of water through branches to the orchard 200 feet away. An overflow pipe was added to the tank and a hose added to route spilled water to a nearby garden.

The two water systems were, at this stage, wholly separate. Any water that was pumped from the wind machine to the tank was used at low pressure in the gardens and orchards; all household water was supplied by the utility-powered submersible pump. Backup hoses from the submersible pump system were routed to the gardens and orchards to take care of any watering needs beyond the capability of the wind-pumped water system. They were never used; once the system was in and operating, it was quickly evident that the wind pump was able to handle *all* of the out-

door watering needs. Indeed, the system exceeded the nearby garden's water requirements, and the owners had to shut down the wind machine manually (via the handcrank in the wellhouse) again and again. Any uncertainty or disbelief on the part of the owners that the added system would handle garden and orchard and, perhaps, some of the household watering needs too, evaporated; they were ready for phase two.

Phase Two

Phase two of the Silver System was the first tie-in of the two systems; a gate valve (GV-1) was added between the pipes for each system (see Fig. 6–19). This serves two functions. First, when utility power is off and the submersible can't work, if there's water in the tank and there's a need for water in the household, by opening gate valve

GV-1, water will flow from the tank directly into the house. It's true that it will be at very low pressure; however, when you need it, water at *any* pressure is hardly "inconvenient."

A secondary function of gate valve GV-1 is a quick and easy way to fill the water tank to any desired level using the submersible pump. This is particularly handy if a forest fire or tornado is coming your way and you've gotten a little advance notice. For this to work, the utility power must be on; if it is, simply opening GV-1 will have the same effect as opening any water faucet, causing water to flow into the tank until the gate valve has been closed.

For a mere twenty dollars in parts—a gate valve, pipe, a union, and a few pipe tees—adding GV-1 does an awful lot! However, it depends on *you* to operate it correctly, so here are a few pointers. If the utility power is off and you want to route low-pressure tank water to the household, turn off the submersible pump motor switch before you open the gate valve. Whether you do or don't do this will not affect water flow, but what's going to happen if utility power comes back on and gate valve GV-1 is still open? The pump will come on, water will flow into the tank, the tank will fill and overflow, and either the pump will eventually burn up (if it pumps the well dry) or your neighbor will complain that his mobile home is floating away! Automatic controls or monitoring equipment can detect this condition and warn you or automatically shut down the pump, but that unnecessarily complicates the installation. On the other hand, if you elect simply to turn off the pump switch, don't forget to turn it back on later when utility power has been restored.

If utility power is on and you open gate valve GV-1 to fill the tank, also observe some basic precautions; if you go off and forget about it, the same thing is going to happen—the tank will fill, overflow, and cause a flood, wasting a lot of electricity and water and maybe even burning up a pump. How fast the submersible pump can fill your tank is, of course, variable; what's its pumping rate in your system? At a 20-gpm rate, for instance, opening GV-1 will put 1,200 gallons of water into a tank in one hour, double that in two, triple that in three. So divide the tank's capacity by the pumping rate to find the amount of time it will take to fill an empty tank; if the tank's not empty, compute the gallonage it will need to reach full. Of course, knowing this doesn't help much if you simply forget. So, set an alarm clock, monitor storage, or install a level sensor in the tank.

Phase Three

Obviously a water system that was sometimes pressurized (on the submersible system) and sometimes nonpressurized (submersible pump off and GV-1 open) was inconvenient. To match the two systems, then, a pressurizing pump (PP-1) was added (see Fig. 6–20); the intention here was to pressurize tank water (when it was available) for household use.

However, the owners did not want to scramble around figuring when tank water was or was not available for household uses; they wanted an automatic system. This created a bit of a problem as four conditions needed to be met:

1. Pressurizing pump PP-1 must be able to sense the presence of water in the tank, operating when it is there and not operating—leaving it to the submersible pump—when it isn't there.

2. Since pressurizing pump PP-1 will have a limited flow rate (this one was rated at $\frac{1}{12}$ HP, 35 psi, and 20 gpm), it should be rigged to work in conjunction with the submersible pump, supplying all of the water needs below a specific gpm figure (its own rating) and receiving assistance from the submersible pump for flow rates above that value.

3. Enough water must be left in the tank at all times to take care of normal nonpressurized water needs such as watering the gardens and orchards.

4. Enough water must be left in the tank to supply blackout, fire, or other emergency needs.

As complex as the requirements seem, satisfying these conditions was not at all difficult (see Fig. 6–20). A level sensor switch (S-2) positioned in the tank takes care of the first condition; an additional pressure switch (S-3) inserted alongside the submersible pump's own pressure switch (S-1) and adjusted to a higher pressure setting takes care of the second condition; and the proper positioning of level sensor switch S-2 in the tank handles both the third and fourth conditions.

Note that pressurizing pump PP-1 is plumbed in *parallel* with gate valve GV-1; this retains the two major features—filling the tank with the submersible pump and having nonpressurized water in the

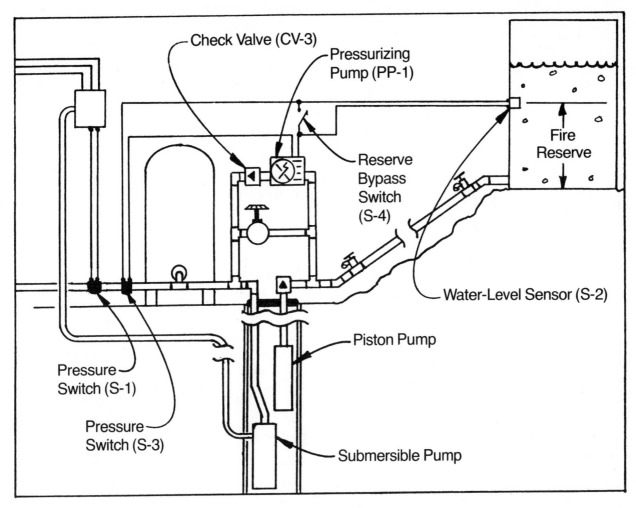

Fig. 6–20 Phase three of the Silver System matches the pressure in both services.

household during blackouts—of the phase two setup. A check valve (CV-3) is added in-line with pressurizing pump PP-1 to prevent a possible reverse flow of water through the pressurizing pump when it is off and the submersible pump is on. Finally, level sensor switch S-2 is positioned in the tank according to the owner's wish to leave some water in it for normal gardening needs and for fire, blackout, and other emergencies. In this instance it is set at the halfway point; in the 2,000-gallon tank this leaves 1,000 gallons in reserve at all times.

Normal system operation is described as follows:

1. If the water level in the tank is *below* the position of level sensor switch S-2 and a faucet is turned on in the house, pressure switch S-1 closes, activates the pump relay, and the submersible pump turns on, supplying water to the system. Pressure switch S-3 also closes, but, since it is in series with level sensor switch S-2, which is open, pressurizing pump PP-1 does not activate.

2. If the water level in the tank is *above* the position of level sensor switch S-2, S-2 closes. Then when a faucet is turned on in the house, pressure switch S-3 will close, pressurizing pump PP-1 will activate, water will flow from the tank through the pressurizing pump and supply household water needs up to 20 gpm (the flow-rate value of the selected pressurizing pump). Initially, pressure switch S-1 may also close—although it is adjusted to a pressure setting that's 5 psi lower than S-3's setting (see diagram)—and activate the submersible pump. However, the combined pressure of the two pumps will quickly force pressure switch S-1 to open, shutting down the submersible pump and allowing pressurizing pump PP-1 to handle the work load. If the household demand rate of flow exceeds the pressurizing pump's capacity, the submersible pump will make up the difference.

3. If the household demand for water is sufficient in duration to cause the water level in the tank to fall below the position of level sensor

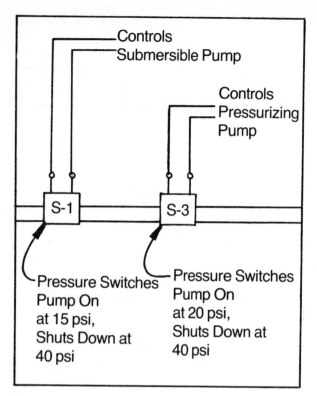

Fig. 6–21 Automatic sequencing of the pumps in the Silver System is assured by adjusting the ranges of the pressure switches.

switch S-2, this switch will open, shutting down pressurizing pump PP-1; this will allow the pressure in the system to fall low enough to close pressure switch S-1, activating the submersible pump to handle further water needs.

4. The reserve bypass switch (S-4) is inserted in the circuit in parallel with level sensor switch S-2, so that the owner, for whatever reason, may defeat the level-sensor switch's function, maintain the activation of pressurizing pump PP-1, and use the emergency stock (1,000 gallons) of water.

Phase Four

A failing of the phrase-three setup is the reliance of both the submersible pump and pressurizing pump PP-1 on utility power; if this power is interrupted, only nonpressurized water, via gate valve GV-1, is available to the house. That's tolerable during normal blackouts but downright frustrating for fire fighting.

This circumstance is easily remedied by replacing pressurizing pump PP-1 with a 12-volt D.C. version (hereafter referred to as PP-2), adding a 12-volt deep-cycle battery to power it during blackouts and connecting to a battery charger to keep the battery topped off when utility power is available (see Fig. 6–22).

No apparent difference may be noted in phase four's functioning over that of phase three. However, if utility power is interrupted, pressurizing pump PP-2 will continue to function, tapping the stored energy in the battery and supplying pressurized tank water to the household on demand. If the water level in the tank drops below the position of level sensor switch S-2, this will deactivate even the 12-volt pressurizing pump; if utility power is still not restored but water is needed, the owner may close reserve bypass switch S-4, and the remaining 1,000 gallons of tank water will be available for pressurized water use as needed. If the system battery is small (in capacity) and unable to pressurize the water for as long as it would take to use the full amount of water in the tank, some of the household water needs may be satisfied by opening gate valve GV-1 for nonpressurized water delivery (as per phase two).

If water is being used in the household and reserve bypass switch S-4 is closed (on), pressurizing pump PP-2 will *not* shut down if the tank should run dry. There are two ways to prevent this failure to shut down. One is to install another level sensor switch at the base of the tank, wiring it in series with level sensor switch S-2 and pressure switch S-3; this will shut down the pressurizing pump as soon as the water runs out. A second solution, which avoids the extra switch and wiring, is simple monitoring. If, indeed, a blackout exists and the owners are cutting into their reserve supply of water, they should be closely watching their water use and they will, if the tank water gets low, shut down the pressurizing pump; if reserve bypass switch S-4 is opened, the pump will stop, since the water level in the tank is below level sensor switch S-2.

While pressurizing pump PP-2 may draw 5 to 15 amps of electricity, the battery charger's rating need not be this large; even when the system is operating under utility power, most of the pressurizing pump's power may be supplied by the battery. Consequently, a 3-amp charger is probably sufficient; any time water isn't being used in the household or the tank water is too low, the pressurizing pump is deactivated and all of the charger's juice will be charging up the battery. However, in any given twenty-four-hour period, the accumulated capacity of the charger should meet or exceed the pressurizing pump's energy

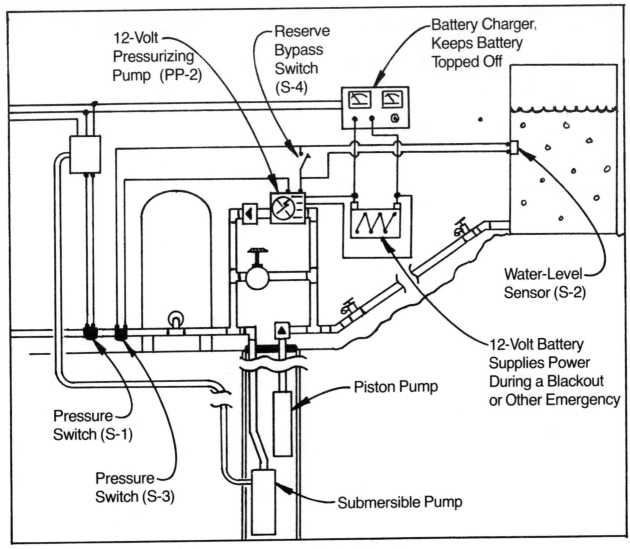

12-Volt
Pressurizing
Pump (PP-2)

Reserve
Bypass
Switch
(S-4)

Battery Charger,
Keeps Battery
Topped Off

Water-Level
Sensor (S-2)

12-Volt Battery
Supplies Power
During a Blackout
or Other Emergency

Piston Pump

Pressure
Switch (S-1)

Pressure
Switch (S-3)

Submersible Pump

Fig. 6–22 Phase four of the Silver System provides blackout protection.

needs. The charger should also be rated high enough to ensure that there will be some energy in the battery should utility power be interrupted at any time of the day or night.

Final Comments

There are many ways to wire up the Silver System so that it may automatically respond to any variety of circumstances and conditions. If you're competent in the matter of electrical wiring or design (or just plain clear thinking), the sky's the limit—have fun. However, realize that the circuits described in this section were derived after a lot of designwork. So in the trash can are a bunch of designs that will work, but not as well as the ones presented. Ad-

mittedly, the main criteria I used were simplicity, versatility, and reliability. If you like sophistication and ornamentation, these circuits will naturally appear a little dry and barren. By all means add all the switches, relays, indicator lights, meters, and alarms you'd like. Good luck!

As simple as the Silver System is, it may not appear that way to the novice. However, get some help installing it if you like its features; after operating it, you'll quickly learn the ins and outs. If you get confused when operating a toaster, photocopy the final diagram (mine or yours) and post it on the wall in the pump house; this will help others—family, friends, guests—to operate the system, too. This will also help if something doesn't seem to be working correctly; you can't troubleshoot something if you can't remember how things are supposed to work. Clearly label all switches—pressure, level sensor, reserve bypass, etc.—in the system and key them to the drawing. Post instructions for operating the system in various modes. In addition, indicate the correct procedures (as given in the text) for restoring the system to its normal operational mode—reserve bypass switch off, submersible pump switch on, etc.—after you've enacted any emergency measures. When siting the switches, keep them high and hidden; the first takes care of inquisitive children and the second should handle button-pushing adults.

OFFSET SYSTEMS

It is sometimes impossible to place pumping equipment directly over the water source. The reasons vary—it may be a condition of terrain, the presence of trees, or limited space in the well house. Whatever the reason, if the equipment is not set directly over the well it is referred to as an "offset" arrangement. The offset is also used for the sake of convenience, permitting an installation that saves electrical wire or locates the water-pumping equipment in a preferred site other than directly at the wellhead.

The versatility of the offset arrangement is examined in the three situations, each representing a unique set of problems and solutions.

Offset One

A typical offset arrangement for the shallow well is used whenever the wellhead is located 5 to 100 feet away from the building in which the pumping equipment is to be mounted (see Fig. 6–23). To connect the two, a pipe is run underground between the pump and some point near the bottom of the shallow well. As long as the head (distance X) does not exceed 15–20 feet (for suction lift of water) and the force pump is designed to lift water by suction as a jet pump or piston pump does, water will flow through the pipe to the pump.

Theoretically, the horizontal distance (Y) in this setup is unlimited. In practice, it is not. The only real effect that it *should* have is to extend the length of time, once the pump is turned on, before all the air is removed from the pipe and water is drawn to the force pump. However, pipe resistance is also a factor since long lengths and high flow rates will cause pressure losses. Larger-diameter pipe and free-flow fixtures do minimize these losses, but unfortunately they also increase the overall volume of air that must be evacuated from the pipe before water is pumped. And there's the additional problem of what to do with all of the air that's pumped into the water lines.

None of this would be a problem if the pump didn't lose its prime—the water in the lift pipe

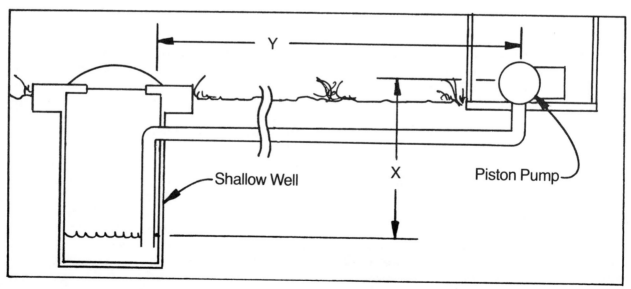

Fig. 6–23 A positive-displacement pump may be offset from the water source.

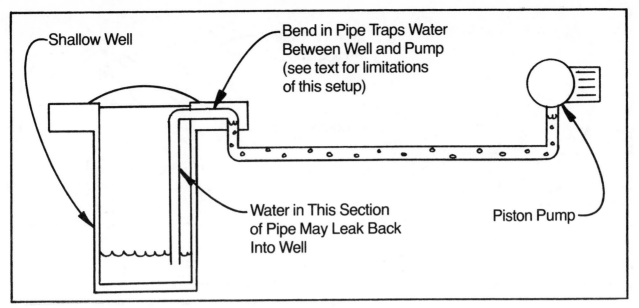

Fig. 6–24 Preventing drainback of water creates other problems.

drawing back into the shallow well when the pump stops—but it can happen. A bend in the pipe at the wellhead (see Fig. 6–24) might help to keep most of the water in the pipe, minimizing the amount of time it will take for the force pump to start lifting water, but this procedure is not recommended for two reasons. First, if the water is normally going to flow freely back into the well, water in the lowest portion of the pipe will simply "siphon" over the plumbing dam anyway. Even if it didn't, the second reason is the clincher: this setup violates a basic principle in pipe layout concerning dips or low points in the pipe runs, which will collect debris, sediment, and prevent complete drainage of the pipe if the need arises, *and* high points, which will trap air.

A "gravity" check valve (see Fig. 4–32) is well suited to this type of installation. If it's installed at the wellhead and oriented correctly, it will prevent backflow in the line and yet, at pump start-up, present a minimum resistance (pressure drop) to suction or water flow. This type of check valve has a clean-out fitting to aid in the removal of debris or deposit formations that might interfere with proper closure or opening of the swing valve after a period of operation. For this reason, the valve should not be buried in the ground or used in those systems where the fittings at the wellhead do not emerge aboveground.

Offset of a shallow-well pump is a good setup if there's a building nearby; at the least, it eliminates the need for constructing a pump house and running the electrical wires to it. However, wiring is cheaper than plumbing; therefore, if the pump equipment is located in a building that wouldn't normally be supplied with water, the extra pipe needed to connect the wellhead and the pump could cost considerably more than the wiring or a very small pump house. If a pump house is required in either situation, it is normally positioned between the wellhead and the usage site to minimize the lengths of pipe or electrical wires.

Offset Two

Another typical offset arrangement is illustrated in Fig. 6–25. In this instance, a small pump house was initially built over the wellhead and housed a water pump powered by a small gasoline engine that would deliver water from a shallow well to a storage tank up on a hill. The original intention was eventually to set up a water-pumping wind machine with the tower positioned directly over the well *and* pump house; indeed, the well had been drilled at what was thought to be the best wind site. However, further investigation disclosed a better wind site some fifty feet to one side. Since the well obviously couldn't be moved, and the wind machine was already purchased, an offset arrangement was chosen.

In practice, the shallow-well piston pump, powered by the wind machine, is located directly at the base of the tower. A suction pipe connects the

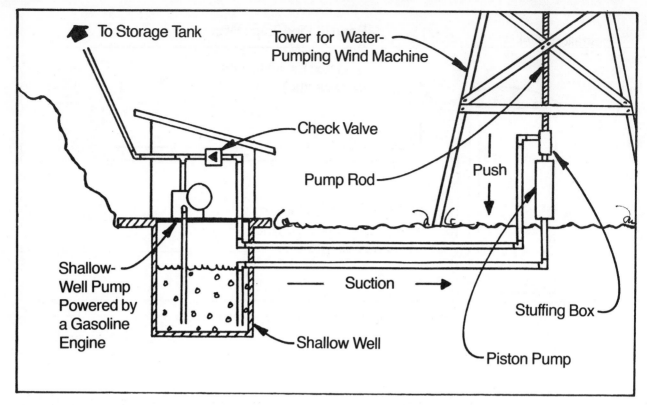

To Storage Tank

Tower for Water-
Pumping Wind Machine

Check Valve

Pump Rod

Push

Shallow-
Well Pump
Powered by
a Gasoline
Engine

Suction

Stuffing Box

Shallow Well

Piston Pump

Fig. 6–25 This offset system features parallel pumping.

shallow well with the pump, whose outlet is connected by a tee to the outlet pipe of the water pump connected with the gas engine; essentially, the pumps are paralleled. When there's wind, the tower pump sucks water from the shallow well and delivers it to storage; during emergencies or a dry period, the gas engine can be fired up to pump water to the tank.

This installation is subject to the same limitations and conditions as the first offset system described. Since this is a hybrid system, care must be exercised in the selection of the equipment so that water cannot be pumped in a loop through the dormant pump back to the well by either system.

Offset Three

Wind machines work best in clear, high places and water inevitably likes to come out of the ground in shaded, low places. Where both conditions—high wind and low water—exist on one piece of property, the landowner is teased with the possibilities but tormented by the obstacles. *Never again!* If the distance between the wellhead and the best wind site does not exceed one-half mile,

there's one offset arrangement that *will* work—the "taut-wire" system, where a steel wire is actually used as a transmission device, transferring power from the wind machine site to the pump located at the well site. No kidding.

This is not some newfangled idea that will break down in long-term usage. It has already passed the test of time, being derived from a system developed by the Amish people for transferring power from waterwheels to remote irrigation systems *and* powering entire shops (drills, lathes, you name it) from waterwheels.

The basic system is adapted to a wind machine. At the wind machine, two lever arms joined at a common pivot are secured to the base of the tower; one of these arms is attached to the wind machine and the taut wire is connected to the other. Since the power in a water-pumping wind machine is designed for the *upward* stroke, the pivot-and-arm arrangement is oriented to rotate clockwise, pulling the wire inward for the power portion of the stroke.

The taut-wire offset works admirably in systems using a shallow well, spring, pond, or lake as a source of water. However, those systems are excluded from further discussion here to simplify the

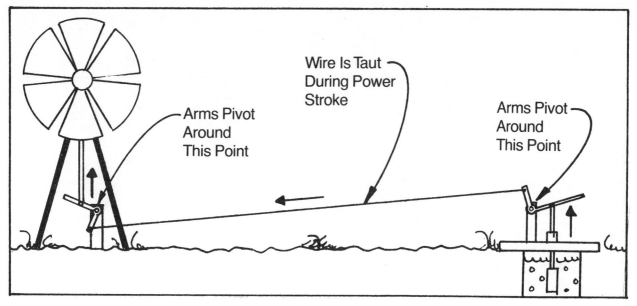

Fig. 6–26 A single wire will transfer power to distant applications.

text. Since the deep-well setup represents the *toughest* test of the taut-wire offset, we'll concentrate on that arrangement; its use with any other water source should be comparatively easy.

A Short-Distance Taut-Wire System

Suppose that the well is only twenty feet distant from the base of the tower. We'd just connect the other end of the wire to one of the arms of a similar pivot and arm device secured in a position directly over the wellhead. The remaining arm, then, would be attached, through suitable linkage, to the pump mechanism—that is, a deep-well piston pump.

Now, let's look at the operation. If the pivot-arm devices mounted at the wellhead and the tower base are positioned exactly as shown in the diagram (see Fig. 6–26), the upward stroke of the pump rod secured to the wind machine will rotate the tower's pivot-arm assembly clockwise, pulling the cable to the left (this view). This motion will rotate the wellhead's pivot-arm assembly counterclockwise; in turn, the piston pump's sucker rod will be lifted up. So in this arrangement we have duplicated the relative movement of the pump's sucker rod and the wind machine's connecting rod just as though they were directly coupled together.

But—this only represents one-half the total movement. In fact, we can next watch the wind machine's pump rod moving downward (see Fig. 6–27), rotating the tower's pivot-arm assembly

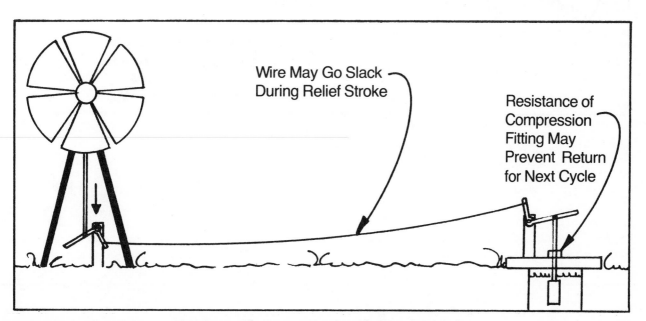

Fig. 6–27 The taut wire may slacken during the portion of the cycle following the power stroke.

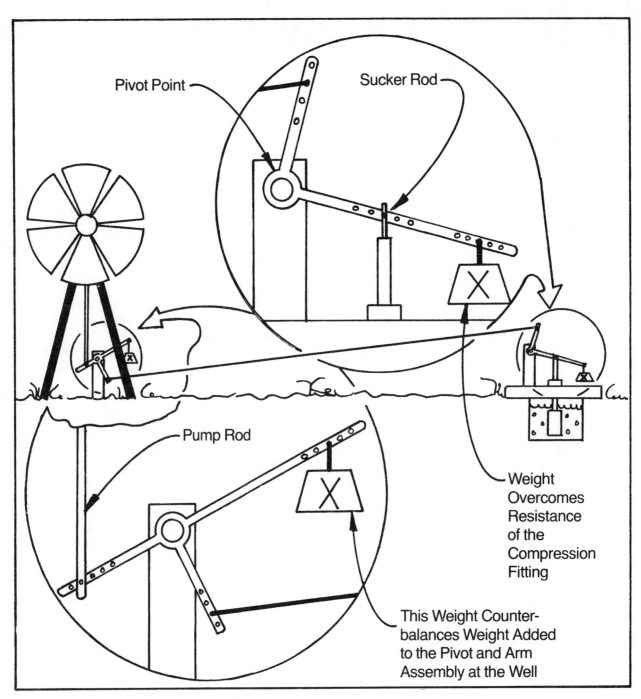

Fig. 6–28 Adding weights to the taut-wire system assures proper functioning.

counterclockwise. However, we might *not* see the wellhead's pivot-arm unit turn clockwise; the tightness of the compression fitting in the stuffing box or pump standard might impede this motion. If this happened, the wire would go slack for this portion of the cycle. The consequence is evident: no further pumping would occur even though the wind machine would be faithfully rotating the tower's pivot-arm unit back and forth.

This problem is easily resolved; by adding a weight to one of its arms, the wellhead's pivot-arm device can be forced to turn clockwise at the end of the first portion of the cycle. Everything should be smooth and graceful through the second portion of the cycle, each of the pivot-arm devices pivoting, and the wire between them as taut as it should be.

This remedy has a shortcoming, and it would be noticed as soon as the first part of the next cycle commenced; if the wind machine doesn't grind to a halt, it will certainly groan in protest. Why? Because in addition to lifting the water in the well, it must also lift all that weight you've added! What's the solution? It's a simple one: just add a weight of corresponding size to the pivot arm device at the tower base (see Fig. 6–28). This balances the two ends of the system so that energy from the water-pumping wind machine is again only applied toward extracting water. Meanwhile, the wire is kept twice as taut as it would be with only one weight; this also minimizes the loss of energy required to "tension" it twice each cycle. Since the power-transfer devices now consist of a pivot, arms, and a weight, let's refer to them as PAW units for convenience.

A Long-Distance Taut-Wire System

Now, if only 20 feet existed between the wellhead and the tower base, this would be the entire system. But where this system *really* shines is when a distance of several hundred feet to several thousand feet separates the two.

The PAW devices don't change as the distance opens between the wellhead and the tower site, but several other factors do. How do we keep the wire off the ground? What happens if the wellhead and the tower site are not in the line of sight? How do we route the wire around trees and buildings, over hills and across gullies? How do we remove the slack in that much wire?

The problems may seem insurmountable with large distances, but they aren't. Let's tackle them one by one.

1. The weights attached to the PAW devices help maintain wire tension, but they'd soon lose this battle without help; a 100-foot wire might require several tons of weights at each end just to keep it from touching the ground. At the very least, the cost of reinforcing the PAW units to handle the dead load would be prohibitive.

The solution to wire tensioning is the installation of wire guides. The Amish accomplished this by securing a small piece of rubber hose to the top of a pole, then slipping the wire through that (see Fig. 6–29). Spaced 60 to 80 feet apart, as many pole guides as necessary were installed between their energy source—a waterwheel—and the wellhead. With a 100- to 150-pound weight at each PAW device, the wire was kept taut.

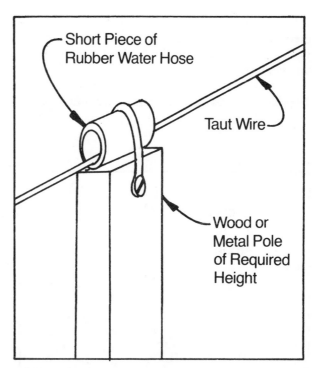

Fig. 6–29 Guide poles support the taut wire over long distances.

2. For the distances involved, a low-level taut wire invariably runs afoul of roads and paths that people or animals might travel. This problem is solved by using pole guides that are high enough to permit humans and animals free passage beneath. Reroute for power poles and major highways.

3. Is there line of sight between the wellhead and tower base? If not, the wire must use change-of-direction, or COD, devices. The pole guides should *not* be used directly for this purpose; with the existing tension, the wire would saw through the guides—wood holes, rubber hose, whatever—within the first few hours of operation.

A good design for the COD device is one similar in appearance to the PAW units (see Fig. 6–30). There are several major differences between the two. One is the length of the arms; those for the COD units can be considerably shorter. A second major distinction between the two is that the COD's axis (pivot point) will normally be mounted vertically (there are exceptions), whereas in the PAW units it's horizontal. A third difference is the relative angle of the arms; at all times the angle between them should be equal to the angle of the direction change. So, a 90-degree angle exists between arms where there's a 90-degree change of direction, the arms are separated by 15 degrees with a 15-degree angle change of direction, and so forth.

A COD with a vertical axis of rotation assists in direction changes that occur in a horizontal plane, such as at the corner of a field or around a house.

However, the COD unit must be oriented with a horizontal axis, as is the PAW unit, if it's to account for direction changes in a vertical plane, such as down a hill or over a rock pile.

In hilly country, right angles and strictly horizontal or vertical changes of direction are rare. Therefore it would seem that a minimum of two COD units are needed to translate power transmission into a direction change that's both horizontal and vertical. However, there's nothing to prevent us from using *one* COD device for this by simply tilting its axis to some angle *between* the vertical and horizontal positions. While some folks might complain about doing this—it *appears* more difficult than compensating for direction changes along the two major planes—in practice, it's easier to do it with a tilt. First, it saves making and installing two COD devices where one will do. Second, it saves having to position the wire's route to handle boxlike angles. And, third, since the tilt-angle COD unit must be adjustable so the installer can select the final angle, sites for the COD units may be chosen along the intended route and the supports for them dug and installed. With a *fixed* vertical or horizontal axis, however, the installation is everything; if the COD units are out of alignment, the side forces on the device will cause uneven wear and unwanted friction. With no adjustability, the entire unit must be repositioned.

Traversing hilly terrain with several thousand feet of wire will usually require the use of several COD units of the tilt-angle type. For this reason, the route must be carefully studied to pick one that uses as few COD devices as possible. A good eye for imaginary angles and hypothetical distances and a slow walk of the route will save work later on. Don't forget the need for pole guides every 75 feet or so.

4. What kind of wire is used? At first, it might seem that we would need stainless-steel cable to handle all the chafing (through guides, at the armholes, etc.), the tension, and weathering. However, this is not the case; high-carbon, single-strand (solid) smooth fencing wire will do nicely. The number 12-gauge size is quite stiff, but it weathers nicely and it's inexpensive.

A Sample Taut-Wire System

Two years ago I suggested the use of a taut-wire system to some folks who had a good well in a gulch, a fine wind site on a hill near their home,

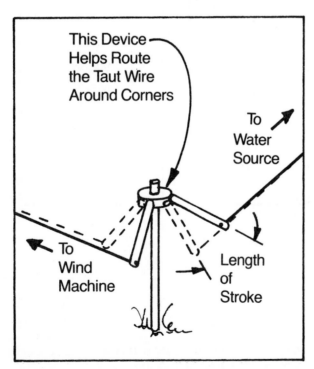

Fig. 6–30 A COD (change-of-direction) device is needed in some taut-wire systems.

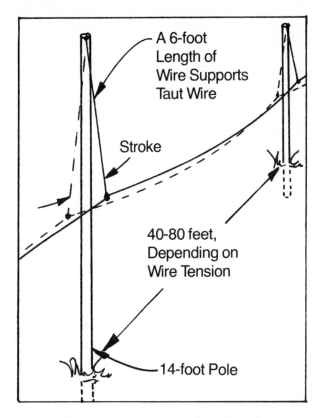

Fig. 6–31   An improved guide pole.

and a real need to set up something of this type. They were fairly remote, had no need for utility power, and were very tired of the noise, expense, and bother (walking almost half a mile) in firing up a gasoline-engine-powered pump for their meager water needs.

They were fascinated by the concept of a taut-wire system and bugged me for design detail. The estimated distance between the tower site and the wellhead was very close to the maximum the Amish used in their installations. For it to work, then, the power losses due to friction would have to be severely reduced.

The first concern was the pole guides. Instead of routing the cable over the top of the poles and through eyelets of any type, I designed a suspended support for the taut wire (see Fig. 6–31). By attaching a length of the same wire to a nail at the top of the pole, the transmission wire was supported and free to rock back and forth. Since a short length of support wire would raise the transmission wire a little bit at the end of each stroke, the length was increased to minimize this. A 14-foot guide pole seemed right; it would allow 6 feet of swing for the support wire, 6 feet of overhead clearance, and 2 feet below ground to fix the pole in place. (I later discovered that many Amish installations utilized precisely this technique for their pole guides. And I thought I was so clever!)

The second area of concern was the COD units. To minimize the effort of construction, I suggested the use of old bicycle rims. With the tire and tube removed, the two ridges around the perimeter will keep the wire from slipping off during the installation stages and account for any slight errors in pivot orientation. With the bearings already mounted in the rim and the threaded axle protruding from each side, the axle could be easily secured in a number of ways and the resultant COD device (see Fig. 6–32) would be able to handle any angle of turn that might emerge.

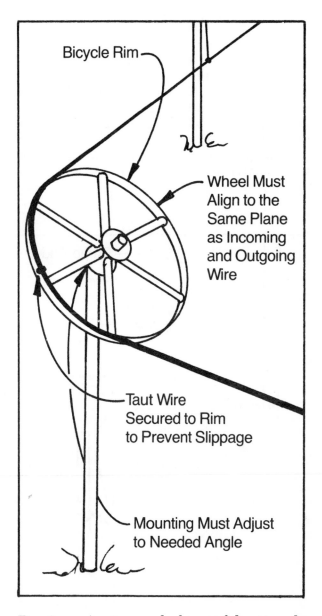

Fig. 6–32   An improved change-of-direction device.

In the process of developing the COD device around a bicycle rim, several other things came to light. One is that the transmission wire could conceivably slip *along* the rim; if the wheel did not rotate, the wire would experience a lot of friction and ultimately fray. To prevent this, it was decided to drill a hole in the rim and actually secure the cable to the rim's edge.

Another problem emerged. The transmission wire could not be secured to the bicycle rim if the COD angle was only a very slight one; the wire must be in contact with a portion of the rim's arc equal in length with the stroke. How, then, could we prevent slippage for slight-angle COD units?

This problem was finally solved by shortening the length of the stroke in the taut wire. With the arms of each of the PAW units equal, the wire stroke was identical to the wind-machine and pump-mechanism stroke. By shortening the length of each of the arms in the PAW units to which the transmission wire was attached (see Fig. 6–33), we cut the wire stroke in half.

At first I wanted to reduce it more—who needed a long stroke? But I realized that if the stroke were too short, the PAW units would need heavier weights. Why? Even with the weights and pole guides, some of the stroke takes out the remaining slack in the transmission wire, and the remainder transfers power. With a shorter stroke, even though it has more torque, *less* of the stroke is available to transfer power since so much is used for tensioning. So either the wire must be pre-tensioned with more weight or the stroke kept long enough to handle tensioning too.

FOUR YEARS LATER

I was busy with other things. The nice folks had thanked me for my time and effort and gone on their way after buying my lunch. Four years went by. Then one day I heard a friend who lives over that way describe an unusual system he'd heard about where a water-pumping wind machine pulled water out of a canyon with a wire! Had these folks done it after all?

Another six months went by before I finally made it over that way, found out where these people lived, and paid them a visit. I received a warm welcome, and after a little chat we walked uphill to the base of the tower. Sure enough, there it was, the big PAW device pistoning back and forth in silent majesty, the taut wire stretching away and disappearing into some trees a few hundred feet downhill. A one-wire fence. Next, we walked down that slope, past pole guide after pole guide. After just six of them we reached the first COD unit, mounted on an 8-foot pole, its axis tilted sharply to shift the wire's direction down and to the left. It was a bicycle rim! It rotated in a small arc, about 10 degrees, back and forth, back and forth. We walked on, past more poles and another COD unit identical with the first, which helped the transmission wire through a right-hand turn this time.

There were twenty-eight poles in all, and I counted six of the COD units. A duplicate of the PAW device I'd seen at the tower's base was bolted over the concrete pad surrounding the wellhead. The stroke appeared to be a little shorter. I asked about that. The power loss was exactly 4 inches of stroke. So, the water moved up the hill a little slower. "But," they said with a smile, "it gets there."

I noticed that they'd used the wire I'd described. "How much wire is there altogether?" I asked. Another big smile. "Exactly 3,314 feet and 4 inches." You could have dropped me with a feather. I did

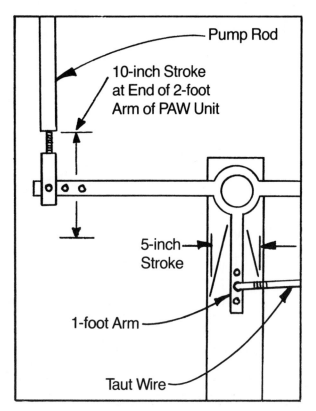

Fig. 6–33   One way to limit the taut wire's stroke.

some hasty calculations in my head. That was over ⅝ of a mile!

I wondered why they'd never bothered to contact me once they'd finished the installation and got it working. It stayed in my mind the whole time I was there. Finally, just as I was leaving, I asked. Both of them stared at me, puzzled. "Why should you be interested in it?" John asked. I didn't understand what he meant. "But," he said, "you do this stuff all the time. There's nothing unique about this," he added, pointing at the wire as it stretched uphill, pulsating as it moved back and forth, stretched and slackened. "We did it just the way you said."

I was astonished. They had thought my hasty drawings four years ago had been the details of a *proven* system I was adapting to their own situation. In fact, I had only been trying to describe the principle! I didn't have the heart to tell them of the risk they'd taken; at ⅝ of a mile, they were more than ⅛ mile beyond the longest Amish setup I'd heard of. It didn't matter; they'd done it, and it worked. And that's the way it happens sometimes. If there's no one around to tell you it won't work, you don't start off with that disadvantage.

THE WATERWATCH

If you, like many others, have decided to use a gravity-fed method of pressurizing your water (good choice), you have no doubt realized by now one shortcoming of the setup: estimating the level of liquid in the tank.

There are two methods that immediately pop into mind: let it go till it runs dry, or hike up the hill and have a look-see. After a couple of jaunts you'll naturally wonder whether there isn't a better way. I don't know about your days, but I have better things to do than play nursemaid to a cistern.

Well, fret not. This situation is readily remedied with a handful of common electronic components. Don't let the word "electronic" intimidate you. This water-level gauge is based on the fact that water is a better electrical conductor than air, and is easily duplicated by almost anyone—even if you've never done more than replace a light bulb. And after completion, this monitor makes it as easy to determine the level of water in the tank as glancing at the living-room wall. Called the Waterwatch, the system is made up of four parts: an in-tank sensor tube, a circuit board, the monitor itself, and the interconnecting wire (see Fig. 6–34). Ready? Let's begin!

The Tank's Sensor Tube

The tank is a logical spot to start. For it, we must build a sensor tube that transmits information about the water level to the monitor; this is fabricated from a length of 1-inch PVC water pipe and eleven stainless-steel, self-tapping screws (see Fig. 6–35).

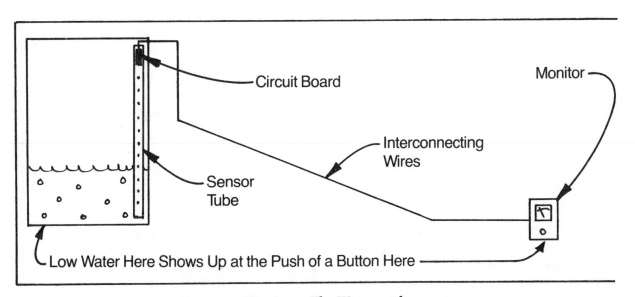

Fig. 6–34 The Waterwatch.

Fig. 6–35 A sensor tube is propped against the side of the tank for which it was designed.

Determine the depth of the water when the vessel is filled, and cut your plastic tube 3 inches longer. Now scribe eleven lines on the pipe, dividing the maximum water level into *eleven* increments with the bottommost point at the level of the tank's outlet and the uppermost at the overflow point (or the top of the tank—see Fig. 6–36). For example, if the water's depth is 33 inches, each division is 3 inches. A 10-foot-high tank, then, would have a scribe mark at each 11 inches (120 inches divided by 11). Now drill a ³⁄₁₆-inch hole at each of the top 10 marks to accept number 10 screws. Drill the eleventh hole at or just below the bottommost mark of the pipe and a quarter turn of the pipe to either side; this will be the "hot" wire.

Still with me? Good. Prepare ten pieces of stranded wire, 20-gauge or so. The first wire is a foot longer than the length of the tube, and each successive wire is shorter by the distance between the holes. Also make an extra (eleventh) wire just a tad longer than your first wire.

With that completed, thread the eleventh wire through the bottommost hole (the offset one), up

the pipe and out the top. Wait! Before pulling it too far, strip the insulation from the trailing end; then lay the bared strands to one side of the hole and *gently* thread the screw into the hole, trapping the wire and at the same time making a good contact. (A word of caution: the thin metal strands are fragile, and easily cut by the sharp screw threads!) Label this wire "hot" for future identification; a knot or a different-color insulation is better than tape, which can slip off.

Continue this procedure by snaking the longest remaining wire into the next hole—through the hole, up the tube, out the top, etc. Repeat this until all wires are firmly fastened in place.

If you experience any problem in getting the wires to move through the tube when all those other wires are in there (this *will* be a problem for tubes over 5 feet in length), cut the tube in half (or into 5-foot intervals if it's longer than 10 feet), slip

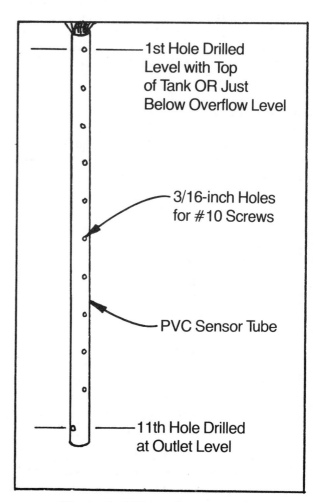

Fig. 6–36 Making the sensor tube.

a coupler onto one of the halves, route all the wires through, and join the tube sections with generous portions of PVC cement.

The Circuit Board

The circuit board is actually the brains of our monitor, even though it rests quietly inside the plastic sensor pipe (see Fig. 6–37). First, locate the ten 39,000-ohm resistors on a 1-inch-wide perf board (see Fig. 6–38). Don't worry, you can't get them backward—they work in either direction. Notice that all the leads from one side are soldered together, forming a common "buss." Now, taking one wire at a time, solder it to the loose end of one resistor. It doesn't matter which wire goes to which resistor, however, *don't* solder the "hot" lead to a resistor.

Obtain a length of twin lead (two wires) long enough to stretch from the tank (sensor) to the monitor. Even for distances of hundreds of feet, this wire can be quite small—small-size speaker wire is ample—since 1 milliampere ($\frac{1}{1000}$ of an amp) is the maximum amount of current that will flow through it. Shop around for it or for especially long lengths; order it from a mail-order outfit for a lower price per foot.

At the tank end, drill a hole in the end of a 1-inch pipe cap just large enough to accept the cable; thread it through and solder one wire to the common leg of the resistors and the other to the "hot" wire.

Now, carefully slide the circuit board into the tube and glue the end cap in place. Apply a liberal covering of silicone sealant around the emerging wires to prevent moisture from creeping into the pipe. While you're at it, also seal the base of the sensor screws, leaving the screwheads exposed; a really good seal is obtained if you back the screw out a bit and squish sealant in the gap, screwing it back down and letting it gush out a bit. If you get sealant on the screwhead, get it *all* off with a paper towel. Glue and seal an end cap to the bottom of the pipe, too. And that's it. Slide the finished product into the tank, anchor it to the side, and you're **halfway finished with the Waterwatch.**

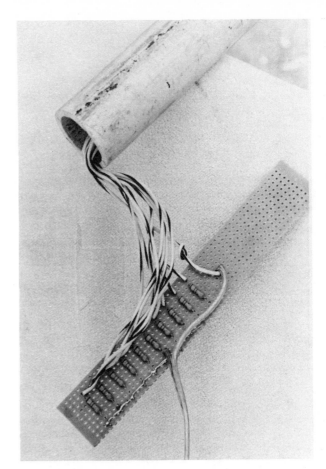

Fig. 6–37 The circuit board is ready to slip into the sensor tube.

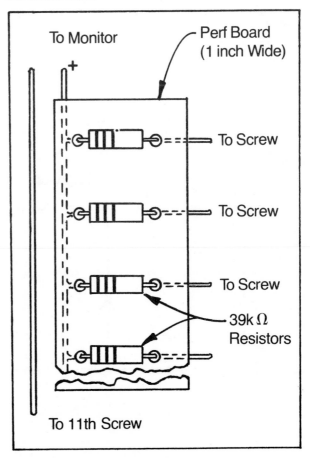

Fig. 6–38 The ten resistors are mounted on perf board narrow enough to fit inside the sensor tube.

Fig. 6–39 A good-looking monitor will look at home on your wall.

The Monitor

The heart of the monitor is a meter that displays the amount of water in the holding tank. I installed mine in a chunk of 2×6 I had on hand; with a little stain and varnish, it finished up quite nicely (see Fig. 6–39). The mounting screws on most meters aren't evenly spaced, so watch this when you're making up your own monitor.

Follow the schematic (see Fig. 6–40) to hook up the monitor's components. The only tricky part of this operation is ensuring that the zener diode (Z-1) has its banded end toward the meter post. If wired backward, the monitor won't work.

Unfortunately, the specified meter reads in D.C. milliamperes. However, you can change the numbers if you wish by carefully removing the protective front and metal plate. With fingernail-polish remover, erase the words "D.C. Milliamperes" and insert the legend "Water." You must be extremely careful not to damage the sensitive needle. If you're really skillful, you can eradicate the numbers and replace them with actual gallonage marks. However, this is hardly necessary; you should know the storage tank's capacity (see Fig.

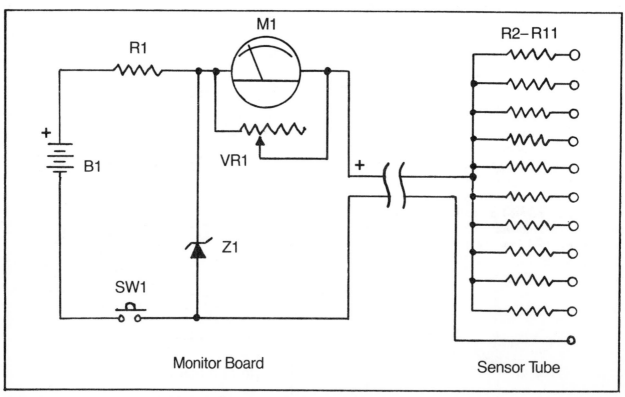

Fig. 6–40   The Waterwatch circuit.

1–7 if you don't). And the purpose of the monitor is to tell you, at a glance, whether the tank is three fourths full, a quarter full, or whatever. If you want to know the gallonage but are clumsy by nature and afraid to open the meter housing, type out a conversion table ($\frac{2}{10}$ full is 180 gallons; $\frac{6}{10}$ is 540 gallons, etc.) and tape it to the monitor's housing.

Putting It All Together

String the cable from the tank to the monitor and connect to the meter, referring to the diagram. A word of wisdom: when routing your wires, keep them off the ground if at all possible, or bury them deep, critters love to chew.

Finally, fill the tank, insert the battery—nestle it into the cavity behind the switch (see Fig. 6–41)—press the "On" button and, with the other hand, adjust the variable resistor (VR-1) until the pointer registers "1" (full-scale). That's it! As the water level drops, the monitor will indicate percentage of water left in the tank—.9 equals 90 percent, .8 is 80 percent, and so on.

Afterthoughts

Although my monitor has performed unerringly for some time now, there is a remote possibility that you may not be able to obtain a full-scale reading when the tank is full. This is due to the fact that the conductivity of water *changes* according to the kinds and amounts of dissolved minerals in it.

The resistivity of well water averages about 10,000 ohms per cubic centimeter—quite acceptable for the gauge. However, rainwater and other forms of soft water can often exceed 100,000 ohms per cubic centimeter, making it impossible to calibrate your meter.

There are two basic approaches to circumvent this dilemma. The easiest is to increase the *conductivity* by adding minerals to the water. Table salt works great; about a tablespoon for every 1,000 gallons should suffice.

Understandably, some readers will be opposed to adding anything to their precious liquid. Their only alternative, then, to poor water conductivity is to increase the *sensitivity* of the sensor. This is handily accomplished with the addition of a few transistors.

Fig. 6–41 The monitor's components will snuggle into the back of the board.

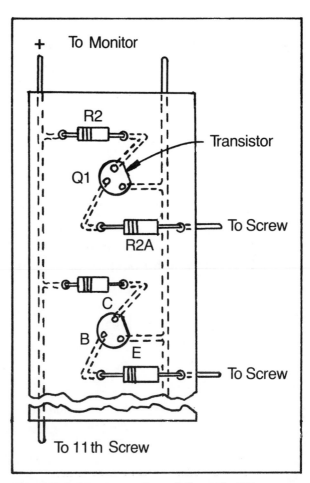

Fig. 6–42 For a mere three dollars, the Water-watch's sensitivity is increased fiftyfold.

An Optional Sensitivity Amplifier

The transistor—the result of silicon wizardry and the progenitor of today's solid-state electronics—is essentially an amplifier. By adding ten of the small semiconductors, the sensitivity of the Waterwatch will increase fiftyfold!

The only modification to the original design is to the circuit board. Follow the pictorial diagram very closely: transistors have three leads, and they must be connected properly. Looking at the diagram (see Fig. 6–42), you'll notice the three leads are labeled E, B, and C. Don't confuse them! (Note: ten additional resistors are also required.)

Other than that precaution, I believe the rest is self-explanatory. Repeat the calibration steps, and if you fail to get the proper reading, reverse the leads to the meter (transistors are polarity-sensitive).

Parts and Cost

All of the electronic parts (see Fig. 6–43) for the Waterwatch are available from your local electronic store, and the rest may be obtained from a hardware store and plumbing shop.

Figure 6-43
Parts List for the Waterwatch

Symbol	Number Required	Description	Stock No.	Price	Where Available*
R1	1	330-ohm, 1/2-watt resistor	271-017	2/19¢	RS
R2-R11	10	39K-ohm, 1/2-watt resistor	271-041	2/19¢	RS
VR1	1	1k-ohm potentiometer	271-333	49¢	RS
SW1	1	On/Off switch	275-609	2/$1.89	RS
M1	1	0-1 milliampere meter	35A6210-8	$7.90	BA
B1	1	9-volt battery	23-464	59¢	RS
Z1	1	6.2 volt, 1-watt zener diode	276-561	2/89¢	RS
	1	Battery clip	270-325	5/99¢	RS
	1	Perf board	276-1395	$1.39	RS
	10	#10 stainless steel, self-tapping screws			H
	1	1″ Schedule 40 PVC pipe, length variable			P
	2	End caps for 1″ PVC pipe			P
Optional Parts for Modification					
Q1-Q10	10	Transistors	276-1603	15/$1.98	RS
R2a-R11a	10	220k-ohm, 1/2-watt resistors	271-049	2/19¢	RS

*Where Available: RS — Radio Shack (local)

BA — Burstein-Applebee
    3199 Mercier Street
    Kansas City, MO 64111

H — Hardware store (local)

P — Plumbing store (local)

GLOSSARY

Acid having a pH higher than 7.0 (pure water).

Air-lift pump a mechanism that uses compressed air to lift water against the force of gravity.

Alkaline having a pH lower than 7.0 (pure water).

Artesian well a dug or drilled well where the water overflows (seasonally or year-round) due to underground hydrostatic pressure. In essence, this is a man-made spring.

Access either the legal right to use a water source, or, in a more general sense, its practical availability.

Appropriative rights the legal right, which is deeded to later property owners, to use water on the basis of "first come, first served."

Ball valve a type of check valve. The flow is determined by the water pressure, which causes a ball to rise or fall within the sphere of the valve.

Black water water that is heavily contaminated, as with sewage, and must be treated extensively before reuse or release to the environment.

Blow test one means of testing the capacity (flow rate) of a drilled well. It involves "blowing" the water out of the well by air pressure and then measuring the rate of refill. While this test lacks accuracy, it is convenient; well drilling may be suspended at any depth to perform this quick test.

Capacity water availability. Applied to storage, it is defined in terms of volume—i.e., thousands of gallons. Applied to a water source, it is usually measured as a flow rate—i.e., gallons per minute.

Casing, well a metal lining for the uppermost portion of a bored well which prevents soil collapse or surface contamination of the well water. In some areas, the entire well is cased; in this instance, the lower portions will have perforated sections to admit water.

Centrifugal pump a water-pumping mechanism that uses centrifugal force to extract, transport, or pressurize water.

CDF Cost per Drilled Foot in bored wells.

Check valve a simple mechanical device that permits the flow of water in only one direction; particularly useful to prevent flow back into a well or through a centrifugal-type pump with high head.

Chlorination a method of disinfecting water by adding chlorine. Either simple (weak) chlorination or super (strong) chlorination may be combined with filtering for the removal of excess chlorine.

Chlorination flush a method of rendering a water system safe from a number of contaminants, mostly biological. A concentrated chlorine solution is added at the water source, taps are opened until all pumps, tanks, pipes and fittings are saturated with the solution, and the system is sealed for the minimum time needed for the concentration to kill all bacteria. The system is then flushed of the chlorine and a coliform count is taken.

Cistern a large vessel, usually either partially or wholly underground, for storing water.

COD device A mechanism that allows changes of direction in taut-wire power-transfer systems.

Coliform a type of bacteria which, in sufficient amounts, can pose a health hazard to human beings if ingested. Standards have been adopted to describe the concentration in a given volume which is considered harmful.

Deep-well piston pump see Piston pump.

Demand system a water system where the pumping mechanism is activated by simply opening a tap. The resulting pressure drop turns on the pump, and water is extracted, transported, and pressurized until the water demand ceases.

Distillation a process of treating (purifying or conditioning) water to remove undesirable minerals, elements, metals, chemicals, biological life, and suspended particles by means of evaporation. Heat is applied and the water evaporates, condenses, and is collected for use, leaving behind most or all of the objectionable materials.

Dowsing the art and science of finding objects. Applied to water, a means to determine the location, depth, and capacity of potential water sources.

Drawdown the level to which water in a well will drop (from a static level) during continuous pumping; useful for estimating well capacity and the effective pumping head, and for correct positioning of the well's pump.

Drive pipe the pipe that delivers water from a source to the inlet of a hydraulic ram.

E. coli a type of bacteria. While not in itself harmful to humans, it is an indicator of the presence of more harmful coliform types; since it is easier to culture than other types, *E. coli* is the specific coliform bacteria counted in tests for water pollution.

Extraction one aspect of water processing; the vertical lifting of water to a higher level.

Float valve a water-control valve fitted with a floating mechanism and positioned near the top of a storage tank so that the high-water level closes it, shutting off water flow.

GPH gallons per hour of water flow.

GPM gallons per minute of water flow.

Gravity flow the movement of water due to gravity. In water systems, this may be used as a method of transporting water.

Gravity pressurization the natural pressurization of water due to gravity. In water systems, this *may* be the sole means of pressurizing water to acceptable flow rates for household and farm usage.

Gray water water that is slightly contaminated. It may be purified with minimal treatment or used directly in some applications, such as gardening, with little or no treatment, depending on the type of contamination. Also used generally to describe systems that are specifically designed to use water several times instead of just once.

Groundwater water that is found below the earth's surface and is available only through springs and wells.

Head the vertical distance (usually measured in feet) separating two levels of water. This may define the total distance water will fall (a stream's entrance versus its exit point on a property); how high water must be pumped (pumping head); how much pressure a gravity pressurization system will supply (gravity head); how much vertical pumping will result in pressurization (closed head) or overflow (open head).

Horsepower (HP) in terms of water, the amount of work required to lift, transport, and pressurize water at varying rates and heads; normally without considering pipe friction, fitting, and other losses.

Hydraulic ram a water-pumping device that uses the energy of falling water to transport a portion of that water to a higher level.

I.D. inside diameter of a pipe. A 6-inch pipe is one with an I.D. of 6 inches.

Induction the lifting of water by inducing a vacuum in a space above the water level, thereby allowing atmospheric pressure to "push" water to a higher point. Also called suction lift.

Jet pump a positive-displacement pump that injects a high-velocity stream of water into a water source for the purpose of lifting the water to a higher level.

Jetting one of several techniques that may be used to reopen a well that has slowed or stopped production. A jet pump nozzle is lowered into the well to pump out debris and sediment stirred up or blasted from the well walls.

Ksc Kilograms per square centimeter. A measure of pressure.

Ksm kilograms per square meter. A measure of pressure.

Leathers those portions of the deep-well piston pump that permit the piston to move up and down in the cylinder without letting water leak back through this interface. Made of leather, these are designed to be the only wearing portion of the pump subject to real wear and therefore requiring periodic replacement.

Mg/l milligrams per liter. A measure of density.

Mpn most probable number. A method of describing the concentration of coliform bacteria in a water sample.

Multiple water use see Gray water.

Pasteurization a method of treating unsafe water by exposing it to high heat (usually from an electric source).

PAW device the pivot arm and weight device used in the taut-wire power transfer system; one is needed at the water source and at the power source.

PE polyethylene, a type of plastic used to make water pipe.

pH a measure of acidity or alkalinity.

Pipe schedules a method of rating pipe for various working pressures, rigidity, ruggedness, and approved applications.

Piston pump a pump that uses the positive displacement of water—i.e., a piston moving in a cylinder—to lift, transport, and/or pressurize water.

Ppm parts per million. A measure of concentrations.

Pressure gauge a pressure-sensitive device that converts pressure into a linear movement of a needle across a calibrated scale.

Pressure switch a pressure-activated electrical switch that closes contacts (turns on) with a loss of pressure, and opens contacts (turns off) at a preset pressure level. Available in a wide range of pressure ratings, these are used extensively in demand systems for automatic pump operation.

Pressurizing pumps a pump whose only function is to pressurize water to desirable levels for usage.

Psi pounds per square inch. A measure of pressure.

Pumping jack a device that converts the rotary motion of an engine or motor into the reciprocating motion necessary to the operation of a piston pump such as that used in a well for water pumping.

Pump standard a device that sits over the drilled well, holds the in-well pump and pipe in position, permits sucker-rod movement (through a pressure seal), and incorporates a handle for hand pumping water from the well.

Pump test one means of testing the capacity (flow rate) of a drilled well. It uses a pump to discharge water from the well at the highest rate possible for a day or more without running it dry—a time-consuming but very accurate procedure.

PVC polyvinyl chloride, a type of plastic pipe used in water systems.

Reciprocating motion a back-and-forth motion, as, a piston moving up and down in a cylinder.

Riparian rights the legal right to use water on a shared or "justifiable use" basis.

Sand filter a simple filter system for removing suspended particles and bacteria from water.

Seasonal stream a stream that normally does not flow year-round.

SLR point a depth determined prior to well drilling at which, if water is still not present, you will "stop, look, and reevaluate" whether to drill deeper or start drilling somewhere else afresh.

Store system a type of water system which separates extraction and pressurization into two independent phases of water processing with storage an integral part of each, thereby allowing utilization of low-yield energy and water sources without compromising even high rates of water usage.

Stuffing box a simple device that performs the same functions as the pump standard without the provision for hand pumping water from the well.

Submersible pump a type of pump designed for in-well use where the motor and pump are combined in a single, sealed unit for direct submersion into the water.

Sucker rod a wood or metal rod used to connect either a wind machine to a stuffing box, or a stuffing box to a piston pump in the well.

Tail pipe a section of pipe situated below a piston pump in a deep well or over a shallow well to permit suction lift of water.

Tail water the "waste" water that exits a waterwheel, water turbine, or hydraulic ram.

Taut-wire system a reciprocating power-transmission system developed for use wherever a water source and an energy source are separated by a long distance.

Transport the horizontal transfer of water from one point to another.

Turbidity water "cloudiness," usually associated with suspended particles.

UV resistance a measure of the ability of a substance such as plastic pipe to resist the effects of prolonged exposure to the ultraviolet radiation of sunlight. Without UV inhibitors, most plastics will discolor, turn brittle, and crack apart unless they are buried in soil.

Water conditioning a process whereby undesirable aspects of water, such as taste, odor, or the presence of certain minerals and elements, are removed or rendered ineffective.

Water processing water development involving one or more of the following aspects: extraction, transport, storage, pressurization.

Water rights the legal right to use water to which you have access. There are two types, appropriate or riparian, and the first step in considering possible water sources should be to find out which type of right applies to your property.

Water table the level at which water first appears during drilling operations, usually described as a given number of feet from the surface for a whole area of the country; variable during the year or during unusually dry or wet years.

Water witching the act of dowsing for water.

Weir a small cutout temporarily placed across a stream which permits, in conjunction with the correct tables, the accurate measurement of the stream's flow rate.

REFERENCES

Aeromotor—P.O. Box 1364, Conway, AR 72032, (501) 329-9811. Windmills, towers, water systems. Check Yellow Pages for distributor nearest you.

American Association for Vocational Instructional Materials (AAVIM)—120 Engineering Center, Athens, GA 30602, (404) 542-2586.

The American Dowser, Quarterly Digest—Headquarters and address for all materials and inquiries is: American Society of Dowsers, Inc., Danville, VT 05828, (802) 684-3417.

Baker—Monitor Division, Evansville, WI 53536, (608) 882-5100. Jacks, pumps, and well supplies.

Bowjon—2829 Burton Ave., Burbank, CA 91504, (213) 846-2620. Windmills, towers, water systems.

Brace Research Institute—Macdonald College of McGill University, Ste. Anne de Bellevue, Quebec, Canada H9X 3M1. Write and ask for a list of all their publications on solar distillers and related subjects.

Cloudburst 2—Edited by Vic Marks. Cloudburst Press of America, Inc., 1716 N. 45th St., Seattle, WA 98103. 1976. Price $5.

Dempster Industries, Inc.—P.O. Box 848, Beatrice, NB 68310, (402) 223-4026. Windmills, towers, water systems.

Development of springs, bored and dug wells, and cisterns—see: "Water for the Farm Home" and *Planning for an Individual Water System* (AAVIM)

Earthmind—4844 Hirsch Road, Mariposa, CA 95338. Send a (long) SASE for current publications list (includes books by Michael Hackleman).

Gray-Water systems—see *Residential Water Re-Use.*

The Homebuilt, Wind-Generated Electricity Handbook—by Michael Hackleman. Peace Press, Culver City, 1975. Available from Earthmind, 4844 Hirsch Rd., Mariposa, CA 95338. Price $10. Tower-raising, wind-electric machine restoration and installation, design notes, standby generators.

Hydraulic ram—Building a hydraulic ram: there are three designs in *Cloudburst 2;* also see Rife Hydraulic Water Rams.

Locating water sources below ground—see: *The American Dowser* and *Modern Dowsing.*

Modern Dowsing, The Dowser's Handbook—by Raymond C. Willey. Cottonwood Press, 2nd printing, September 1976, from Esoteric Publications, P.O. Box 1529, Sedona, AZ 86336. Price $5.

Planning for an Individual Water System—by AAVIM (see: American Association for Vocational Instructional Materials for complete address), 3rd revised edition, 1973. Price $6.95.

Residential Water Re-Use—by Murray Milne, Report No. 46, Sept. 1979, from Water Resources Center, University of California, Davis, CA 95616. Price $10.

Rife hydraulic water rams—Rife Hydraulic Engine Manufacturing Company, 132 Main St., Andover, NJ 07821. Send 25¢ for information.

Solar distillers—*Description of the Construction of a 50 Sq. Ft. Wooden Roof-Type Solar Still in Barbados,* Technical Report No. T-1, Feb. 1962, by T. A. Lawand. This booklet is available from Brace Research Institute (see Brace for complete address). Price $1.25.

Standards for concentrations of minerals, etc., in water—varies from state to state; obtain current standards from your local Dept. of Health or local library. Example: excerpts from the California Health & Safety Code & Administration Code are published in pamphlet form titled "California Domestic Water Quality and Monitoring Regulations." Copies may be obtained from Dept. of Health, Sanitary Engineering Section, 2151 Berkeley Way, Berkeley, CA 94704.

Towers, wind machine—see: *The Homebuilt, Wind-Generated Electricity Handbook* for types, raising procedures, etc.

Treatment of unsafe water—see: *Planning for an Individual Water System* (AAVIM)—by distillation, see: Solar distillers.

Water for the Farm Home—by Cumberland Country Reader, Cumberland Press, P.O. Box 588, Crossville, TN 38555. 1978. Price $2.

Water Supply Sources for the Farmstead and Rural Home—Farmers Bulletin #2237, Revised December 1971. U. S. Dept. of Agriculture, Agricultural Engineering Research Division, Agricultural Research Service. For a copy, write: Superintendent of Documents, U. S. Govt. Printing Office, Washington, DC 20402. Stock #0100-1527. Price 15¢.

Water test results—see: Standards for concentrations of minerals, etc.

Wind and Windspinners—A "Nuts-'n-Bolts" Approach to Wind-Electric Systems—by Michael Hackleman. Peace Press, Culver City, 1974. From Earthmind, 4844 Hirsch Road, Mariposa, CA 95338. Price $10. Basics of wind, electricity, batteries, and step-by-step building of an S-rotor.

Wind machines, water-pumping—see: Aeromotor, Baker, Bowjon, and Dempster.

INDEX